WORD ACCENT IN MODERN SERBO-CROATIAN

WORD ACCENT IN MODERN SERBO-CROATIAN

Thomas F. Magner

The Pennsylvania State University

and

Ladislav Matejka

University of Michigan

The Pennsylvania State University Press
University Park and London

Copyright © 1971 by The Pennsylvania State University

All rights reserved
Library of Congress Catalog Card Number 77-145826
International Standard Book Number 0-271-01138-6
Printed in the United States of America

To

Gudrun and Irma

TABLE OF CONTENTS

PREFACE

CHAPTER ONE	Vukovian Accentual Norms	1
	1. The function of accent marks	4
	2. Words with and without accent	8
	3. An accented text	12
CHAPTER TWO	Phonological Interpretations of the Vukovian System	15
	1. The phonological role of tone	20
	2. The phonological role of stress	23
	3. Place of accent	26
	4. Phonological relevance of the accentual position	28
	5. Other typographic arrangements	32
CHAPTER THREE	History of the Serbo-Croatian Word Accent	38
	1. Comparative observations	44
	2. Accentual notation in early writers	49
CHAPTER FOUR	Observations of Serbocroatianists	62
CHAPTER FIVE	Testing of Prosodic Distinctions	75
	1. Method of testing	78
CHAPTER SIX	Evaluating Test Performance	95
	1. Test of postaccentual quantity	99
	2. Test of accentual quantity	107
	3. Test of tone	111
	4. Test of accentual position	116

WORD ACCENT

CHAPTER SEVEN	Cumulative Test Scores	121
	1. Postaccentual quantity	127
	2. Accentual quantity	132
	3. Tone	136
	4. Place of accent	139
CHAPTER EIGHT	Local Voices	141
	1. Accentuation of the local voices	142
	2. Postaccentual quantity in the local voices	146
	3. Accentual quantity in the local voices	149
	4. Tone in the local voices	151
	5. Place of accent in the local voices	153
	6. A Belgrade voice	157
	7. A Zagreb voice	160
	8. Communication within the classroom	163
	9. Variations in accentuation of local voices	168
	10. Test of the specialists	169
CHAPTER NINE	General Conclusions	174
	1. Concluding observations about postaccentual quantity	178
	2. Concluding observations about accentual quantity	181
	3. Concluding observations about tone	183
	4. Concluding observations about place of accent	186
APPENDIX I	Accented Readings	193
APPENDIX II	Bibliography	206

PREFACE

The idea for an investigation of the accentual system of Serbo-Croatian was born during a conversation between the two authors one Fall morning in 1965 as they drove leisurely through the countryside north of Zagreb. Both Matejka and Magner were in Yugoslavia on Fulbright research fellowships for the academic year 1965-1966. Matejka was concerned with Croatian and Serbian recensions of Church Slavic while Magner was studying the kajkavian dialects of the small cities in the kajkavian area. On this particular trip Magner had planned to make a short visit to Začretje and Krapina, important points for any kajkavian investigation, both located short distances to the north of Zagreb. As the two authors rode through the pleasant Zagorje countryside, the conversation covered the usual range of topics one would expect from two colleagues in the field of Slavic linguistics. One topic, however, proved more interesting than others and recurred throughout the day in their discussions; that was the puzzling situation of the Serbo-Croatian accent. One of the authors, perhaps because of previous residence in Belgrade and Zagreb, was extremely skeptical about the whole accentual system described by Vuk Karadžić and contained in all the standard grammars and reference books; he felt that the Vukovian system has little relationship to the accentual reality of those two cities and probably to other parts of the country as well. The other author who was doing research in Yugoslavia for the first time was well acquainted with the Vukovian system as presented in the handbooks and had had no cause to doubt its validity. Both authors, intrigued by a situation which could produce skepticism in some and unquestioning belief in others, decided to investigate the accentual situation in urban Yugoslavia in as an objective a way as possible. The results of this investigation are contained in the following pages.

In attempting to arrive at an understanding of the accentual reality of the Serbo-Croatian area of Yugoslavia, there were at least

WORD ACCENT

two approaches open to us. One approach would be to describe the accentual situation in individual cities and regions, then try to make a statement about their prosodic common denominator. Another approach would be to assume as a working premise that the Vukovian accentual system, as given in grammars and reference works, was in fact the actual system of Serbo-Croatian speakers, then test the speakers against this system. We followed the latter approach and tested some 1,600 speakers, mostly high school students, on their ability to perceive the prosodic distinctions characteristic of the Vukovian system. During the investigation an interesting change in attitudes took place: after traveling many hundreds of miles through the cities and villages of the Serbo-Croatian speech area, the skeptical author was forced by the facts of the investigation to modify his skepticism and to admit that in certain areas the Vukovian system did indeed function while the author who started out with total belief in the system suffered a series of shocks as he met, face to face, with an accentual reality which deviated significantly from the Vukovian dogmas of the textbooks. The results of our work may not permit us to enunciate any "God's truth" about Serbo-Croatian prosody, but they do permit us to counter grammatical folklore with experimental data, and to make reasoned judgments about the present status of word accent in the Serbo-Croatian language.*

The authors are very grateful to the many Croatian and Serbian linguists, dialectologists, accentologists, and language teachers who gave freely of their counsel and time during the investigation. They are particularly grateful to the directors of those high schools *(gimnazije)* who courteously received these odd foreigners with their tape recorder and test forms and permitted them to test in various classes. And they remember with particular pleasure the many young Serbs, Croats and Moslems who cooperated enthusiastically in the language game which these foreigners brought into their classrooms.

*Preliminary discussions of this investigation have appeared in Ladislav Matejka, "Generative and Recognitory Aspects in Phonology," *Phonologie der Gegenwart*, ed. Josef Hamm, Graz-Wien-Köln: Hermann Böhlaus, 1967, pp. 242-253; and in Thomas F. Magner, "Post-Vukovian Accentual Norms in Modern Serbo-Croatian," *American Contributions to the Sixth International Congress of Slavists*, Vol. I: *Linguistic Contributions*, ed. Henry Kučera, The Hague: Mouton, 1968, pp. 227-247.

CHAPTER ONE

VUKOVIAN ACCENTUAL NORMS

Ima naš jezik jednu osobinu koja mu daje posebnu ljepotu, koja ga čini neobično melodioznim, pa u tome nadmašuje i sam talijanski jezik, - to je naglasak. . . . No naglasak ne služi našem jeziku samo kao ukras nego kao sredstvo da njime razlikujemo dvije riječi.

Stjepan Babić

The Serbo-Croatian system of "four accents" was first described by Vuk Karadžić (1787-1864) in his *Srpski rječnik* of 1818 but his presentation was deemed incomplete and ambiguous, and it was largely through the craftsmanship of his student, Đuro Daničić (1825-1882), that the canonical statement of the Vukovian system achieved its present-day elegance.[1] Though both Vuk and Daničić were of the 19th century, they live on in modern Yugoslavia in a symbolic way: Vuk has become a mythic figure of such proportions that one can rightly say that Yugoslav Serbocroatianists operate "in the shadow of Vuk," while Daničić endures in his

---

[1] A book-end list of references will give bibliographical details about those books and articles which are important to this study or which are referred to more than once; for such works abbreviated citations will be made within the text, e.g. Brabec (*Gramatika*, p. 18), Ivić ("Prozodijski sistem," p. 34). Otherwise (as in footnote 3) a complete citation will be given at the bottom of the appropriate page.

accentual formulations which have become a type of natural law for Yugoslav philologists.[2]

The sprawling lands through which Vuk wandered, collecting his texts and songs, have greatly changed: the bucolic kingdom of Serbia, the Croatian *reliquiae reliquiarum,* the Dalmatian littoral, the Bosnian *pashaluk,* the tiny princedom of Montenegro have been transmuted along with Slovenia and Macedonia into modern Yugoslavia. The country now has a population of some 20 million of which about 15 million speak Serbo-Croatian as a native language; at the time of Vuk's death, a little more than 100 years ago, the number of Serbo-Croatian speakers was about 5 million.[3] Where Vuk saw sleepy towns, there are now bustling cities; urbanization moves apace in Yugoslavia with the result that this onetime peasant country now has 50 percent of its population in urban centers. The language and accentology which Croatian and Serbian children meet in their schools is that of Vuk (*cum* Daničić), refined and elaborated by Tomo Maretić and other disciples, both Croatian and Serbian. This Vukovian accentology was based upon Vuk's own speech (he was born in Tršić in western Serbia) which reflects the more general dialectal type of eastern Hercegovina (now part of Montenegro), the home of Vuk's ancestors. Modern Serbo-Croatian is, in its own self-image, an updated version of Vuk's 19th century peasant speech and the canonical accentuation is based on the rhythms of rustic Serbia and Hercegovina.

The Vukovian system, as stabilized by Daničić, has four accents which are designated by four accent marks: ̏, ̀, ̑, ́. These marks are shorthand devices which designate a combination of prosodic features:

    ̏ indicates a falling tone on a short vowel in the accented position of a word;

---

[2] In this book the adjective "Vukovian" will refer to the accentual system established by Karadžić and brought to completion by Daničić.

[3] Jagić's estimate minus S-Cr. speakers in Hungary; see Vatroslav Jagić, "Članci iz Književnika (1866)," *Djela Vatroslava Jagića* IV, ed. Petar Skok, Zagreb: Jugoslavenska Akademija, 1953, p. 216.

` indicates a rising tone on a short vowel in the accented position of a word;
ˆ indicates a falling tone on a long vowel in the accented position of a word;
´ indicates a rising tone on a long vowel in the accented position of a word.

Thus, there are two tones, one rising and one falling, which coincide with accentedness; vowel length or its absence in the accented syllabic is the component which makes for the four accents rather than two. Other accent markings can be and have been devised (e.g. vowel length of the accented vowel can be indicated by a macron or a double vowel) but the traditional marks are widely understood and indeed have a certain economy of their own. As examples of the four accents we can use Daničić's favorite examples:

Short fall	Short rise	Long fall	Long rise
slȁva fame	màgla mist	prâvda justice	gláva head

Vowel length after the accent is marked with a macron, e.g. G sg. glávē. The operating rules for this Vukovian system are the following:

(1) The falling accent (ˈˈ or ˆ) occurs only on the first syllable of a word, e.g. prȉjatelj, "friend," pûtnīk, "traveler."
(2) Monosyllabic words can have only a falling accent, e.g. pȍp (G sg. pòpa), "priest," krâlj (G sg. králja), "king."
(3) No accent can occur on a final syllable.
(4) The rising accent (ˋ or ´) can occur on any syllable except the final, e.g. vòda, "water," tráva, "grass," dubìna, "depth," napísati, "to write," Dalmatínac, "Dalmatian."
(5) Length (ˉ) can occur on any syllabic nucleus except before the accent, that is, it occurs either as part of the accent (prâvda, gláva) or after the accent, e.g. ùčenīk, "pupil," G pl. ùčenīkā.

4   WORD ACCENT

As Ivić ("Functional Yield," p. 301) points out, "in monosyllabic words there are two prosodic possibilities, in bisyllabic eight, in trisyllabic twenty, and so on." He demonstrates these possibilities in the following scheme, using the letter *a* to symbolize "any vowel in function of syllable nucleus."

    Monosyllabic: â, ȁ
    Bisyllabic: âa, âā, ȁa, ȁā
                     áa, áā, àa, àā
    Trisyllabic: âaa, âāa, âaā, âāā
                     ȁaa, ȁāa, ȁaā, ȁāā
                     áaa, áāa, áaā, áāā
                     àaa, àāa, àaā, àāā
                     aáa, aáā, aàa, aàā

Thus *prâvda* would be âa, *ȕčenīk* would be ȁaā, G pl. *prèdstāvnīštāvā*, "representations," would be àāāāā, while the 10-syllable form *internacionalizíraju*, "they internationalize," would be aaaaaaaáaā.

1. *THE FUNCTION OF ACCENT MARKS*

The Vukovian system of accent marks has become a standard tool used by lexicographers, dialectologists and grammarians for denoting prosodic distinctions which serve to differentiate lexical items or inflectional and derivational forms in Serbo-Croatian. In dictionaries, textbooks and reference works a S-Cr. word like *pȁra*, "steam," is graphically distinguished from *pàra*, "money," the explicit assumption being that a correctly articulated distinction will result in the production of two distinct words within every context regardless of sentence intonation and other factors such as speed, loudness, modulation and subjective emphasis.[4] Thus, for example, only the difference between short falling and short rising accents is assumed to distinguish two sentences such as

---

[4] Brabec (*Gramatika*, p. 20): "The sentence accent does not change the nature of the accent of the word itself."

or

1a. *I danas pàra igra ulogu.*   Even today steam plays a role.
1b. *I danas pàra igra ulogu.*   Even today money plays a role.

or

2a. *Da li je òrao na tom brežuljku?*   Has he been plowing on that hill?
2b. *Da li je òrao na tom brežuljku?*   Is that an eagle on that hill?

3a. *Voda je prèvrela.*   The water is too hot.
3b. *Voda je prèvrela.*   The water boiled over.

Preservation of a meaningful distinction is expected even if the word accent should coincide with the initial or final pitch of sentence intonation.[5] If the word alone is used as a sentence, it is expected to be capable of carrying interrogative or declarative or, for that matter, any other intonation while still preserving its accentual integrity as a word, e.g.

Pȁs?   "Is that a dog?"
Pȁs.   "That is a dog."
Pâs?   "Is that a belt?"
Pâs.   "That is a belt."

In the normative lexicography of Standard Serbo-Croatian prosodic marking plays an important role in distinguishing one lexical item from another, e.g.

WORDS DIFFERING IN TONE

short falling (̏)   versus   short rising (̀)

| *pȕčina* | surface of sea | *pùčina* | large crowd |
| *prȁšnīk* | pistil | *pràšnīk* | powder-hole |

---

[5] Miletić ("Uticaj," p. 222) has shown, however, that the tonal element of the word accents can be affected by sentence intonation to the extent that the rising word tone can become falling and the falling tone rising.

WORD ACCENT

✓prèdati	to be afraid	prèdati	to hand over
pòd(j)elica*	charity	pòd(j)elica	piece of land
✓ùmiti	to reason	ùmiti	to wash
pòuzak	rather narrow	pòuzak	connecting link
pŕtiti	to load	pŕtiti	to remove snow
sȑčan	brave	sȑčan	pertaining to heart

        long falling (ˆ)   versus   long rising (´)

✓Lûka	Luke	lúka	port
✓mâjka	mother	májka	grandmother
lîčīm	I paint	líčīm	I resemble
cȓnīm	I blacken	cŕnīm	I become black
✓pûstīm	I empty	pústīm	I become empty

DIFFERENCE IN ACCENTUAL QUANTITY

        short falling (˝)   versus   long falling (ˆ)

✓pȁs	dog	pâs	belt
✓grȁd	hail	grâd	city
lȕk	onion	lûk	arch
pȕstīm	I free	pûstīm	I empty
bȅg	bey	bêg [ekavian]	flight
✓Vlȁsi	Vlachs	vlâsi	hair

        short rising (`)   versus   long rising (´)

zòra	dawn	Zóra	Zora [woman's name]
pèro	pen	Péro	Pero [man's name]
pomètati	to arrange	pométati	to disturb
slàgati	to tell a lie	slágati	to stack up
sèdeti [ek.]	to sit	sédeti [ek.]	to become gray

*Forms with (j) indicate both variants in use in Standard S-Cr: ekavian *podelica* and jekavian *podjelica*.

DIFFERENCE IN PLACE OF ACCENT

gùščetina	goose meat	guščètina	big goose
tèlešce	little calf	telèšce [ek.]	little body
p(j)èvačica	cuckoo	p(j)evàčica	songstress
sùnčanica	sun beam	sunčànica	sun-stroke
òsobnīk	private property	osòbnīk	personnel file
dùhovskī	spiritual	duhòvskī	pertaining to Pentecost

DIFFERENCE IN POSTACCENTUAL QUANTITY

sa sùprugom*	with the husband	sa sùprugōm*	with the wife
plȁmen	fiery	plȁmēn	flame
òpisan	descriptive	òpīsān	described
srednjòškolskī	high school (adj.)	srednjòškōlskī	high school student (adj.)

DIFFERENCE IN NUMBER OF ACCENTS

belocr̀ven [ek.]	whitish red	bélo-cr̀ven [ek.]	white and red
srpskohr̀vātskī	Serbo-Croatian	sr̀psko-hr̀vātskī	Serbian and Croatian

ACCENTEDNESS VERSUS UNACCENTNESS

ȍko	eye	oko	around
krȃj	end	kraj	by the side of
m(j)ȅsto	place	m(j)esto	in place of

The Vukovian system of prosodic notation is employed in normative presentations of Serbo-Croatian morphology. Thus, the grammatical meaning of a form is often distinguished from that of

---

*Dalibor Brozović has provided the authors with a similar contrast in the jocular saying: *Sprijateljio sam se sa sùsjedōm i zato sam se posvadio sa sùsjedom,*" I got friendly with my neighbor [female] and for that I got into an argument with my neighbor [male]."

another form in the same paradigm by a single prosodic distinction or by various combinations of tone, accentual and postaccentual quantity and by the place of accent. A few of the thousands of possible examples are the following:

    G sg. *sèla*, "village"   N/A pl. *sȅla*, "villages"
    G sg. *pöljä*, "field"   N/A pl. *pòlja*, "fields"
    N sg. *Ivo*,   V sg. *Îvo*
    G pl. def. *mlâdīh*, "young"   G pl. indef. *mládīh*
    2nd sg. imper. *bdȉ*, "be awake"   3rd sg. pres. *bdî*, "he is awake"
    3rd sg. pres. *će*, "he'll"   3rd pl. pres. *ćē*, "they'll"
    1st sg. aor. *brȁh*, "I picked"   1st sg. imperf. *brȃh*, "I was picking"

In normative grammars the prosodic differentiation of inflectional forms is classified according to parts of speech and grammatical categories, and subclassified by number of syllables and other formal characteristics. The accent of the dictionary form (i.e. nominative singular, infinitive, etc.) usually serves as the point of departure in classifying the forms of an inflectional set. The obvious result of such a classificatory approach is the production of an impressively diverse catalogue of prosodic types. For example, several hundreds of such types are listed in Stevanović's 1964 grammar.* Although his collection consists essentially of a reclassification of the Vuk-Daničić corpus, supplemented by marginal details, it is presented as a description of contemporary standard usage. Actually, such blind acceptance of the Vukovian accentual heritage characterizes most grammars of Standard Serbo-Croatian, although the various catalogues of accentual types may differ in the degree of comprehensiveness.

2. WORDS WITH AND WITHOUT ACCENT

A word in Standard Serbo-Croatian is normally expected to be characterized by one word accent. There are, however, certain

---

*In *Srpski akcenti* Daničić has 252 accentual types of nouns alone!

compound words which are said to have two accents, e.g. nâjstàrijī, "the oldest one," nâjbȍljī, "the best one," nâjgȍrnjī, "the highest one." Some compound words with two accents are even claimed to be semantically distinguishable from the corresponding compounds with a single accent, e.g. sȑpsko-hȑvātskī, "Serbian and Croatian," vs. srpskohȑvātskī, "Serbo-Croatian."[6]

Certain types of words are considered to be accentless and to form an accentual unit either with the following or the preceding word or words. The accentless words, which usually constitute an accentual unit with a preceding word, include functional forms such as the question particle *li*, present form of the auxiliaries (e.g. *sam, si, je* . . . ; *ću, ćeš, će* . . . ; *bih, bi* . . .), the short forms of the personal pronouns (e.g. *mi, me; ti, te; mu, ga*, etc.), and the reflexive pronoun *se*. They are called enclitics because they most frequently occur in enclitic position, e.g. *vidio sam ga* = vȉdiosamga, "I saw him." But in certain syntactic environments the "enclitic" can actually appear in proclitic position by forming a unit with the following accented word, e.g. *promenio se da ga ne poznaš* = proméniose daganepòznaš, "he has changed so that you won't recognize him."[7] Furthermore, some enclitics cease to be accentless if they are used sentence initially, e.g. *Jȅ li dȍšao*, "has he come?" As a matter of fact, all enclitics will probably be accented if quoted or mentioned as single words, e.g. *Forma "mȉ" data je kao prim(j)er,* "the form 'mi' is given as an example."

The words, which usually form an accentual unit with the following word or words, include conjunctions (e.g. *jer, da, kad*), connectives (e.g. *i, ni*), the negative particle *ne* and prepositions (e.g. *od, iz, između*). They are called proclitics, although, in certain cases, they are expected to take over the accent from the following word.

The normative grammar thus distinguishes:

1. Accented and unaccented proclitics (e.g. *pȍd rūku / pod víno*).
2. Accented and unaccented enclitics (e.g. *Jȅ li dȍšao / dȍšao je*).

---

[6] Cf. *Pravopis*, p. 78 and 742.
[7] Stevanović (*Savremeni*, p. 162).

3. Enclitics in enclitic and proclitic position (e.g. pòznāš ga / da ga ne pòznāš).
4. Nouns, adjectives, verbs, pronouns, numerals and adverbs capable of occurring in enclitic position without being called "enclitics" (e.g. pòd rūku / nà Novū gòdinu / nè vidīm / kòd mene / nà treći / ì čēsto).

As a rule, the accentual shift from one word to the preceding one can take place only if the second word is a noun, adjective, pronoun, adverb, numeral or verb with a falling accent. The accent can shift when the preceding word is a proclitic, that is, a word which is classified as *unaccented* but *accentable*. As a result, the unaccented word takes over the accent of the following word and becomes the accent carrier of the entire phrase which then exists as a single accentual unit (i.e. a "phonological word"), e.g. ùgrād, "into the city."

When describing this phenomenon, Yugoslav grammarians usually make the observation that such "accent jumping" (*skakanje*) no longer takes place consistently and that often the word with a falling accent maintains it while the preceding proclitic (preposition, conjunction or connective) remains unaccented. Thus Brabec (*Gramatika*, p. 21): "One notices a tendency in the literary language for the accent to be shifted more infrequently to the proclitic, especially a polysyllabic proclitic, and to connectives: *preko môra* instead of *prȅko mōra*, *u jȅzeru* instead of *ù jezeru*, *ni bràtu* instead of *nì bratu*, *kad rȅčēm* instead of *kàd rečēm*, *da vȉdīm* instead of *dà vidīm*, *dâni i gòdine* instead of *dâni ì godine*. The accent is regularly shifted to the prefix or to the negative particle *ne*: *pòmisliti - mȉsliti*, *nè vidīm - vȉdīm*." Hamm (*Grammatik*, p. 33) states that "more and more frequently" (*immer häufiger*) the accent remains on the noun in such prepositional phrases, e.g. *za kȕću* for classical *zà kuću*, *u grâd* for *ù grād*.

Stevanović repeatedly points out that the shift often does not take place even if all relevant conditions are fulfilled. In his view the retaining of accent by individual words is "an ever more frequent phenomenon, especially in the regions and cultural centers of the eastern part of the Serbo-Croatian language territory."

(*Savremeni*, p. 162.) He therefore concludes that the shift as well as the retention can be regarded as a *književna norma* (p. 223).*

By introducing this concession in their otherwise total acceptance of the Vuk-Daničić prosody, Stevanović and his fellow grammarians are doing two things: 1) partially modernizing the accentual canons by basing norms on practice, and 2) creating some basic contradictions in the prosodic system.

If accent retention is accepted as an optional part of the system, it is now possible to have falling accents in the interior of the phonological word, e.g. *u grâd [ugrâd]*, *preko môra [prekomôra]*, *od brȁta [odbrȁta]*. This would be a violation of one of the basic tenets of the Vukovian canons: falling accents can occur only on the initial syllable of a word, whether lexical or phonological. The new optional norms can be illustrated by using phrases with the preposition *bez*, "without," and the nouns *brȁt*, "brother," *stȁrac*, "old man," *pȍlje*, "field," and *grâd*, "city." In the case of *skakanje* the new accent would be a short rising in the phrases with *brat* and *starac* (Type A), short falling in the phrases with *polje* and *grad* (Type B).

	unshifted	shifted
Type A	bez brȁta [= bezbrȁta]	bèz brata [= bèzbrata]
	bez stârca [= bestârca]	bèz stārca [= bèstārca]
Type B	bez pȍlja [= bespȍlja]	bȅz polja [= bȅspolja]
	bez grâda [= bezgrâda]	bȅz grāda [= bȅzgrāda]

*The Croatian grammarian, Mate Hraste, strongly disagrees: "Departure from this norm [*skakanje*] will call forth other departures which are already in evidence, and that can lead to two or even three official accentuations: an eastern, a western and a southern." See Mate Hraste, "O potrebi prenošenja akcenta na prijedlog," *Jezik* 5(1963-1964), p. 143.

If the preposition itself has two syllables, like *preko*, "through," it can receive a short rising accent only on the second syllable (Type A), a short falling only on the first (Type B).

	unshifted	shifted
Type A	preko brȁta [= prekobrȁta]	prekò brata [= prekòbrata]
	preko stârca [= prekostârca]	prekò stārca [= prekòstārca]
Type B	preko pȍlja [= prekopȍlja]	prȅko polja [= prȅkopolja]
	preko grâda [= prekogrâda]	prȅko grāda [= prȅkogrāda]

3. AN ACCENTED TEXT

To illustrate how Yugoslav linguists treat the accentuation of texts we have selected an accented schoolchild's essay which appeared in a Yugoslav textbook. The textbook version has been checked and corrected by an accentologist; an English translation follows the text below. The obvious characteristic of this type of accenting is that, in accordance with Yugoslav tradition, the accentual focus is on the word; phrase and sentence intonation, and their effects on word accent, are not considered.

Stârī drâgī pût

Mòj pût òd kuće dò škōlē nìje dȕg—svèga pètnaest minȗtā hȍda. Zȁprāvo trȋ púta vȍdē od mòjē kȕćē dò škōlē, ȁli jâ ȕvijek odàberēm jèdan pût: pût kòjī vȍdī uz prúgu. Tȋm pútem ȉdēm svȁkōg dâna, pa ga mògu opísati. Mògla bih ĭći ȕlicōm uz kukùruzna pòlja i uz lȉvade. Ȁli jâ ȕvijek pôđēm uz prúgu jer će me nà tom pútu pràtiti šàrenī lȅptīri, a zȋmi cvȓkūt pròmrzlīh vrâbācā. Ako bȕdē kȉšilo, nà tom će pútu bȉti i blȁtnjavo.

Na pútu uz prúgu tráčnice će me ùvijek privláčiti, a ònē dáljine, gdje tráčnice nèstajū, zamĩšljat ću kao kràjeve ìz pr̃īčā. Néću tàda mĩsliti na kàmēnje o kòjē se spòtičēm, već ću u míslima lètjeti za vagónima bȓzōga vlāka. I tàkō, dok bùdēm mĩslila, glĕdat ću pòlja i lĩvade, brĕgove i plànine, jezèra, rijèke i môra. U mòjōj će se màšti isprèplitati slĩke iz zĕmljopīsnīh ùdžbenīkā, Andersēnovīh bájkī i pr̃īčā iz "Tĩsuću i jèdnē nòći." Nȁjzād, kad se bùdū prȅda mnōm, sàsvīm nènādāno, pojávila vèlikā vráta škòlskē zgrȁdē, jā ću prèstati da màštām. Prènijet ću se ù svōj svakìdašnjī̄ škòlskī život i ùčit ću—ùčiti o ljúdima, o krajèvima, o pròšlòsti i sàdašnjosti.

A na pòvratku ìz škōlē mòje ćē slĩke o dàlekīm zèmljama i ljúdima bìti odrèdènijē, šarènijē i ljȅpšē. Tàda ću glĕdati vlàkove kòjī pròlazē i razmĩšljat ću o krajèvima kùdā tī vlàkovi ìdū. Tàkō će tô bìti svàkī dân. Mĕni tâj pût ù škōlu i òd škōle kùći nìkada nêće bìti dòsādan. A kad ljȅti bùdēm ùbirala izmèđ dr̀venīh prȁgōvā pokòjī cȑvenī màk, òsjećat ću žĩvo kolìkō vòlīm svôj stárī svakìdašnjī pût.

The Favorite Path

My path from home to school isn't long; it's only a fifteen-minute walk. Actually there are three paths from home to school, but I always take the same one: the one that goes along the railroad track. I go along that path every day, and thus I can describe it. I could choose the road which goes near the corn fields and meadows. But I always go along the railroad track because on that path I will be accompanied by colorful butterflies and in winter by the chirping of chilled sparrows. In rainy weather that path will also be muddy.

On that path by the railroad I will always be fascinated by the tracks and I will visualize the far-away distances, where the tracks disappear, like story-book realms. Then I won't be thinking about the stones that I stumble on, but in my thoughts I will be flying after the cars of the express train. And so, while thinking about these things, I will see fields and meadows, hills and mountains, lakes, rivers and seas. In my imagination there will be intermingled pictures from geography books, Anderson's fairy tales, and stories from "A Thousand and One Nights." Finally, when the big door of the school building appears suddenly before me, I will stop my day-dreaming.

I will enter into the everyday school life and I shall study—study about peoples, about places, about the past and the present.

On the way home from school my images of distant lands and peoples will be sharper, more colorful and more beautiful. Then I will watch the trains that pass by and think about the places they go to. And so it will be every day. For me that path to and from school will never be boring. And in the summer when I pick red poppies from in between the wooden ties, I will feel again how much I love my old path which I take every day.

CHAPTER TWO

PHONOLOGICAL INTERPRETATIONS OF THE VUKOVIAN SYSTEM

> *The inventory of Standard Serbocroatian totals 29 qualitatively distinct phonemes, and if we add the phonemes distinguished by prosodic features the amount of phonemes swells to 47.*
>
> Roman Jakobson

The Vukovian diacritic system provides for six prosodic distinctions of each vowel. According to Daničić's interpretation (*Srpski akcenti*, p. 1), the first *a* in the words 1. *glava*, 2. *pravda*, 3. *magla*, 4. *slama* is pronounced in four different ways because of the accentual modification, i.e. *gláva, pråvda, màgla, slȁma*. Thus, the *a* is distinct prosodically although it is considered to be identical qualitatively. On the other hand, the second *a* in all four examples is considered to be the same both prosodically and qualitatively. Since postaccentual vowels have to be distinguished in terms of length and shortness, Daničić's vocalic system is equipped with thirty-six distinctive values combining five vowels and the syllabic *r* with the superimposed prosodic characteristics, e.g.

ä à â á ā a

ë è ê é ē e

ï ì î í ī i

ö ò ô ó ō o

ü ù û ú ū u

r̈ r̀ r̂ ŕ r̄ r

Theoretically, each of the thirty-six vowels is expected to be capable of distinguishing words from each other. Daničić insists on using the diacritic markers not only to differentiate individual words semantically but also to denote a word's proper pronounciation from a deficient one. In his view, the Serbo-Croatian speaker would not know whether the place name *Perast* should be pronounced *Pèrast* or *Pérast,* if he knew the name only from literature which did not use the relevant accentuation. By implication, two types of word pairs came into the picture: the type with two existing members such as (to use Vuk's example) *jàrica,* "wheat sown in spring," in contrast to *järica,* "young goat," and the type with only one member meaningfully used in Serbo-Croatian.

After one and half centuries the system of thirty-six vowel values, defined in Vuk's and Daničić's terms, continues to play a crucial role in the descriptions of Standard Serbo-Croatian on both theoretical and pedagogical levels. *Gramatika hrvatskosrpskoga jezika* by Brabec, Hraste and Živković repeats essentially the traditional claim about identical words distinguishable only by prosodic modification. "There are words," the authors state, "which have identical forms but which with different accents have different meanings." (p. 19) They illustrate this identity of forms which, however, are prosodically distinct, by word pairs such as *päs - pâs* ("belt" - "dog"), *gräd - grâd* ("hail" - "town"), *prègledati - preglédati* ("to examine [pf.]" - "to examine [impf.]"), *kúpiti - kùpiti* ("to buy" - "to collect"), etc. Although the authors of the *Gramatika* feel that accent in Serbo-Croatian is unstable, difficult to learn and to determine with certainty, they insist on the importance of mastering the prescribed code of standard accentuation. It is not the differentiating role, however, but the aesthetic value which is particularly emphasized, because, in the authors' view, "length and accent make the language musical and beautiful." (p. 18).

The necessity to observe accent and quantity for aesthetic reasons also permeates the thoughts of Ljudevit Jonke in his *Književni jezik u teoriji i praksi* (p. 222). Although he mentions pairs such as *pàs - pâs* or *ràzgledati - razglédati*, he puts euphony before phonological considerations because, in his view, "accent is an essential embellishment of the standard language." Serbo-Croatian without accent, he feels, "overpowers us with monotony and lack of expressiveness, with cacophony and dullness." (p. 222). Jonke complains rather bitterly that both accent and quantity are not used as they ought to be, and he blames school and communication media for failure to promote the prescribed traditional system of prosodic rules (pp. 218-219).

Babić agrees with the necessity to observe the quantitative and accentual distinctions defined by Vuk and Daničić; he is convinced, however, that the importance of accent and quantity consists in their role in differentiating meaning.[1] He illustrates this point in sentences which differ from each other only by markers of accent and/or quantity. Thus, the diacritics serve to prevent not only word homophony but, implicitly, sentence homophony as well, e.g.,

Smátrat će te ròbom.	He will consider you a male slave.
Smátrat ćē te ròbom.	They will consider you a male slave.
Smátrat će te ròbōm.	He will consider you merchandise.
Smátrat ćē te ròbōm.	They will consider you merchandise.

[1] Stjepan Babić, *Jezik,* Zagreb: Panorama, 1965, p. 161: *Naglasci i dužine u našem su jeziku vrlo važni jer imaju razlikovnu službu.* See also Babić, "U čemu je ljepota hrvatskosrpskog jezika," *Jezik* 4 (1963-1964), pp. 123-124.

Some of Babić's sentences juxtapose word pairs such as *rádio - râdio, smìjē - smȉjē, rúža - rûža, lúkē - Lûkē, vúci - vûci, Jéla - jȅla, upòznājū - upòznajū, strȁžare - stražáre, mȁčke - mȃčke, mláda - mlâda,* etc. Fundamentally in agreement with the norms codified by Vuk and Daničić, Babić presents his pairs with the implication that the user of Standard Serbo-Croatian should be able as a speaker a) to select the form semantically, b) to produce the prescribed accentual distinction, c) as a hearer, to identify it acoustically, d) and to interpret it accordingly.

In his 1964 grammar Stevanović embraces the accentual system as it was defined by Vuk and Daničić and promotes all four accents and quantity to the status of "phonological elements." In his view the meaning of individual words depends on these phonological elements so that they are comparable to any other phoneme (*Savremeni,* p. 156). To illustrate the phonological function of his "elements," Stevanović used word pairs, some of which are directly borrowed from Vuk, e.g. *jàrica* ("spring wheat") - *jȁrica* ("female goat"); he does not make it clear, however, whether, for example, the *a* in *jàrica* is one phoneme or two phonemes or, perhaps, one phoneme plus one "phonological element." (p. 157).*

The status of the Vukovian four accents as phonemes is also discussed in A. Peco's paper, "Valeur phonologique des accents serbocroates." "Such examples," he says, "as *Brána* ("woman's name"): *brâna* ("harrow"): *bràna* (aorist of *branati,* "to harrow"): *Brȁna* ("man's name") clearly show that accents are precisely the signs which carry semantic distinction and consequently have phonological value (p. 456).

Peco distinguishes three basic types of accentual oppositions:

1. qualitative opposition (e.g. *jàrica - jȁrica; lúka - Lûka*);
2. quantitative opposition (e.g. *bêg - bȅg; Kósa - kòsa*);

---

*Junković asserts that a prosodic distinction is as important as the distinction between vowels of different quality: "In the čakavian dialect *sûd* and *sūd* are two distinct words in the same sense as *sûd* and *sâd,* and in štokavian *pâs* and *pȁs* are different in the same sense as *râd* and *rôd.*" Zvonimir Junković, "Napomene o naglasku," *Jezik* 1(1969-1970), pp. 4-5.

3. opposition of accented and unaccented words (e.g. ȍko - oko; krâj - kraj);

In addition, he distinguishes:

4. opposition in place of accent (e.g. màlina - malìna; Édina - Edína);
5. opposition of quality-quantity (e.g. krȕniti - krúniti).

The very concept of opposition, however, is used in Peco's article without any clarification. The units which are expected to oppose each other are not specified. One does not know whether they are the vowels or syllables or, perhaps, the entire words. In some instances Peco refers to the syllables, whether accented or unaccented; sometimes, however, he mentions only vowels, each of which can be modified by one of the four accents. If the distinctive units, appearing in opposition, are vowels, Peco's opposition in place of accent would actually be a double opposition: the *a* with short rising accent in *màlina* ("raspberry") would be in opposition to the unaccented *a* in *malìna* ("trifle"), while the unaccented *i* would be in opposition to the *i* with short rising accent.

Particularly unclear is Peco's opposition of accented and unaccented words as, for example, the noun ȍko ("eye") vs. the unaccented preposition oko ("around"). The two words are viewed by Peco as distinct because the initial ȍ with short falling accent is opposed to the initial o without accent (i.e. ȍ vs. o). Peco, however, does not tell us what to do with the accented preposition ȍko in ȍko brda ("around the hill") and with the unaccented noun oko in zà oko ("for the eye"). It is obvious that both the noun *oko* and the preposition *oko* are capable of carrying accent; each of them is either accented or unaccented depending on the accentual rules of syntactic concatenation, e.g.

	Accented *oko*	Unaccented *oko*
Preposition:	ȍko brda	oko sèla
Noun:	dèsno ȍko	zà oko

If, however, the form *oko* is quoted alone, it has to be accented, whether it means "around" or "eye" so that the preposition *oko* and the noun *oko* simply cannot display any accentual opposition as isolated words. For that reason, the two sentences.

1. *Forma 'ȍko' data je kao prim(j)er.* The form "around" is given as an example.

2. *Forma 'ȍko' data je kao prim(j)er.* The form "eye" is given as an example.

are homophonous and semantically ambiguous since in both cases the form *oko* is virtually bound to carry short falling accent.

1. THE PHONOLOGICAL ROLE OF TONE

The first analysis of Serbo-Croatian accent in phonological terms appeared in 1930 in Jakobson's lecture on accent and its role in the phonology of word and syntagma (*"Die Betonung"*). According to Jakobson's observations, accent in the štokavian dialects, and, by implication, in Standard Serbo-Croatian is tonal in its nature; it employs phonologically the contrast between high pitch and low pitch rather than voice-loudness. Thus, in Jakobson's view, it is tone which phonologically characterizes word accent in Serbo-Croatian while stress is considered to be predictable and therefore redundant.

With regard to the syllabic structure of the Serbo-Croatian word Jakobson distinguishes two types of accent. One type (which corresponds to the Vukovian falling accent) normally affects the onset of the first syllable of the word; the second type (which corresponds to the Vukovian rising accent) can appear on any syllable of the word with the exception of the last one. As Masing had done earlier (*Die Hauptformen,* pp. 58-61), Jakobson points out that rising tone extends to the following syllable, thus becoming transsyllabic (*"übersilbig"*). It is only this second type with its high pitch which is viewed by Jakobson as phonologically relevant.

He would, therefore, mark accent only in those words which in Vukovian terminology have rising accent and would leave unmarked all other words with the implication that they have predictable accent on the onset of the first syllable. Thus *Brána : brâna : bràna : Bräna* would appear as *Br̍ána : brāna : brana : Br̍ana* with the vertical line denoting high pitch and with the horizontal line for quantity.

In 1949 in his article, "On the identification of phonemic entities," Jakobson describes the inventory of Standard Serbo-Croatian as totaling 29 qualitatively distinct phonemes. In his view, however, "if we add the phonemes distinguished by prosodic features the amount of phonemes swells to 47." (p. 421). The additional eighteen phonemes are explained by his assumption that "prosodic features divide any vowel, as well as *r*, into four distinctive varieties: high-toned long, high-toned short, low-toned long and low-toned short." (p. 422). High tone and length constitute the marked characteristics, e.g.

	1	2	3	4
High-tone	-	-	+	+
Length	-	+	-	+

Jakobson's inventory of 47 phonemes underwent a further expansion to 51 phonemes in Brozović's *"O fonološkom sustavu suvremenog standardnog hrvatskosrpskog jezika"* which describes not only the "Serbian" but also the "Croatian" variant of contemporary standard Serbo-Croatian (p. 34). Basically in agreement with Jakobson's insistence that only rising accent and quantity (but not stress) are the phonologically relevant prosodic features, Brozović enumerates 26 syllabic phonemes in the "Croatian" version, of which 24 suffice to characterize the "Serbian" version;*

---

*"*To je ukupno 26 slogotvornih fonema za hrvatsku varijantu, odnosno 24 za ekavsku zonu srpske varijante i za klasični jezik.*" (p. 34).

the syllabic phonemes are represented by Brozović as follows
[1 = rising intonation; 2 = length]:

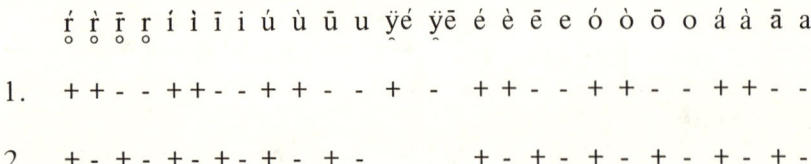

1.	+ + - - + + - - + + - - + - + + - - + + - - + + - -	
2.	+ - + - + - + - + - + - + - + - + - + - + - + -	

Quite a different method of counting Serbo-Croatian phonemes is used by Shevelov (*Prehistory of Slavic*, p. 596). In his view Serbo-Croatian actually employs three subsystems of vowels: under stress, in pretonic syllables, and in postaccentual syllables; the most complete system appears under stress where 24 vowel phonemes can be distinguished since "each of the six vowels may occur under four tones: ̏ ̀ ́ and ̂. There is no opposition," he says, "in pitch in postaccentual syllables so that instead of ȉ : ì : í : î, etc., one finds only an opposition of ĭ : ī, etc., the number of phonemes thus reducing to twelve." The lowest number of phonemes appears in the third Shevelov subsystem which is used in the pretonic position where only 6 vowel phonemes are used without any opposition in quantity and pitch.

Trubetzkoy in his *Grundzüge der Phonologie* is essentially in agreement with Jakobson's original interpretation of Standard Serbo-Croatian accent although he formulates certain points differently. He particularly emphasizes that the implementation of free accent (which corresponds to the Vukovian rising accent) requires two syllables: its onset is on one syllable and its decay on the following one. Free accent, as Trubetzkoy interprets it, is characterized by its musical properties and by the absence of any significant expiratory reinforcement in distinction to the predictable accent (corresponding to Vukovian falling accent) which, according to Trubetzkoy, has a predominantly expiratory character. Since the falling accent is normally bound to the first syllable of the word or of an accentual unit, it merely denotes a boundary while free tonal accent can by its very position differentiate two members of the word pairs such as, to use Trubetzkoy's examples (p. 191),

PHONOLOGICAL INTERPRETATIONS 23

pjèvačica ("cuckoo") vs. *pjevàčica* ("songstress")
ràzložiti ("to explain") vs. *razlòžiti* ("to take apart")

Trubetzkoy, moreover, underlines the fact that free tonal accent is not affected by syntactic concatenation in distinction from predictable expiratory accent which may retreat from the first syllable of the word to the proclitic.

The difference between the phonological tonal accent and the predictable stress accent in Serbo-Croatian was elaborated by Isačenko.[2] Basically, he agrees with Masing's observation (*Die Hauptformen*) about the bisyllabic character of the rising accent but points out that bisyllabic accent (*"Zweigipfelakzent"*) should not be interpreted as an ictus on one syllable followed by an ictus on the successive syllable. Such an interpretation is viewed by Isačenko as a projection of the stress system into the tonal system by a foreigner who has in his mother-tongue stress but not tone and willy-nilly reinterprets the contrast between high and low as a contrast between strong and weak (p. 175).

2. THE PHONOLOGICAL ROLE OF STRESS

The role of tone as compared with that of stress remains the most controversial problem in Serbo-Croatian accentology. One school of thought insists on the prominence of tone and, implicitly, on the contrast of voice-pitch, whereas the other school of thought emphasizes the dominant role of stress (force) and, implicitly, the contrast of voice-loudness. Accordingly, either tone is viewed as phonologically relevant and stress phonologically redundant, or vice versa. In distinction from Jakobson and Trubetzkoy, Trager insists in his 1940 article ("Serbo-Croatian Accents and Quantities") that "phonemically Serbo-Croatian has two accentual systems, one of stress and one of quantity" (p. 30). In Trager's terminology 'accent' refers to both stress and quantity and 'stress' is

---

[2] A. V. Isačenko, "Zur phonologischen Deutung der Akzentverschiebung in den slavischen Sprachen," *Travaux du Cercle linguistique de Prague* 8 (1939), pp. 173-183.

viewed as the manifestation of voice-loudness with increasing and decreasing intensity and of voice-pitch with rising and falling frequency. "The main contrast of stress," Trager asserts, "is between falling and rising, not between loud and weak."* Nevertheless, he considers the tonal difference of falling and rising pitch as non-phonemic, merely an automatic accompaniment of difference in voice-loudness. It is the loudness which in his view plays the phonemic role while the non-phonemic, concomitant pitch phenomena "vary greatly with individuals and with the sentence intonation, and are in every case conditioned, never independent."

Thus, the Vukovian falling accent becomes in Trager's interpretation falling stress which is phonetically characterized by a sudden decrease in loudness during the pronounciation of the vowel so that "there is no loudness left when the end of the syllable is reached." On the other hand, the Vukovian rising accent becomes in Trager's interpretation rising stress which phonetically "begins fairly loud and usually increases in loudness slightly through the syllable, so that at the end the loudness is as great or greater than at the beginning." "The loudness," Trager adds, "does not fall until well into the syllable succeeding the loud-stressed one."**

---

*Cf. also Trager's "The theory of accentual systems," *Language, Culture, and Personality,* ed. by Leslie Spier, Wisconsin: Menasha, 1941, p. 132: "In the case of stress, all the emphasis is laid on physical considerations of loudness, and of the supposed "logical" consequences of such physical phenomena." Cf., moreover, p. 138: "There are pitch differences usually accompanying these stress differences, but they are not essential, and may vary greatly, while the stresses are determining and non-conditioned by pitch, length, or other factors. . . . The usual descriptions of this system, calling the stresses 'tones' and 'intonations,' miss the point that the element involved is stress, because they do not recognize the possibility of the existence of stress contours."

**Trager's presentation of prosodic details is supplemented by several distributional rules some of which radically depart from the observations of all other investigators. He claims, for example, that "every word of more than three syllables must have rising stress but no word may have more than one rising stress." This apodictic rule places Trager's rising stress on thousands of Serbo-Croatian words which traditionally are denoted by falling accent, e.g.,

Vukovian	Trager	
Cărigradanin	Cárigradanin	
Vȋnkōvčāni	Vȋ·nko·vča·ni	
zâmjenica	zá·mjenica	etc.

Trager's insistence on the phonemic role of loudness in contrast to Jakobson's emphasis on tone has its echoes in several more recent studies of Serbo-Croatian accents. In 1958 Hodge in his investigation of prosody in Serbo-Croatian utterances ("Serbo-Croatian stress and pitch") concluded that Serbo-Croatian has three degrees of stress and four pitch phonemes:

> "There are three degrees of stress in Serbo-Croatian: weak (here unmarked), secondary /'/ and primary /'/. There are four pitch phonemes: low /1/, mid /2/, high /3/ and extra-high /4/. Each utterance consists of one or more phonemic phrases. Each such phrase contains at least one primary stress...." (p. 43).

In addition, Hodge analyzes long vowels in Serbo-Croatian as double vowels so that his entire graphical representation differs strikingly from the traditional notation, e.g.

Vukovian	Hodge
razùmēm	$^2ra^3z\acute{u}m\acute{e}^1em$
da plâtīm	$^2da^3pl\acute{a}^1atiim$

Essentially the same approach underlies Bidwell's observations about accent in Serbo-Croatian. "If one accepts Hodge's analysis of long vowels as double vowels," he writes, " 'rising tone' may be analyzed as a double stress extending over two syllables (in some cases a single stress on the second half of a long vowel, while 'falling tone' is a single stress on the first half if the vowel is long."[3] Bidwell, however, does not insist that such a solution is the only possible one. "If," he continues, "one regards long vowels as units however, it is necessary to posit at least one additional phoneme, namely a phoneme of rising tone." Thus, in his first phonemic

---

[3] Charles E. Bidwell, *Slavic Historical Phonology in Tabular Form*, The Hague: Mouton & Co., 1963, p. 18.

solution Bidwell emphasizes the phonological role of stress while in his second solution he raises tone to a phonemic status.

3. PLACE OF ACCENT

August Leskien in his *Grammatik der serbo-kroatischen Sprache* (p. 123) uses geminated letters to denote the word's accented vowel, whether long or short, and in this way, divides the syllable carrying the accent into two fractions. Two semi-circles or dots over the double-letter specify length and shortness respectively. The difference between falling and rising accent is indicated by the position of the *gravis*; it is placed over the first letter (i.e. the initial fraction of the accented syllable) to denote the Vukovian falling accent whereas rising accent is denoted by the *gravis* placed over the second letter (i.e. terminal fraction of the accented syllable) e.g.,

Vukovian	Leskien
grâd	*grȁăd*
rúka	*rŭŭka*
krăva	*krààva*
žèna	*žèèna*

Since Leskien is not concerned with the phonological primacy of tone over stress or stress over tone, he assumes that both pitch and loudness participate in falling as well as in rising accents and sees the difference in the position of accent within the syllable, that is, whether the initial or the terminal fraction is accented.

The interpretation of falling and rising accents in terms of the accentual position within the syllabic structure also plays a prominent role in the study of Leskien's student Leonhard Masing, *Die*

PHONOLOGICAL INTERPRETATIONS 27

Hauptformen des serbisch-chorwatischen Accents (1876). In Masing's interpretation, "rising tone" presupposes two successive syllables and is, therefore, denoted by two diacritics (two dots) in distinction to the monosyllabic falling accent which is denoted by one diacritic (a vertical line), e.g.

Vukovian	Leskien	Masing
nȍsīm	nòòsīm	nǒsīm
dònosīm	dòònosīm	dǒnǒsīm
gláva	glǎǎva	glāvà
prâvda	prǎǎvda	prāvda
màgla	mààgla	mǎglǎ
slȁma	slààma	slǎma
ȍrao	òòrao	ǒrao
òrao	òòrao	ǒrǎo

The rising tone of bisyllabic accent is explained by its dependence on the falling component; therefore, it is considered to be secondary in distinction to the falling tone, the primary one.* Hence, Masing's interpretation is exactly opposite to Jakobson's and Trubetzkoy's claim that only rising accent in Serbo-Croatian is independent, free and functionally relevant in distinction to falling accent which can occur on the first syllable only and is, therefore, predictable and phonologically redundant.

---

*Cf. p. 92: "Der fallende Ton is also, principiell betrachtet, der bestimmende, der steigende aber der abhängige, secundäre Bestandtheil des serb.-chorw. Accents."

4. PHONOLOGICAL RELEVANCE OF THE ACCENTUAL POSITION

After more than one century the bisyllabic character of rising accent and its graphic representation as well as the role of the first and second fraction of the accented syllable still continue to stimulate both phonetic and phonological investigations of Serbo-Croatian accent.

Pavle Ivić in his "Prozodijski sistem srpskohrvatskog standardnog jezika" (1965) considers only place of accent and quantity as phonologically relevant in Contemporary Standard Serbo-Croatian (p. 136). According to his interpretation, there are not four accents but only a single one with two positional variants, the initial, traditionally called "falling," and the medial, called "rising." The initial variant appears within one syllable and is therefore monosyllabic, whereas the medial variant is bisyllabic since its implementation requires two successive syllables. This single accentual phenomenon with two variants is called by Ivić "cardinal point of height." In his view it is basically of tonal nature while intensity (loudness), which is typical of dynamic stress, may appear as a concomitant factor (p. 137).

According to Ivić, a vowel under short accent, whether it is traditionally called rising or falling, neither rises nor falls; the tonal contrast between them is displayed only if the successive syllable is taken into account: in the case of "short falling accent," the pitch of the successive syllable is considerably lower, whereas the pitch of the syllable following "short rising accent" is almost the same or only slightly higher (p. 136). Thus the accentual difference is viewed as a contrast between two syllables rather than a contrast within the syllable initiating the accent. It follows that the accentual difference between *màgla* and *slàma*, explained by Daničić in terms of the different pronunciation of the first *a* in each word, would be explained by Ivić in terms of the contrast between the first and the second *a* in each word.

As far as "long falling accent" is concerned, the basic contrast between two successive syllables has, according to Ivić, a supplementary feature in a sharp decline in the terminal fraction of the first syllable in distinction to the "long rising accent" which gently and gradually rises (p. 136). In both cases, however, the contrast between two successive syllables is considered by Ivić as more important than the accentual characteristics of a single syllable nucleus.

Ivić's phonological interpretation is based on a meticulous acoustic-phonetic investigation executed in cooperation with the instrumental phonetician Ilse Lehiste. The first report on this investigation (*Accent in Serbocroatian*) explicitly states that it was "impossible to locate the distinctive characteristics of accent within the syllable nucleus traditionally assumed to carry the accent." (p. 131). According to the author's findings, "the fundamental frequency movement within the short accented syllable appeared completely redundant." "There was," as they put it, "very little difference between the phonetic quality of the realizations of stressed vowels with rising and falling accents." (p. 87). In their view, "the feature which was constantly present and appeared to carry the main burden of distinction was the relationship between the stressed and the posttonic syllable." (p. 132). Thus, the traditional names as well as descriptions of Serbo-Croatian accent were in many respects actually found to contradict the phonetic reality registered by the spectrograph. The short rising accent did not appear as either rising or quantitatively distinct from short falling accent which in turn did not appear falling at all. The traces burned on the spectrogram paper by the stylus provided data, the interpretation of which runs counter to the conclusions of the founding fathers of the four accents in Serbo-Croatian. Together with the traditional interpretation of Serbo-Croatian accents the authors also flatly rejected Jakobson's attempt to describe Serbo-Croatian accent in terms of prosodic features dividing any vowels, as well as *r*, into four distinctive varieties: high-toned long, high-toned short, low-toned long and low-toned short. In their view, "the treatment of the long accents as high and low tones appears equally unwarranted as in the case of short accents." (p. 132).

Moreover, the acoustic-phonetic analysis by Lehiste and Ivić concludes with the claim that "in a hierarchy of suprasegmental features, duration is presently more significant than either intensity or fundamental frequency." (p. 134). In fact, this observation about the role of duration is projected by the authors into the history of the neo-štokavian accent shift. In their view, "the phonological nature of the accent shift, which was obviously a complex process, seems to have consisted largely of a change in the relative duration and in the relative importance of duration in the hierarchy of the suprasegmental system. . . . " (p. 134).

In accordance with his view about the phonological role of place of accent and quantity, Ivić marks only the place of accent (by a vertical line) and quantity (by a horizontal line). The vertical line is always placed on the syllabic border: it denotes monosyllabic accent ("falling" in Vukovian terminology) if it is placed initially; in all other positions, it denotes bisyllabic accent ("rising" in Vukovian terminology), unless the case is somewhat special. Thus *Brána : brâna : bràna : Bräna*, used by Peco as a proof of the phonological status of the four accents in Standard Serbo-Croatian, would be distinguished by Ivić by means of a single accent in its two positional variants and by the difference in quantity, e.g., *Brā'na : 'brāna : bra'na : 'Brana*.

As far as the shift of accent on the proclitics or its absence is concerned, Ivić's graphic representation ("Prozodijski sistem," p. 139) distinguishes both variants, e.g.,

	Vukovian	Ivić
unshifted	*na vȍdu*	*na'vodu*
shifted	*nȁ vodu*	*'na vodu*
unshifted	*na sȁblju*	*na 'sablju*
shifted	*nȁ sablju*	*na'-sablju*

Since the unaccented proclitic is considered to be a dependent part of the following accented form, Ivić's vertical line, preceded by a space and the unaccented proclitic, actually denotes monosyllabic ("falling") accent in the medial position. Ivić's monosyllabic ("falling") accent also has to be used medially if it denotes superlatives which in Vukovian notation appear as *nâjdônjī, nâjbôljī,* various compounds such as *poljoprĭvreda, samoùprava, Jugoslâvija* as well as forms such as *Austrâlija, komunĭst, agitâtor,* etc.

An acoustic-phonetic analysis was also used as a basis for the phonological interpretation of Serbo-Croatian accent by Peter Rehder (*Beiträge*). His phonetic description of the spectrographic data are essentially parallel to the measuring executed by Lehiste and Ivić. He also found that fundamental frequency, underlying tonal difference, was more relevant than intensity underlying the difference in stress. Nevertheless, his phonological conclusions differ substantially from Ivić's concept of place of accent and of the two positional variants: monosyllabic and bisyllabic. While Ivić and Lehiste put a special emphasis on the claim that the Serbo-Croatian word accents "have a larger domain that the stressed syllable nucleus" (p. 133), Rehder insists that a single syllable nucleus is in fact the domain of the phonological distinction between tonal rise and fall (p. 189). The distinction is viewed by him not as a syntagmatic contrast but as a paradigmatic polar opposition so that, in fact, he interprets the prosodic characteristics as inherent features, presupposing that the feature *in praesentia* is distinguishable from its opposing member *in absentia*. Rehder's systematization in terms of binary opposition of rising and falling features strongly resembles Malmberg's interpretation of Swedish accent. Malmberg is also convinced that "the intensity difference, even if there is one in most cases, is not sufficient to function as the basis for word accent distinctions."[4] And, therefore, he is inclined "to regard the place of the peak within the stressed vowel and the direction of the melody curve (mainly falling or rising) which follows this difference, as the distinctive feature for word accent opposition."[5] At the same time, Malmberg explicitly rejects the bisyllabic theory which regards the intensity of the postaccentual syllable as

---

[4] B. Malmberg, *Structural Linguistics and Human Communication*, Berlin: Springer, 1967, p. 108.
[5] *Ibid.*, p. 109.

an essential feature of the word accent. "Linguistically untrained people," he stated in this connection, "often speak of different stress on the second syllable of the word when they are asked to characterize the difference they make between two words differing in accent."[6]

5. OTHER TYPOGRAPHIC ARRANGEMENTS

The role of two successive syllables in the explanation of Serbo-Croatian accent clearly dominates the typographic rearrangement of the Vukovian heritage by Browne and McCawley.[7] Pursuing Masing's observations from 1876 about the bisyllabic character of rising accent, the authors radically depart from all other notations by denoting only the second of the two involved syllables, e.g. rūk-'a [Vukovian rúka]. Thus the neo-štokavian shift is graphically reversed into its pre-shifted stage. Falling accent remains unmarked unless it is changeable into rising accent by the shift on the proclitic: in such a case it is denoted on the first syllable. Consequently, there are two types of word with "falling" accent, unmarked or marked on the first syllable, while "rising" accent is never marked on the first syllable of the accented form. The following table provides a comparison of the Browne-McCawley notation with that of Vuk-Daničić, Jakobson and Ivić.

Vukovian	Jakobson	Ivić	Browne-McCawley
đȁvo	davo	'davo	davo
brȁt	brat	'brat	br'at
ȍd davola	od davola	'od davola	od-davola
òd brata	¦od brata	od'-brata	od-br'ata

[6]*Ibid.*, p. 108.
[7]E. W. Browne and J. D. McCawley, "Srpskohrvatski akcenat," *Zbornik za filologiju i lingvistiku* 8(1965), pp. 147-151.

Although Browne-McCawley's marking technique accurately denotes the possibility of the accentual shift and its consequences, it is not equipped to denote the absence of the expected shift.[8] Thus Browne-McCawley's ingenious systematization is actually anachronistic and more suitable to describe Serbo-Croatian in the school-manuals than Serbo-Croatian used by the majority of contemporary speakers of Serbo-Croatian. Thus, for example, the application of Browne-McCawley's notation in *na-j'ezeru, pred-K'ārlōvcima, u-l'ādicima* is valid only for the forms with shifted accent, which would appear in Vukovian notation as *nà jezeru, prèd Kārlōvcima, ù lādicima,* but not for the much more frequent forms *na jȅzeru, pred Kârlōvcima, u lâdicima.*

In a letter to the authors Browne suggests that a juncture marker #, placed between the proclitic and the following accented form, would take care of the unshifted variant (e.g., #Od#br'ata#, #Od#boga#). "This means," he writes, "that the semi-separated words get no accent of its own, but nevertheless doesn't function as a part of the main word as far as the rules for assigning and interpreting are concerned." This looks like a reasonable provision, but it would cause hopeless ambiguity if it were applied to the case such as

    Vukovian   Browne-McCawley

1. *oko dȁvola*   #*oko*#*davola*# ('around the devil')

2. *ȍko dȁvola*   #*oko*#*davola*# ('the eye of the devil')

Moreover, there would be numerous problems in denoting, for example, *nâjgôrnjī* 'the highest,' *nâjbȍljī,* 'the best,' *poljoprȋvreda,* 'agriculture,' *primoprȅdaja,* 'transmission,' *samoùprava,* 'self-management,' *Jugoslávija,* 'Yugoslavia,' *studȅnt,* 'student,' *lingvȉst,* 'linguist,' *komunȉst,* 'communist,' *diletȁnt,* 'diletante.'[9] It is

---

[8]This deficiency was also noted by Bidwell; see Charles E. Bidwell, "Accent Patterns of the Serbo-Croatian Noun," *Folia Linguistica* II, 1/2, p. 22, ftn. 7.

[9]Cf. Magner ("Post-Vukovian Norms"), p. 232.

apparent that a juncture or rather a system of junctures would solve certain deficiencies of Browne-McCawley's notation but many forms, daily used in Contemporary Serbo-Croatian, would have to be "swept under the rug" to retain the brilliant design.

P. Garde's analytic notation of Serbo-Croatian accent is also beset with problems caused by "falling" accent and its interpretation. In his paper "Les propriétés accentuelles des morphèmes serbo-croates," Garde marks "rising" (bisyllabic) accent on the second of the two affected syllables, while "falling" (monosyllabic) accent is marked on the initial syllable of the accentual unit, whether the accent turns by *skakanje* into rising accent or falling, e.g.

Vukovian	Browne-McCawley	Garde
grâdu (D sg.)	*grādu*	*gra̍du* (p. 157)
bràta	*br'ata*	*bra̍ta* (p. 160)

In his book *Accent* (1968) Garde explicitly claims that the real carrier of rising (bisyllabic) accent is the second of the two involved syllables while the first syllable carries only an echo. Thus Garde, in distinction to the traditional view, assumes that 1) the last syllable of the word in Standard Serbo-Croatian can bear accent, 2) the first syllable cannot bear rising accent although it can carry falling accent or an echo of rising accent, and that 3) a long vowel can precede an accented vowel in Contemporary Standard Serbo-Croatian. Since Vukovian *bràta* (G sg.) and *grâdu* (D sg.) are denoted in Grade's predictive typography as *bra̍ta* and *gra̍du,* the shift on the proclitic in accordance with Garde's general rule produces the acceptable form *òd brata* but the faulty ('non-grammatical') form *okò grāda* while the current forms which in Vukovian notation would appear as *òko grāda* or *oko grȃda* cannot be denoted by Garde's graphical provision at all. Thus, Garde's notation is not only inadequate for marking the absence of the expected shift but in many instances it is bound to generate an accentuation which is impossible in any kind of Serbo-Croatian whether standard, substandard or regional.

Regardless of various degrees of exactness, all analytic notations, which distinguish monosyllabic and bisyllabic accent in Serbo-Croatian, are primarily concerned with the difference in the position of the accent within the syllabic structure of the word (or morpheme) and within the accentual unit comprising more than one word (or morpheme). Accordingly, the accentual modifications are interpreted as concomitant characteristics and not as autonomous values (i.e. phonemes). In fact, McCawley and Browne do not employ the concept of phoneme at all while Garde includes into the phonemic inventory of Standard Serbo-Croatian only quantity but not accent. In his view the Serbo-Croatian vowel phonemes display quantitative opposition which makes it possible to identify paradigmatically a short vowel in the absence of its long counterpart whereas Serbo-Croatian accent can be identified only syntagmatically by means of a contrast juxtaposing a syllable (or mora) with the rest.[10] Thus Vukovian *pàs* ("dog") and *pâs* ("belt") would be considered by Garde to represent a minimal pair which displays a quantitative opposition of inherent features. On the other hand, Vukovian *òrao* ('he plowed') vs. *òrao* ('eagle') would be interpreted as two phonemically identical strings which are accented in different places and do not represent a minimal pair at all.[11]

The traditional interpretation, following Vuk-Daničić, would see the difference between *òrao* and *òrao* in the ability of the Serbo-Croatian speaker to pronounce the initial *o* in *òrao* differently than the initial *o* in *òrao*; accordingly, the hearer is expected to distinguish *ò* from *ò* and from all other vowels on the basis of the acoustic correlates of the articulatory distinctions. In Garde's interpretation, however, *òrao* and *òrao* would be phonemically identical and different only accentually by the fact that in each of

---

[10] ... l'accent, qui se caractérise par son unicité dans une unité grammaticale donnée correspondant à peu près au 'mot,' a pour rôle d'établir à l'interieur de chaque mot un contraste sur le plan syntagmatique entre une syllable (ou une more) et toutes les autres," P. Garde, "Fonctions des oppositions tonales dans les langues slaves du Sud," *Bulletin de la Société de Linguistique de Paris* 61 (1966), p. 42.

[11] Cf. P. Garde, "La fonction contrastive de l'accent," *Accent*, Paris: Presses Universitaires de France, 1968, pp. 3-11.

them a different syllable bears the accent so that each of them displays a different contrast between accented and unaccented syllables (i.e. òrao vs. orȁo = 1. the initial syllable is accented in contrast to the two following syllables, vs. 2. the medial syllable is accented in contrast to the initial and final syllables.)

The attempts to interpret accent in Standard Serbo-Croatian in terms of accentual position focus on the fact that each word in Standard Serbo-Croatian normally has only one primary accent regardless of the number of syllables so that the accented syllable (or its fraction) appears in contrast to all other syllables of the word (or accentual unit). Those who are convinced that tone is the dominant characteristic of Serbo-Croatian accent view, in effect, the accented syllable (or its fraction) as the highest one, higher than all other syllables of the entire accented unit; on the other hand those who feel that Serbo-Croatian accent is dominated by stress implicitly interpret the accented fraction as the loud*est* (strong*est*) one, louder (stronger) than the rest of the entire accented unit. Thus, accent is conceived as the *superlative* value (of frequency and/or intensity) assigned to a specific position in each accentual unit and expected to be interpreted accordingly.*

Since the accented fraction does not necessarily coincide with the domain of a single segmental phoneme, any discussion of accentual position involves the notion of the syllable (or the mora), of its nucleus and boundaries, and also the very concept of the accentual unit (i.e. whether the accentual unit embraces one word or morpheme or more than one word). Implicitly, therefore, morphological and syntactic considerations become an essential part of those accentual studies which focus on the place of the accent. In most of such studies the graphic re-interpretation of the four

---

*Cf. H. G. Lunt, "On the Study of Slavic Accentuation," *Word* 19 (1963), pp. 84-85: "For the most part the languages in question can be treated—descriptively and historically—in terms of the three features called tone, force and quantity (or voice-pitch, voice-loudness and subjective duration, with the physical correlates of frequency, intensity and time . . .) . . . it seems worth while to repeat what ought to be obvious, that these are not the inherent features observable in a minute vertical slice of a spectrogram that practically speaking represents no time factor, but rather the features whose very definition requires comparison of two or more fractions along the time axis. A given fraction is high*er*, strong*er* or long*er* than another fraction."

Vukovian accents is primarily motivated by the need to simplify the description of the accent in its grammatical role in the entire system and particularly in the inflectional and derivational processes. In fact, in the majority of recent accentual studies, the entire emphasis has been on the re-interpretation rather than the verification of the Vukovian four accents: the century-old accentual norms are taken at face value without any systematic effort to determine their relevance to contemporary usage. And yet even a cursory reading of the activities and methods of Vuk and Daničić will suffice to show that the Vukovian accentual codes contain a large component of impressionistic phonetics. Prescriptive grammarians and language-planners have been trying for more than a century to impose the Vukovian system on the Serbo-Croatian language; they have succeeded magnificently in implanting it in dictionaries, textbooks, grammars and reference manuals. The Vukovian system has a textbook reality; whether it exists among the speakers of Serbo-Croatian is a basic question which demands the attention of all scholars interested in Slavic and/or Serbo-Croatian accentology.

CHAPTER THREE

HISTORY OF THE SERBO-CROATIAN WORD ACCENT

> *Nach meiner Überzeugung wird man mit der slavischen Lautlehre nicht gut weiter kommen, wenn man nicht die Quantitäts- und Betonungslehre des Serbischen energisch bearbeitet . . . Die Erkenntniss würde oft erleichtert, manche Zweifel leichter gehoben, wenn man nicht fast ausschliesslich mit Vuks Aufzeichnungen zu arbeiten hätte. So ausgezeichnet sie sind, so ist es doch selbstverständlich, dass nicht ein Mann alle Manningfaltigkeit eines grossen Sprachgebietes kennen und beherrschen konnte.*
> *August Leskien*

The Vukovian system of Serbo-Croatian accentuation played a pivotal role not only in synchronic studies of modern Serbo-Croatian but also, as Leskien clearly shows, in diachronic investigations of Serbo-Croatian in its relationship to Proto-Slavic, to Balto-Slavic and/or to Indo-European.[1]

---

[1] August Leskien, *Untersuchungen*, 1893, p. 610. See also Ivić (*Die serbokroatischen Dialekte*, p. 11): "The Serbo-Croatian dialects have long commanded the attention not only of Yugoslav linguistics but also of foreign linguistics because of the importance the Serbo-Croatian dialects have both from a Slavic as well as a general linguistic standpoint. It is well known how much the comparative grammar of the Slavic languages and the study of linguistic structures have from the beginning relied on the material of Serbo-Croatian dialects."

The nineteenth century comparativists generally interpreted word accent in Serbo-Croatian as a relic of extreme importance for the reconstruction of the Indo-European linguistic past. Karl Brugmann in his famous comparative compendium emphasized the striking similarities between accentuation systems preserved in the South Slavic languages and Russian on the one hand[2] and Lithuanian on the other. In his view, "Lithuanian and a part of the Slavic languages show freedom of accentuation, and there can be no doubt that this method of accentuation extends back to Proto-Baltic and Proto-Slavic."[3]

Hermann Hirt goes even further: "The Lithuanian accent," he says, "is often in harmony with the proto-Slavic accent and there can be no doubt that this Lithuanian-Slavic accentuation corresponds in part to the Indo-European. . . ."[4] With regard to comparative studies, he considered Serbo-Croatian especially valuable:

> "Serbo-Croatian provides for our task the richest material, since it contains the old accent relationships practically unaltered. It allows us not only to determine the place of accent but also to ascertain all the types of accent from the changes in quantity, thereby yielding practically complete agreement with Lithuanian."[5]

Such observations about the striking similarities between the Serbo-Croatian and Lithuanian word accent led to the postulation of the Balto-Slavic linguistic family as an intermediate stage between the disintegration of the Indo-European proto-language and the autonomous development of the Slavic and Baltic branches. The concept of a common Balto-Slavic proto-language, however, was rejected by Antoine Meillet and his followers. Meillet was

---

[2] "The languages of special importance are the South Slavic languages (Serbian-Croatian-Slovenian and Bulgarian) and the Russian dialects. These represent on the whole the prim. Slavic accentuation." K. Brugmann, *Elements of the Comparative Grammar of the Indo-Germanic Languages,* New York: Westermann, 1888, p. 561.

[3] *Ibid.,* p. 556.

[4] H. Hirt, *Der Indogermanische Akzent,* Strassburg: Trübner, 1895, p. 55.

[5] *Ibid.,* p. 75.

willing to admit that Baltic and Slavic underwent parallel development and that such parallelism has as a natural consequence the creation of a few identical forms but, according to his view, "those innovations do not point to any period of common development."[6] "Baltic and Slavic," he emphasizes in his survey of Indo-European dialects, "provide a fine example of two parallel, but long autonomous developments."[7] And he adds in the footnote: "Moreover, there is no decisive proof that there was ever a Balto-Slavic national unity comparable to the unity of Indic and Iranian."[8]

In accordance with this view Meillet tried to study Serbo-Croatian word accent and the Slavic prosodic characteristics without postulating an intermediate Balto-Slavic stage. In 1908 he wrote: "In spite of the very numerous deviations which have in part been explained, the accent of certain Baltic and Slavic dialects still reflect the Indo-European tone."[9] Later, in 1915, he elaborated on this thesis with the following statement:

"Each independent word in Common Slavic had one syllable which differed from the others and which is represented today by the accented syllables of Russian and Serbo-Croatian (with regular displacements). This accent could fall on any syllable of the word. In a bisyllabic word, it could be either on the first syllable or on the second. Thus, we have:

Russian	Serbo-Croatian	Bulgarian
gríva "mane"	grȉva	gríva
vodá "water"	vòda (from vodȁ, maintained in Čakavian)	vodá

This phenomenon alone would lead us to assume that the Slavic accent is the successor of the Indo-European tone. Furthermore, the place of the Slavic

---

[6]Antoine Meillet, *The Indo-European Dialects,* Alabama: Univ. of Alabama Press, 1967, p. 65.
[7]*Ibid.,* p. 67.
[8]*Ibid.*
[9]*Introduction à l'étude comparative des langues indo-européennes,* Paris: Hachette, 1908, p. 114.

HISTORY 41

accent corresponds to that of Greek and Vedic tone, as in Russian *nébo,* "heaven," S-Cr. *nëbo* which agrees with Sanskrit *nábhah,* Greek νέφος. If a correspondence is often lacking, it is because in many cases phonetic and morphological changes have displaced the tone."[10]

Meillet's doubts about the Balto-Slavic linguistic unity and his attempt to link the Slavic linguistic development directly to the Indo-European proto-language became one of the outstanding topics of the comparative disputes in the twentieth century.[11] The most outspoken rejection of Meillet's concept was formulated by Jerzy Kuryłowicz who reached the conclusion that the Slavic and Baltic intonation systems are not inherited from Indo-European but are descendants of a prosodic system which was established first during the Balto-Slavic common period:

"There is no historical connection between Baltic and Greek tones. Neither of the two systems was inherited from the Indo-European epoch."[12]

Thus, the interpretation of Serbo-Croatian word accent and of Baltic and Slavic prosodic characteristics divided the community of comparativists into several camps deriving word-accent either directly from Indo-European without any special Balto-Slavic stage

---

[10] *Le slave commun,* 2nd. ed. revised by A. Vaillant, Paris: Librairie ancienne Honoré Champion, 1934, p. 159.

[11] See Porzeziński, *Rocznik slawistyczny* 4, 1911, p. 1: "Since the beginnings of comparative linguistics the assumption has been held that Baltic and Slavic form a very special unity within the family of Indo-European languages. The many analogies and correspondences in the linguistic development of (Baltic and Slavic) speech seemed to provide eloquent testimony for this assumption and thus the earlier existence of a Balto-Slavic language came to be viewed as an established fact." See also J. Rozwadowski, *Rocznik slawistyczny* 5, 1912, p. 1: "The problem of the mutual relationship of the Baltic and Slavic languages . . . no longer existed in Indo-European linguistics since the time these languages have been thoroughly studied. Thus, it was ascertained many years ago that both these groups form within the boundaries of and among the Indo-European languages a more precise entity, a group of a higher order; that is to say, at one time there existed a so-called Balto-Slavic proto-language which was spoken by the linguistic ancestors of the historical Balts and Slavs and out of which in the course of time two linguistic types came to stand apart: the Proto-Slavic and the Proto-Baltic."

[12] "L'indépendance historique des intonations baltiques et grecques," *Bulletin de la Société de linguistique de Paris* 35, 1934, p. 33.

or from Indo-European via Balto-Slavic[13] or, finally, directly from Balto-Slavic without Indo-European.

Characteristic for the dispute is André Vaillant's response to Kuryłowicz's revolutionary conclusions, when he states:

"The tones of Greek and Balto-Slavic have the same Indo-European origin, still quite recognizable despite the changes which are hardly surprising since the phenomena (tones) are particularly unstable and since the languages developed independently."[14]

While Kuryłowicz considers the incompatibility of the Balto-Slavic and Greek prosodic systems to be the best proof that they do not reflect the accent of the common Indo-European proto-language,[15] Christian Stang insists on their mutual relationship and their Indo-European prosodic background.[16] Like Kuryłowicz, however, he emphasizes the striking parallel between Baltic and Slavic intonational systems and concludes: "It seems that the basis for the two old intonations—acute and circumflex—is the same in both groups of languages."[17] Still he does not view the Balto-Slavic base as a single proto-language: "By 'Balto-Slavic,' " he says, "I mean not an absolutely homogeneous language, but a dialectal area which is so homogeneous that it is capable of carrying through common linguistic changes. . . ."[18]

---

[13] Rajko Nahtigal, *Slovanski jeziki*, 2nd. edition, Ljubljana: Univerza v Ljubljani, 1952, p. 19: "Common Slavic has inherited already from the Indo-European and Balto-Slavic period a qualitative musical accent consisting mainly of the rising and falling (peak of) tonality, similar to the Greek acute and circumflex. . . ."

[14] "Le problème des intonations Balto-Slaves," *Bulletin de la Société de linguistique de Paris* 37, 1936, p. 115.

[15] J. Kuryłowicz, *L'accentuation des langues indo-européennes*, Cracow: Polska Akademia nauk, 1958, p. 169: "Phonology furnished definite proof that there cannot be a question of two continuations of one and the same accentual system (Indo-European). If such a system existed, it cannot be demonstrated by historical languages. The incompatibility of the Balto-Slavic and Greek systems is the strongest argument for their recent and independent origins."

[16] Ch. S. Stang, *Slavonic Accentuation*, Oslo: Universitetsforlaget, 1957, p. 14: "I am in spite of all inclined to subscribe to the idea of a connection between the Baltic and the Greek intonations. . . ."

[17] *Ibid.*, p. 173.

[18] *Ibid.*, p. 174.

The assumption of a relatively recent origin of Slavic intonations was most skeptically received by Illič-Svityč who summarized his own observations about Indo-European accentuation with a claim that certain parallel prosodic features in Baltic and Slavic languages could very well represent a surviving Indo-European archaism which was not preserved in the Indic and Greek prosodic systems.[19] In accordance with this view Serbo-Croatian word accent would be, in fact, a remarkable continuation of the most archaic stages of the Indo-European proto-language and as such it would actually represent a more precious relic than the nineteenth century comparativists had ever dared hope.

In his observations about Slavic prosody Shevelov is also in favor of linking Serbo-Croatian word accent to the Indo-European proto-language:

"Indo-European had quantitative opposition in vowels: length vs. brevity. . . . In addition, Common Slavic long vowels were characterized by certain pitch or tone patterns also called intonations. The two original types of pitch are still discernible in those modern Slavic languages which retain syllabic intonations as distinctive features of their phonemic systems: Serbo-Croatian and Slovenian."[20]

Although the controversy about the degree of antiquity of the Serbo-Croatian word accent still continues, there is almost general agreement that Serbo-Croatian word-accent is an archaic survival of the Proto-Slavic prosodic system. According to Roman Jakobson, "The Vukovian system of prosodic correlations is in its structure completely identical with the late Proto-Slavic system."[21] The footnote to this statement points out that this striking identity was suggested to Jakobson by Trubetzkoy himself.

An almost general agreement about the Proto-Slavic source of Serbo-Croatian word accent, however, did not discourage

---

[19] V. M. Illič-Svityč, *Imennaja akcentuacija v baltijskom i slavjanskom,* Moscow: Akademija Nauk, 1963, p. 162.

[20] Shevelov, *A Prehistory of Slavic,* Heidelberg: Winter, 1964, p. 38.

[21] R. Jakobson, "Die Betonung und ihre Rolle in der Wort- und Syntagmaphonologie," *Selected Writings,* I, 's Gravenhage: Mouton, 1962, p. 131.

Helmuth Lüdtke from making his own observations that the Proto-Slavic prosodic system actually does not survive in any contemporary Slavic language and that Serbo-Croatian word accent is, in fact, a late innovation which goes back neither to Proto-Indo-European nor to Proto-Balto-Slavic or Proto-Slavic but to early Serbo-Croatian in its development as an independent language.[22] In many respects, Lüdtke's speculations about the recent origin of Serbo-Croatian word accent bring to mind Kuryłowicz's revolutionary way of interpreting Balto-Slavic word-accent as an innovation rather than as an inheritance from the Indo-European protolanguage. Thus, if all theories are taken into account, Serbo-Croatian word accent can be either recent or ancient, either created during the autonomous stages of its development or inherited from Proto-Slavic which in turn inherited it either from Balto-Slavic and Indo-European or from Balto-Slavic without Indo-European or from Indo-European without Balto-Slavic.

1. COMPARATIVE OBSERVATIONS

The reconstruction of the Serbo-Croatian accent is usually based on the comparative evidence furnished by other Slavic languages. In this connection, the contemporary distribution of Russian word stress is considered to be a particularly good indicator of the original accentual position, Slovenian word-accent is used to demonstrate that the South Slavic accentual development produced different results in some areas, and modern Czech quantitative distinctions are cited to show how the old tonal differences developed in some instances into distinctions in vowel quantity. The mutual

---

[22] H. Lüdtke, "Das prosodische System des Urslavischen und seine Weiterentwicklung im Serbokroatischen," *Phonetica* 4 (supplement), 1959, p. 153: "By a comparison with Lithuanian, and by comparing the evidence of Serbo-Croat, Czech, and Russian it is possible to reconstruct the older Proto-Slavonic prosodic system, which includes stress, quantity, and two distinct tones (acute : circumflex) in long syllables.—This system is not continued in any of the modern Slavonic languages, not even in Serbo-Croat—contrary to what has been held hitherto. Wherever tone correlations are found today (i.e. Serbo-Croat, Slovenian, Slovincian), they are an outcome of later and separate development."

relationship of various prosodic characteristics is best displayed in connection with the process of opening the old closed syllables based on diphthongs ending in a liquid (i.e. TårT/TerT/TålT/TelT). This process resulted in pleophony in Russian and other East Slavic dialects (i.e. Tårt > ToroT); on the other hand, in the South Slavic and southern West Slavic dialects it produced liquid metathesis combined with vowel lengthening (i.e. Tårt > TraT, etc.). The Russian pleophonic sequence can carry word accent either on the first vowel (e.g. T́oroT) or on the second vowel (e.g. Toŕ oT); the first situation is said to reflect the proto-Slavic circumflex (also called "falling pitch," "Schleifton," or "intonation douce"), whereas the second situation is assumed to show a reflex of the proto-Slavic acute (also called "rising pitch," "Stosston" or "intonation rude"). In corresponding examples Czech usually has short and long vowels respectively while Slovenian developed falling accent in the first situation and rising accent in the second situation. Serbo-Croatian, however, usually has long falling accent and short falling accent respectively in such situations. In other words, the ancient tonal difference between proto-Slavic circumflex and acute was not actually preserved in Serbo-Croatian but rather developed into a quantitative difference, e.g.

PROTO-SLAVIC	SERBO-CROATIAN	SLOVENIAN	CZECH	RUSSIAN
CIRCUMFLEX	vrân "raven"	vrân	(ha)vran	vóron
ACUTE	vrȁna "crow"	vrána	vrána	voróna
CIRCUMFLEX	brêg "hill" (jekavian brȉjeg)	brêg	břeh	béreg
ACUTE	brȅza "birch"	bréza	bříza	berëza (= ber'óza)

Thus, in Serbo-Croatian the proto-Slavic acute yielded a short falling accent which came into *quantitative* opposition with the long falling accent derived from the proto-Slavic circumflex, e.g.

PS ACUTE > SC ˝ vs. SC ˆ < PS CIRCUMFLEX

There are, however, certain cases where the Standard Serbo-Croatian long falling accent corresponds to Slovenian rising accent, Czech length and Russian stress on the second vowel of the pleophonic sequence. Moreover, in corresponding cases some čakavian, kajkavian and štokavian (Slavonian) dialects display a special type of long rising accent which dialectologists (following Ivšić) denote by ˜, e.g.,

Standard SC	Čakavian	Slovenian	Czech	Russian
krâlj "king"	krãlj	králj	krāl	koról'

These particular reflexes are usually interpreted as an inheritance from a special proto-Slavic neo-acute which originated in late proto-Slavic as a consequence of accentual retraction in connection with the development of the reduced vowels (i.e., "jers").[23] In Serbo-Croatian dialects the reflexes of the proto-Slavic neo-acute came into tonal opposition with the long falling accent derived from the proto-Slavic circumflex, e.g.

PS NEO-ACUTE > SC ˜ vs. SC ˆ < PS CIRCUMFLEX

Historical dialectology usually considers the Serbo-Croatian rising reflex of the Proto-Slavic neo-acute to be an archaic feature which in the past had characterized the common base of Serbo-Croatian dialects. Subsequently, however, the rising reflex of the Proto-Slavic neo-acute merged with the long falling accent in the

[23]Cf. Stang, *Slavonic Accentuation*, pp. 21-22: "Neo-acute on a long vowel is only represented in Čakavian, Kajkavian and certain archaic Štokavian dialects by a separate intonation, differing both from the old acute, which had been shortened, and from the circumflex. This is the intonation which in Čakavian is symbolized by ´: *pĩšeš, krãlj*, and which Ivšić in his description of the Posavina dialect and Kajk. dialects has symbolised by ˜."

HISTORY 47

majority of štokavian dialects, including the Vukovian dialectal base, e.g.,

Proto-Slavic	Russian	Czech	Slovenian	Čakavian	Štokavian (Standard)
OLD ACUTE	voróna	vrāna	vrána	vrȁna	vrȁna
NEO-ACUTE	koról'	krāl	králj	krãlj	krâlj

Thus, these štokavian dialects transformed the tonal distinction between the rising accent (< PS neo-acute) and the falling accent (< PS circumflex/PS old acute) into quantitative distinctions while a new rising accent (which might be called a neo-neo-acute) developed as a consequence of a thoroughgoing accentual retraction in these same štokavian dialects. In this process the word accent, or at least its onset, moved onto the preceding syllable, thus producing a new rising accent, short or long depending on the quantity of that previously unaccented syllable,[24] e.g.

ACCENTUAL POSITION

PRESERVED Russian		PRESERVED Čakavian	RETRACTED Štokavian
vinó	"wine"	vīnȍ	víno
davát'	"to give"	dāvȁt	dávati
sestrá	"sister"	sestrȁ	sèstra[25]

An accent on the first syllable, which could not move, remained as a falling accent unless an adjacent proclitic provided the necessary

---

[24] Cf., Kuryłowicz, L'accentuation, p. 219: "The retraction of the accent from the second syllable of a word to the initial syllable produced on it a new rising tone, thus depriving the ancient rising tone of its phonological value in its distinction to the ancient falling tone. The new phonological opposition: falling tone (< ancient circumflex or ancient neo-acute) vs. rising tone (new) is now limited to the initial syllable."

[25] Cf. Shevelov, A Prehistory p. 41.

conditions for a shift and for a corresponding change, *brȁt*, "brother," *òd brata*.

This retraction of accents brought about a situation in which certain forms, once differentiated by the place of accent, are differentiated by tone in Standard Serbo-Croatian, e.g.

	BEFORE RETRACTION	AFTER RETRACTION	cf. Russian
G sg.	*selä*	*sèla*	*selá*
N pl.	*sëla*	*sëla*	*séla* (= *s'óla*)

Since all rising accents in Standard Serbo-Croatian result from this particular process of accent retraction (*prenošenje*), the tonal distinction between falling and rising accents, prescribed for Standard Serbo-Croatian, cannot actually be directly traced to any Proto-Slavic tonal distinction. As shown above, the Proto-Slavic tonal distinctions turned in Standard Serbo-Croatian into quantitative characteristics of the falling accent which appeared in tonal opposition to a new rising tone, developed only as a restricted local innovation, e.g.

PS CIRCUMFLEX/PS ACUTE/PS NEO-ACUTE > SC FALLING
vs. SC RISING < štokavian retraction

It is assumed that the process of accent retraction had taken place by the fifteen century though it could have taken place earlier. The transformation of the old reflexes and the retraction of accent was a complex process which apparently had several stages still traceable in contemporary Serbo-Croatian dialects, yet resisting an exact chronological specification because of the lack of written accentual records.[26] One of the crucial problems is the

---

[26] M. Moguš has set up four stages in order to present the development more precisely. See his article, "Za novu akcenatsku klasifikaciju u dijalektologiji," *Zbornik za filologiju i lingvistiku* X (1967), pp. 125-132. For a discussion of the accent-shifting process see M. Hraste, "O kanovačkom akcentu u Hrvatskoj," *Filologija* I (1957), pp. 71-74.

chronological relationship between the rise of the third acute (by means of retraction) and the merger of the rising reflex of Proto-Slavic neo-acute with long falling accent.

The problem is further complicated by the fact that tone, quantity and place of accent were subjected to differing developments in various dialectal areas so that, as Shevelov puts it, "in two adjacent villages, with otherwise identical phonemic systems, one dialect may have retained the historically inherited system of intonations while the other may have eliminated it completely."[27] In the last analysis perhaps the most satisfactory general statement about the background of the Serbo-Croatian accent is Belić's observation: "our accent contains in itself characteristics which it received in the Proto-Slavic epoch of its development and, in addition, it has characteristics which developed during the Yugoslav epoch. . . ."[28]

2. ACCENTUAL NOTATION IN EARLY WRITERS

The priest, Bartuo Kašić, who published his grammar of Serbo-Croatian in 1604, pointed out the importance of the accents in a passage which is worth quoting in full.*

"On Tone and Apostrophe

Since one cannot read clearly without tone or accent, their number must be set forth concisely. Essentially, there are three [accents].

1. Acute is designated by ´, [for example,] $\acute{a}$: its function and meaning are to raise the tone of the syllable over which it is placed.

2. Grave is designated by `, [for example,] $\grave{e}$: its function and meaning consist in lowering the tone of a syllable in such a way that where this accent appears the sound is deeper than where none appears. (Its use will demonstrate the truth of this statement better.) Jacob Gretserus notes this well in

---

[27] Shevelov, *A Prehistory*, p. 40.
[28] *Osnovi* I, p. 149.
*Kašić's remarks have been translated from the Latin original which appeared in Karl-Heinz Pollok, *Der neuštokavische Akzent und die Struktur der Melodiegestalt der Rede,* Göttingen: Vandenhoeck und Ruprecht, 1964, p. 141.

Chapter 22 of *Accents,* where he says δεὸς should not be read with the final syllable raised, as though it were δεός, but lowered. From that the distinction between the grave and acute accents is sufficiently clear; so we have [the grave accents] in the following words: *Sedlò,* 'saddle;' *Veslò,* 'oar,' and *Tìh,* 'calm.'

3. Protracted or circumflex has traditionally been designated by ˆ, [for example,] *ô:* its function and meaning is to indicate that one must raise and lengthen the tone either of a diphthong which is made up of two vowels or of a double vowel or of a syllable which retains the same pronunciation as a diphthong after one of the vowels has been left out, as in *Mnoox,* 'multitude;' *Meed,* 'honey,' or *Mnôx* and *Mêd.*

4. It must be kept in mind, however, that we sometimes place two accents in the same word, and sometimes not even one."

Kašić himself was a čakavian speaker from the island of Pag; this fact may explain such examples as *sedlò* (čakavian *sedlö,* standard S-Cr. *sèdlo* < *sedlö*). According to Ivšić (*Prilog,* p. 138), Kašić used the signs ˊ and ˝ indiscriminately to indicate long accents, e.g. *méso [mêso], mòst [môst].*

Đuro Daničić examined manuscripts and books produced in the early centuries (the 13th through the middle of the 17th) and found that accents were indicated in one or more of five possible ways: 1) by geminate vowels, 2) by geminate consonants, 3) with the accent mark ˋ, 4) with the accent mark ˊ, 5) with the accent mark ˆ (only in one work).[29] Not surprisingly, the marking of accents is not consistent in any particular writer nor is there any uniformity as between writers; what does impress the reader is that many of the writers were quite conscious of differences in vowel length, both under and after the place of accent. Here are some examples from two štokavian writers of the 17th century:[30]

Ivan Bandulavić (1613)

(˝) *krúh, stottina, vùna, mùdrost, nebbo, óko*
(ˋ) *ogganj, subbotta, zorra, immam, sello, gorre* [Gsg.]
(ˆ) *dán/dàn, glâs, grád, gráda* [Gsg.] , *ljúdi, súdaac, paas*

---

[29] Daničić, *Srpski akcenti,* p. 240.
[30] *Ibid.,* pp. 243-317.

HISTORY 51

(´)   národ, peetak, dúša, dánaa [Gpl. dánā] , ljúdij [Gpl. ljúdī] , sinóvaá [Gpl. sinóvā]

Jakov Mikalja (1649)

(῀)   gràd, gradda [Gsg.] , brat, bratta [Gsg.] , bák/bàk, babba, ribbár [rȉbār]
(`)   ječma, róbak, ròsa, muhha, suzza, slàgati
(ˆ)   bán, bóg, dúb/dùb, gráda [Gsg.] , krimák [kȓmāk]
(´)   sábor, súdac, gláva, slágati, vrríbá [Gpl. vŕbā] , kónjà [Gpl. kónjā]

In asking his readers not to conclude that the four accents did not exist in these documents just because on occasions both longs and short accents were indicated in the same way. Daničić says that these differences are not well indicated today [1872] and that even Vuk was not consistent in the matter of the accents. Thus,

". . . Vuk who founded our present method of accentuation completely differentiated between the two longs but ignored the difference between the two shorts (although he was well acquainted with the difference and wrote well about it) except in those words in which all the sounds are the same (jàrica = 'wheat,' jȁrica = young goat). He ignored this distinction between the shorts not only in the first edition of his dictionary (1818) but even in the second edition of his proverbs in 1849."[31]

The first writer to distinguish the four accents seems to have been Šime Starčević whose grammar appeared in the year 1812.[32] Starčević left the short fall unmarked, e.g. nebo [= nȅbo] , but used three signs for the other accents: ῀ for short rise, e.g. dobròta [= dobròta] , ` for long fall, e.g. glàs [– glȃs] , and ´ for long rise, e.g. písati [= písati] . To indicate postaccentual length he used his sign for long fall, e.g. mlàdi [= mlâdī] . His description of the accents is novel: the difference between the long fall and long rise is that the latter is longer in duration; he refers to tonal characteristics only in reference to the short rise which he describes as glas

---

[31] Ibid., p. 241.
[32] Cf. Vladimir Anić, "Akcenat u gramatici Šime Starčevića," Radovi, Razdio lingvističko-filološki (4), Zadar: Filozofski fakultet, 1968, pp. 70-71. See also Jakobson, "Die Betonung," p. 129f.

uzdignuti i barzo spuštani, "a sound raised and quickly lowered," which seems to combine a description of both the short rise and the short fall.

Vuk Karadžić in the grammatical foreword to his 1818 dictionary used for the first time the sign ˝ for the short falling accent. Vuk's early marks are not those of his later works and in this 1818 work are not without considerable ambiguity. His distinction between the two short accents (˝ ,ˋ) seems almost to be an afterthought and he uses it, not consistently, only to designate pairs such as *pȁra,* "steam," *pàra,* "money"; otherwise, a form such as *brat,* "brother," is marked as *bràt* (= *brȁt* in its later marking). One cannot help but wondering, though, how well actually Vuk perceived this distinction, *if at all.* If he was indeed conscious of the difference but, because of his experience with the insubstantiality or heterogeneity of the distinction over the Serbo-Croatian speech area, he deliberately did not "force" the distinction, then we may well praise him for not codifying a minor distinction.

In the grammatical sketch which appeared in the foreword to his 1818 dictionary Vuk made the following statements about accents:[33]

"In the Serbian language there are four different accents and here are the four marks designed for them: ˋ, ´, ˆ, ˝.

The first (ˋ) is on that letter, where the sound is pronounced sharply, e.g. *vòda, vràna, vùna, zèmlja, premètati, prèmetnuti, tìca, pìši, kr̀st, pr̀st,* etc.

The second (´) is on that letter, where the sound is actually drawn out, e.g. *grána, óvca, séka, rúka, víkati, dúša, ríkati, vesélje, tŕkati, sŕna,* etc.

The third (ˆ) is on that letter where the sound comes out round, e.g. *glâd, blâgo, têlo, bîr, sûnce, krûg, rôj, pâmtiti, tr̂n, kr̂v, tr̂k, cr̂njka,* etc.

The fourth (˝) is on that letter where the sound is so stretched out that the lengthening passes over even to the other letters which come after it [the first accented sound] , e.g. *nȃvo*; (and everywhere in the Gpl.) *deset ljȗdi, pet ovȃca, sviju nȃroda,* etc. . . .

In time grammars will specify the type and place of accents for words; but here we can give some additional information about the accents so that they can be correctly identified.

---

[33] *Srpski rječnik* (1818), photo-offset republication, Belgrade: Prosveta, 1966, p. xxxvi ff.

1) The articulation of the first sign (`) is double, which can especially be recognized in similar words, e.g. *bacati* is pronounced more sharply when it means *stechen* than when it means *werfen*; likewise *ora* is pronounced more sharply when it means *die rechte Zeit* than when it means *die Nuss*; likewise *jarica*, 'a young goat,' is pronounced more sharply than *jarica*, 'wheat,' etc. For that reason in such words I have placed two marks (") where the pronunciation is more sharp, as may be seen in [the items] *bacati, jarica, para*, etc.

2) With the third accent (̂) one must remember: a) whenever this accent is on a second, third or fourth syllable, then the sharp accent (`) can also be on a preceding syllable, e.g. *òvčâr, ràtâr, ràdôst, gospòdâr, gòtovljênje, goròpadnîk, vòjvodovânje*, etc. For that reason I have not everywhere placed the sharp accent on the first syllable when this accent [̂] is on the second, as for example *ovčar, ratar, rvač, radost, ranjenje, nošenje, motanje, gnjecovan, goletan, građanče*, etc. b) this accent is on the penultimate syllable of all words made from imperfective verbs with [the suffix] *nje*, e.g. *gòtovljênje, rijênje, vòjvodovânje*, etc. Thus in such words it would not be necessary to write this accent (since its occurrence is everywhere known), just as I have not indicated it in those words which have a preceding ´ accent, e.g. *písanje, strúganje, dosađívanje, otkupljívanje, ljúbljenje*, etc. c) one could really say this accent is double in those words where there are two in the same word, e.g. *pâmćênje, sûdîm, râdîm, šârâm, vêžêm*, etc. (in such verbs).

3) The fourth accent (̑) is also double, which can be most easily determined in similar words, e.g. *nas ima sedam druga* and *svaki imamo po deset lijepi druga* (spindles for weaving yarn): here in *deset lijepi druga* the sound is not as extended as in *sedam druga*, but rather is pronounced *drûgâ*; likewise in the pronunciation: *viđeli smo na nebu 10 dûga*, and *donijeli smo svaki po 10 kačni dûgâ; deset grâna*, and *dopao rânâ*, etc.

4) The accent does not remain the same on every syllable but changes, e.g. *vòda, vòde, vòdi, vòdu, vòdo, vòdom, vòdi, vòde, vôda, vòdama; sòkô, sokòle, sòkole; lònac, lónca* (but *rònac, rònca!*), *lônci, lônâcâ, lôncima; písati, pîšêm, písâše; jùnâk, junáka, jùnâče, junâka*, etc.

In his exposition of the accents and their use in the dictionary Vuk has been criticized on at least three scores:[34] 1) his restriction

---

[34] For an analysis of the virtues and deficiencies of Vuk's 1818 system of accentuation see Ljub. Stojanović, *Život i rad Vuka Stef. Karadžića*, Belgrade-Zemun: Makarije, 1924, pp. 131-132, 142-143; and Pavle Ivić, *Pogovor* in the 1966 reprint of Vuk's dictionary *(op. cit.)*, pp. 71-78.

of the use of the accent mark " to 'minimal' pairs, e.g. *pȁra, pàra,* while other words with that accent are marked with `, e.g. *vràna [vrȁna];* 2) his decision not to indicate the place of the ` accent when it was followed by ˉ, e.g. *Dubrȏvnik [Dùbrōvnīk], vekovânje [vekòvānje], budalisânje [budàlisānje], buljubašovânje [bùljubašovānje];* 3) the confusion resultant in his use of ^ and ˉ, e.g. *drȗga [drúgā], drūgá [drūgȃ];* the ambiguity of the sign ^ can be seen clearly by considering some of the genitive plural forms in Vuk's noun paradigms, e.g. *žȇna [žénā], knjȋga [knjígā], pȗšāka [púšākā], ljȗdi [ljúdī], pȏlja [pólja], imȇna [iménā], sȇla [sélā], jȇlena [jélēnā], zmȋja [zmíjā].*

The difficulty of distinguishing between the short rise and the short fall is perhaps the most noticeable characteristic of early writings about the accents. Even as late as 1853 Šunjić is able to distinguish them only by placing nouns and verbs with the short accents into a preposition/prefix context and seeing whether the accent moved or remained:[35]

"As I studied the problem for a long time, it seemed to me that the distinction is so subtle and that it is so difficult to set up any rule for this distinction that I often remained in doubt as to whether an acute or a grave accent sounded above this or that syllable of my native Illyrian speech. Finally, after long testing and with the resources of my native language, which alone seems to have preserved the original character of ancient Greek and Latin speech, I clearly recognized the distinction. I perceived and discovered that in verbs and nouns an acute accent is not moved from its place if a preposition is added, while, on the contrary, with the addition of prepositions, a grave accent is not only drawn back from the first syllable of the word to the preposition, but also, and this is to be carefully noted, the grave accent is changed into an acute.

This will be clear in the Illyrian words: *dı̏ca (djeca),* 'children,' and *tı̏ca,* 'bird.' The first syllable of each is short, but anyone who produced the first syllables, *di* and *ti,* with the same accent would make children laugh. So also *pı̑sak,* 'sand,' and *pı̑sak,* 'reed:' the first syllable of each word is long. Quantity

---

[35] M. Suñić [Šunjić], *De ratione depingendi rite quaslibet voces articulatas seu de vera orthographia cum necessariis elementis alphabeti universalis,* Viennae, 1853; the excerpt above was translated from the Latin selection which appeared in Pollok, *op. cit.,* pp. 146-147.

does not, however, constitute the distinction, but the accent of the first syllable of the first word *pìsak* is acute while that of the first syllable of the second word *pȉsak* is grave; in both words the *i* is long.

If you are caught in doubt as to which of these should be assigned an acute in the first syllable and which a grave, put *od* or *iz* before them, and your ear will tell you that in *ód tice*, pronounced as a whole, the accent recedes from the first syllable to the preposition *od*. However, the pronunciation *ód dice* is not possible, since the syllable *di* retains its accent which is, in fact, acute. . . . The same holds true of the words *pìsak* and *pȉsak*. So also in the verbs *vódit*, 'to lead,' *gónit*, 'to drive,' *lóvit*, 'to hunt,' no matter which prefixes you use, the accent sounds over the same first syllable of the root, e.g. *na-vódit*, 'to lead to,' *u-vódit*, 'to lead into.' The ear warns us that the case is different in the verbs *plàvit*, 'to moisten,' . . . , *stàvit*, 'to place,' *pìti*, 'to drink,' and *mèsti*, 'to sweep.' If, for example, you place *po* before these verbs, not only is the accent drawn back from the first syllable but also this accent, formerly grave, becomes an acute on the syllable *po*, e.g. *póstavit*."

Šunjić's examples indicate that his acute and grave accents correspond to Vuk's rising and falling accents respectively. It seems curious that he would have difficulty in distinguishing between the accents of *pìsak* (the ikavian equivalent of ekavian *pésak*, ijekavian *pijèsak*, "sand") and *pȉsak* (*pisak*, "reed," also in ijekavian and ekavian) since it is usually felt that the accentual difference on long syllables is easily perceivable.[36] More examples of *skakanje* in prepositional phrases might have shown us whether his statement about the grave accent receding to the preposition as an acute was in fact accurate. In the Vukovian system the recessive accent can be, depending on rather complex conditions, acute (i.e. rising) or grave (i.e. falling); thus, Vukovian *brȁt*, G sg. *brȁta*, *òd brata*, but *bȏg*, G sg. *bȍga*, *òd boga*. In the Vukovian system the recessive accent on the prefix becomes, as in Šunjić's system, rising (i.e. acute). e.g. Vukovian *stàviti, pòstaviti* (= Šunjić's *póstavit*). But, of course, it could well be that Šunjić's observation was very exact, namely, that the recessive accent on both prepositions and prefixes was acute (i.e. rising) in his dialect and perhaps in many štokavian dialects and that Daničić's dicta (e.g. *òd brata - òd boga, nà vatru - nà*

---

[36] Cf. Ivić, *Die serbokroatischen Dialekte*, p. 107.

vodu) were based on archaic survivals or on his language planner's zeal for historical consistency.

In his 1859 book Mažuranić devoted 18 pages to a discussion of quantity and accent.[37] Like Karadžić and Daničić, he distinguished four accents: two short, and two long. Unlike them, he defines accent as a prosodic characteristic of a syllable *(slovka)* rather than of a letter or a vowel. In discussing the nature of the four accents he says nothing about tone but rather defines the differences in terms of length and stress location. Thus, for him the two short accents differ in that the accent of *vòda* is not as abrupt and is somewhat more drawn out than that of *kȍlo*. The long accents differ in that such syllables have twopart *(dvostruk)* vowels and that for one long accent the stress occurs on the second part, e.g. N sg. *gláva = glaàva*, while for the other long accent the stress occurs on the first part, e.g. A sg. *glâvu = glàavu*.[38]

In any event it was Đuro Daničić who made the final adjustment of the accent markings for Serbo-Croatian, presenting them in his *Mala srpska gramatika* (1850) and using them consistently in his revision of Vuk's dictionary (2nd. edition, 1852). One modern change introduced in the 20th century is the use of the macron (¯) for postaccentual long vowels instead of the earlier ˆ, e.g. G. pl. *vrâbâcâ* [thus Vuk-Daničić], "sparrows," present-day *vrâbācā*, Daničić produced a series of accent studies, later published together as *Srpski akcenti* (1925), which provide the accentual "bible" for all grammarians and textbook writers. Curiously enough, Daničić seems never to have written anything about the characteristics of the four accents other than saying that they were different and that two were short and two were long. In fact, he never used names for the accents but referred to them only by means of accent marks. In 1851 he wrote (*Srpski akcenti*, p. 1):

---

[37]Antun Mažuranić, *Slovnica Hèrvatska,* Zagreb: Karl Albrecht, 1859, pp. 8-25.

[38]Mažuranić used " and ' in the Karadžić-Daničić fashion but his signs for the long accents were just the opposite; for him ˆ was a long rise, thus *glâva*, while ' was a fall, thus *gláva*. To avoid confusion, we made the respective adjustments: *gláva* (= Mažuranić's *glâva*), *glâvu* (= Mažuranić's *gláva*).

"In the Serbian language there are four accents: the first *a* in the word *glava*, for example, is pronounced one way, the [first *a*] in *pravda* another way, the [first *a*] in *magla* a third way, and the [first *a*] in *slama* a fourth way. Of these four accents the first two are long, while the second two are short; the first is indicated by the mark ´, the second by ˆ, the third by ` , while the fourth has received little attention up to now: it has been marked in the same way as the third [`], except in similar words, which are distinguished only by means of these accents, as for example *jarica*. This word means 'wheat' which is sown in the spring when its first *a* is pronounced like the a in *magla* [màgla], but when the first *a* is pronounced like the *a* in *slama* [slȁma] it means a 'young goat.' In such examples [i.e. *slȁma, jȁrica*] this fourth accent was indicated by the mark ̏; I shall use it also in other words [which require it]."

It was Leonhard Masing, a student of Leskien, who made a unique contribution to Serbo-Croatian accentology in his Leipzig doctoral dissertation of 1876 *(Die Hauptformen)*. On the basis of his observations of two principal informants, Miloje Vlajić from Žarkovo (near Belgrade) and Stefan Radošević from Mrkopalj (to the east of Rijeka) Masing concluded that the S-Cr. accents are either 1-syllable accents (̏, ˆ) or 2-syllable accents (` , ´). Thus, the so-called rising accents extend over two syllables, each with an ictus and each reaching or maintaining the same tonal level, e.g. *kraljica* (kraljica), *narodi* (naarodi). The falling accent is limited in its characteristics (tone, ictus) to one syllable; it is, Masing says, essentially the same as the second part of the two-part rising accent. The falling accent can occur on any syllable, including the last; the rising accent can occur only on a syllable before a falling accent and thus cannot occur on the last. Masing summarizes his conclusions as follows (p. 92):

"1) The elements, from which the principal accent is formed, are a falling and a rising tone.
2) The falling tone can appear in any syllable of the word, in the last as well as in the first or any medial syllable.
3) The rising tone has secondary meaning: it appears only in the syllable directly preceding the falling tone; it must, however, always be there.
4) It therefore follows that the falling tone can only be articulated in the first syllable of the word when it [the falling tone] is not accompanied

and supported by the rising tone and is thus autonomous; in this syllable there can be no preceding rising tone since there is, after all, no [preceding] syllable on which it could be formed. It is thus also clear why the rising tone never can appear on the last syllable of an independent word: since it always only accompanies and supports the falling tone immediately following, it cannot advance toward the word-end further than the penultimate syllable, since otherwise there would be no room remaining for the falling tone.

Thus, in the final analysis the falling tone is the determining element, while the rising tone is the dependent, secondary component of the Serbo-Croatian accent."

Ivšić (*Prilog,* pp. 147-149) thinks that Masing's interpretation reflects the foreigner's typical aural impression of the nature of the rising accent:

"The syllable under the accent ´ and the accent ` is pronounced differently than the syllable under the accents ῀ and ", such that the expiratory strength is divided equally on the entire syllable . . . and because of this the force with which we pronounce the following syllable is greater than that with which we pronounce the end of the syllable under the accents ´ and `. For that reason the foreigner who starts learning our language is generally more aware of the syllable after the accents ´ and `, so that he thinks that the 'real' accent is on that syllable, while the expiratory force deceives others in the question of pitch. This cannot happen after the syllable under the accents ῀ and " because the expiratory force on the syllable under ῀ and " is so great *already in the beginning* that it has a greater impact than the expiratory force of the 'unaccented' syllable. . . . If the short syllable after the accents ´ and ` has such an impact on us, it is clear that, for example -ē in *rúkē* and *vòdē*, will seem longer than -ē in *prâvdē* and *ko͂rē*. Just because of such pronunciation of the syllable after the accents ´ and ` L. Masing constructed his bisyllabic accent *(Zweisylbenakcent)* . . . . O. Broch agrees with Masing and he thinks that this higher pitch that is found at the end of the syllable under the accents ´ and ` also extends to the following syllable, either on the whole following syllable or at least on its first part (*Slavische Phonetik,* p. 324). Broch also speaks about the expiratory strength of the accents ´ and ` but he leaves unresolved the question of whether the expiratory force of those accents extends to the following syllable and even sometimes reaches its peak there (p. 315). In all this I can say that the overall (auditory) impression is greater for the syllable under the accents ´ and ` than the syllable after the accent ´ and `, that is to say, that the expiratory force is greater and the pitch of the voice is higher."

Belić (*Osnovi* I, p. 153) thinks that Masing has presented an accurate picture of the tonal characteristics of the rising accent but he disagrees with Masing's perception of the stress component:

"Masing is a foreigner to our language and he gave a very flimsy picture of the external side of our accents. But there is something which cannot be achieved through instruments or by descriptions of foreign pronunciation, something which can only be sensed in our accents. That is what Masing calls ictus and which we call the stress or expiratory stress of the accent. That force is so slight and tenuous in our accent that it can only be sensed. In the words žèna, kràljica, národ, dòmovi and similar ones the stress is on the accented syllable in our dialects which have the complete development of our modern accentuation. Masing had informants from such areas and thus in the matter [of stress] his observations are not exact. . . . But Masing is nevertheless correct on one thing. In the matter of the musical or tonal direction he noted exactly that very often the syllable behind the accent is in respect to the height of tone the same or sometimes even higher than the accented syllable."

Hraste (*Filologija* I, p. 73) in discussing dialects in which the štokavian shift is still in process in that they show forms with both the old and new accents (e.g. trávä, vòdê), makes the following remarks about the theory of the 2-syllable nature of the rising accents:

". . . Rešetar thought . . . that in the history of our accentuation the 2-syllable accent was a transition phase before the complete shift of the accent one syllable forward toward the beginning of the word. Already in 1876 L. Masing wrote about the 2-syllable nature of the new-štokavian accents (` and ´) . . . Lj. Kovačević in a review of that work . . . proves that, contrary to Masing's view, those accents are not 2-syllable but 1-syllable. . . . T. Maretić says that it is completely proved that the words vòda, rúka have two accents, that the *a* in each of those words is accented, and thus he agrees with Masing's theory only he modifies it as did Kovačević . . . to the extent that our words do not carry two identical tones of the same height and strength but that the second syllable of Masing's "2-syllable accent" (the *a* in vòda and rúka) is weaker and deeper than the first. Although it is not easy to agree completely with Masing in regard to all štokavian dialects, there is no doubt whatsoever that we do have dialects, especially where the new accentuation collides with the old, in which it is difficult to determine which syllable has the stress accent. I myself have been in such uncertainty in certain dialects, especially in the Split dialect."

In their recent instrumental study of speakers from the Novi Sad area, Lehiste and Ivić (*Accents in Serbocroatian,* pp. 132-133) reached conclusions which support part of Masing's observations:

"While the distinction between the two long accents might thus conceivably be based on information contained in the accented syllables themselves, in the case of the two short accents this information is decidedly insufficient. The feature which was constantly present and appeared to carry the main burden of distinction was the relationship between the stressed and the posttonic syllable. In the case of both the short and the long falling accents, the posttonic syllable had a fundamental frequency that was *either the same or higher than that of the preceding syllables* [our italics]. . . . It appears therefore necessary to recognize that the word accents have a larger domain than the stressed syllable nucleus."

In reading the remarks of earlier grammarians about accents one is impressed by the diversity of views regarding the nature of Serbo-Croatian accent. The reason for such diversity is clear: the grammarian, lexicographer of writer on the language came from a particular dialect region and either gave too much weight to the features of his own speech or, being unsure of himself because of his dialect, too much weight to views presented on the subject of accents in other sources. There was only one writer whose views endured and that was Vuk Stefanović Karadžić whose dialect became the base for the modern Serbo-Croatian language. And yet Vuk's statements on accents and his use of an accentual notation were not sufficiently precise to insure acceptance for posterity. Credit for the fact that the Vukovian accentual system was perfected and almost enshrined in the culture of literate Serbs and Croats goes to his young student from Novi Sad, Ðuro Daničić, who attached himself to Vuk and labored with him to create a viable language system for his countrymen. Daničić, whose knowledge of linguistics was in the opinion of Leskien not particularly strong, almost single-handedly established accentual canons which are accepted to this day.[39] In his detailed articles about Serbo-Croatian accents Daničić tried to provide an exact accentuation for all classes of words in the language. Though his services merit commendation, writes Jagić, it is unfortunately true that he gave a picture of an accentual homogeneity which never, in fact, existed.[40] On the surface Daničić's accentual contributions were a triumph of language planning since they have been accepted officially for over a century.

---

[39] A. Stojićević, "Leskien o Daničiću," *Daničićev zbornik,* Belgrade-Ljubljana: Srpska Kraljevska Akademija, 1955, p. 125.

[40] Jagić, *Istorija slavjanskoj filologii,* reprint of 1910 St. Petersburg edition, Leipzig, 1967, p. 739.

CHAPTER FOUR

OBSERVATIONS OF SERBOCROATIANISTS

> "Mora se priznati, da je pravilno naglaša-
> vanje u našem najteže pitanje za svakoga,
> pa i za profesora hrvatskoga jezika, ako se ak-
> centskim pitanjem nije posebno bavio ili ako
> nije iz krajeva (Bosna i Hercegovina), u kojima
> se dobro i pravilno naglašuje svaka rieč."
>
> Mate Hraste

There are two types of observations which we would like to consider: statements by those specialists on Serbo-Croatian who maintain that the Vukovian accentual system functions today as an essential part of the language, and statements by specialists who point to one or more aspects of the Vukovian system which do not function today or which function imperfectly. Unquestioning affirmation of the Vukovian system can easily be found in various grammars and reference books, or in articles such as "The Beauty of the Serbo-Croatian Language" by Stjepan Babić, a docent at the University of Zagreb.[1] After pointing with pride to the "liveliness and variety" brought to the language by its four accents, Babić then states that the accents serve not merely as melodic decoration but function to distinguish words.[2] He cites the following forms

---

[1] Babić, "U čemu je ljepota hrvatskosrpskoga jezika," *Jezik* 4 (1963-1964), pp. 117-125.
[2] *Ibid.*, p. 123.

which look similar but which are distinguished in pronunciation by means of their accent:

lȕk	"onion"	lûk	"bow, arch"
pȁs	"dog"	pâs	"belt"
trȅšnja	"cherry-tree"	trêšnja	"shaking"
kȕpiti	"to gather"	kûpiti	"to buy"
slȁgati	"to lie"	slâgati	"to put in order"

Babić relates that a colleague was asked by children in a streetcar why they were not allowed "to blow"; the children had concluded this from the sign *NE PUŠITE U KOLIMA.* If one reads the sign, writes Babić, with the accentuation *nè pušite,* then the meaning is "don't smoke"; if it is pronounced *ne púšite,* then the meaning is that derived by the children, "don't blow." Babić goes on to show the more subtle accentual distinctions of his language, those represented in minimal contrasts of short accents and long accents, e.g. *pàra,* "money," *pâra,* "steam"; *rádio,* "worked," *râdio,* "radio."

Babić, then, represents those "true believers" who hold that the Vukovian accentual system is real and operative in the Serbo-Croatian language. But even a casual reading of the Yugoslav literature, concerned with language and linguistics, will show quite clearly that there are, particularly in the cities, major deviations from the Vukovian system. Aleksandar Belić, for example, describes how migrants from other regions have affected Belgrade's accentuation.[3] There are those who come from the region of the Kosovo-Resava dialect which maintains the older place of accent (e.g., *sedîm,* "I sit," for Vukovian *sèdīm*) but has lost postaccentual length (e.g. G pl. *lȍpata,* "shovels," for Vukovian *lȍpātā*). Then there is the influence of the Timok dialect which has shortened longs but retained the pre-shift accent (e.g. *sedȉm* for *sèdīm*). Also influential are incoming speakers with the *šumadijski* accent, particularly the *kanovački* type which lengthens vowels originally short (e.g. *sélo,* "village," for *sèlo, dúkat,* "gold coin," for *dùkat*). "As can be seen from this," Belić continues, "the accent presents

---

[3] Belić, "Pozorišni jezik," *Naš jezik* VI, sv. 5-6 (1939), pp. 134-135.

much greater difficulties than the sound segments because the accent has a greater number of different systems and a greater number of particular deviations." Belić claims that Belgrade's "cultured circles" still maintain the Vukovian system with, however, "significant deviations, especially in the maintenance of the short-rising accent in two-syllable words and in the maintenance of unaccented lengths."[4] Actually, it is clear from his writings that Belić, though he was an acute observer of linguistic phenomena, did not wish to contemplate the possible consequences of the collisions of accentual systems but staunchly proclaimed the integrity of the Vukovian system, though he adds the Delphic statement: "Only that system is not everywhere the same."[5]

In writing about the problems of teaching Serbo-Croatian to high school students in Sisak (Croatia), Mate Hraste was most discouraged in the matter of accentuation:[6]

"Meanwhile the question of the accent is the most difficult. It must be admitted that proper accentuation in our language is the most difficult question for everyone, and even for a professor of the Croatian language, if he has not specialized in accentology or if he is not from the regions (Bosnia and Hercegovina) where each word is accented well and correctly."

Reading Branko Miletić's description of the short accents, one would be able to predict a certain amount of confusion in the communication process. Of the short fall he writes:[7]

"In reference to the melodic movement there are principally two types: 1) the falling in the central dialects (Bosnia and Hercegovina, Mačva, Dubrovnik and elsewhere) and 2) a level in Belgrade and in other eastern regions. The first (the falling) pronunciation is more typical, much more widespread and probably more archaic. Besides these two basic types there exist transitional types of the ˵ accent with a lesser or greater level of falling melody."

---

[4] Belić, "Srpskohrvatski književni jezik," *Naš jezik* I, sv. 3 (1933), p. 68.
[5] Belić, "Pozorišni jezik," p. 135.
[6] Hraste, "O govoru grada Siska," *Jubilarno izvješće Državne realne gimnazije u Sisku,* 1919-1944, Sisak, 1944, p. 65.
[7] Miletić, *Osnovi fonetike srpskog jezika,* Belgrade: Naučna knjiga, 1960, p. 88.

And of the short rise:

"In all our dialects the accent ` has most usually a rising melody which is either: 1) completely rising from the beginning to the end, or 2) only partially rising, while one part of the melody is level. In such cases the accent ` becomes, consequently, similar to the accent ``.''

Miletić further notes that this "drawing together" of the two short accents has resulted in the loss of a distinction in some dialects. For example, in Belgrade two-syllable words with an original short rise now have a short fall if the final syllable is also short, e.g. žèna for Vukovian žèna, sèstra for Vukovian sèstra.

Dalibor Brozović distinguishes impressionistically three types of *spori* (short rise) accent: 1) a northeastern (Srijem and neighboring areas), 2) a central (Bosnia and Hercegovina), and a southeastern (Dalmatia). He considers the central variety to be ideal for the accentual standard but admits that it is the hardest to acquire. This central accent is such, according to Brozović, that if it is pronounced correctly in a word such as *kompòzītor,* the acoustic impression will not differ essentially (*bitno*) from that of the pronunciation *kompôzitor;* "the difference," he explains somewhat vaguely, "is more in the degree, more in quantity than in quality."[8]

According to Lehiste and Ivić (*Accent in Serbocroatian,* p. 61), "it is well known among Yugoslav linguists that there exist noticeable dialectal differences in the realization of phonemically identical accents." Presumably, then, various regions might each have distinct pairs such as òrao, "plowed," and òrao, "eagle," prèvrela, "too hot," and prèvrela, "boiled over," etc., but the members of the pair of one region might be interpreted differently when heard in another region. Thus, if a speaker from Region A were to articulate prèvrela and prèvrela in Region B, his audience might interpret his forms as prèvrela and prèvrela respectively; while an audience in Region C might hear the forms as prèvrela and prèvrela. Given this inter-dialectal variation in the short

---

[8] Brozović, "Akcentuacija tudica na *-or* u hrvatskom jeziku," *Jezik* 3 (1954-1955), p. 123.

accents, one would expect some difficulty in establishing a country-wide accentual norm and indeed there seems to have been no effort by Daničić or his followers to establish a phonetic norm for the short accents. A major question which then faces foreign scholars is this: what trust can one place in the many studies of accents produced by Yugoslav investigators who themselves come from various regions and whose perceptions are influenced by their regional accentual codes?

The bulky 1960 *Pravopis* performed a real service in indicating the normative accentuation for many thousands of words but, by its extensive citing of accentual doublets (and triplets), it also introduced a new confusion. Here, for example, are a few of the many forms which the *Pravopis* sanctions with either short accent:*

bèrēm/bérēm, čòv(j)ek/čòv(j)ek, Círil/Ćîril, ĭdēm/ídēm, hŕpa/hȑpa, mȁrka/màrka, kȑčma/kŕčma, pòluga/pòluga, krȅčiti/krèčiti, rjȅčnīk/rjèčnīk (/rjȇčnīk), sȍkōl/sòkōl, v(j)ȅsnīk/v(j)èsnīk (/v(j)ȇsnīk); this choice is also possible for the bisyllabic indefinite forms of many adjectives, e.g. *nȍv, nȍva/nòva; pȕn, pȕna/pùna; slȁb, slȁba/slàba, stȁr, stȁra/stàra;* etc.

There are also many doublets for the long accents, e.g.

bânka/bánka, bânov/bánov, ćâle/ćále, G sg. *dêla/déla, dvôjka/dvójka, gȓlce/gŕlce, prêrov/prérov, prôđa/próđa,* D sg. *rûci/rúci,* A sg. *stênu/sténu,* G pl. *tônā/tónā,* and a large number of bisyllabic infinitive forms, e.g. *cvrêti/cvréti, cȓpsti/cŕpsti, drêti/dréti, dûpsti/dúpsti, klêti/kléti, lêći/léći, mrêti/mréti, prîći/príći, prôći/próći, râsti/rásti, skûpsti/skúpsti, snâći/snáći, snêti/snéti, spâsti/spásti, sprêći/spréći, trêsti/trésti, tûći/túći, ûći/úći, vêsti/vésti, vrêći/vréći, vȓsti se/vŕsti se, vûći/vúći.*

*Members of these accentual doublets are not identified as to their provenience and users of the *Pravopis* are advised (page 6) to make a selection *prema vlastitoj volji,* "at their own discretion." The possibility arising from such a situation is that a user of the *Pravopis* may make no selection but use the members of a doublet interchangeably.

In addition, there are doublets involving short and long accents, and also optional changes in the place of the accents, e.g. dòlac/dôlac, škòla/škôla, prèmetnuti/premètnuti, etc. Though the compilers of the *Pravopis* are to be commended for their attempts to record wide-spread accentual variants, one clear result of their work is to portray a certain instability in the Vukovian system.

Deviations from the Vukovian system raise real problems for teachers of the language as Vaso Tomanović notes:[9]

". . . it has been confirmed that a gradual process of the losing of unaccented lengths (long vowels) is taking place in the language, that they are being lost particularly in the cities and so the question could be raised: to what extent should the pronunciation of these lengths be required. Of course the length of a vowel in the first syllable after a rising accent should be pronounced, because the length is in a relationship with the rising accent which continues its musical tone even onto the following syllable."

Words like "required," "should be," "ought to be" are common in such comments about accent problems but yet to be faced is the practical question as to how vowel length, for example, can be "required" of students who may not have phonemic vowel length in their speech.

The well known Slavist, Josip Hamm, also notes the disappearance of postaccentual length in urban speech. He writes:[10]

"In general, lengths after the accents are being lost more and more. And in this there is nothing surprising. The language of city residents and workers, which in our time is the main bearer and creator of cultural and consequently of literary and language achievements, differs quite significantly, both in tempo and in other aspects, from the language of farmers in the southern regions, from their very simple, melodious and drawling speech which 150 years ago and 115 years ago Vuk Stefanović Karadžić and Đuro Daničić codified accentually, intonationally and in quantity."

---

[9] Vaso Tomanović, "Akcenat srpskohrvatskog književnog jezika i njegova nastava u školi," *Jezik* 3-4 (1959-1960), p. 98.

[10] Hamm, *Kratka gramatika hrvatskosrpskog književnog jezika,* Zagreb: Školska knjiga, 1967, p. 34. Masing observed this phenomenon in 1876: one of his informants (Miloje Vlajić from Žarkovo near Belgrade) would say sàčūvam (Vukovian sàčúvām), nàpišem (Vukovian nàpíšēm), etc.; *Die Hauptformen,* pp. 61-62.

As examples of the shortening of postaccentual length "in everyday urban speech" ("u svagdašnjem gradskom govoru") Hamm cites verbal forms such as *pîtam, glȅdam, pîšem, gòvorim, kùpujem* which in the Vukovian standard would be *pîtām, glȅdām, pîšēm, gòvorīm, kùpujēm*.[11] A similar observation was recently made by Slavko Pavešić in the Croatian language journal, *Jezik*.[12]

"In the speech of the urban population and that of the great number of educated people (who are not from the area where lengths are pronounced in the vernacular) lengths are not spoken outside the accented syllable."

Pavle Ivić points out that the dialects of the cultural centers of Croatia and Serbia impose special restrictions on the occurrence of vowel quantity (*"Prozodijski sistem,"* p. 137). For example, the "dominant dialect" of Belgrade only permits *one* length in a word and that can occur as part of the accent (ˆ, ´) or immediately after a short rising accent (`). Thus, there are only the following possibilities in bisyllabic words:

	Vukovian	Belgrade "dominant dialect"
	prâvda	*prâvda*
	gláva	*gláva*
	jùnāk	*jùnāk*
but		
	kàmēn	*kàmen*
	prâvdōm	*prâvdom*
	glávōm	*glávom*

Vukovian contrasts such as G sg. *vína* - G pl. *vínā*, G sg. *rȉbāra* - G pl. *rȉbārā*, G sg. *vojníka* - G pl. *vojníkā*, I sg. *lûkom* - I sg. *Lûkōm*, and others, would simply be homophonous in these dialects, viz. *vína-vína, rȉbara-rȉbara, vojníka-vojníka, lûkom-Lûkom*.

[11]*Ibid.*, p. 98.
[12]Pavešić, "O promjeni norme u jednoj gramatici," *Jezik* 1 (1968-1969), p. 25.

Ivić is concerned because textbooks do not inform students about this matter and so lose their confidence. He writes:[13]

"There is another difficulty in the school-programs in connection with the accents, a difficulty which plays a role not only in particular dialectal zones but practically on the whole territory of Serbia and Vojvodina, and also in a greater part of Croatia. This difficulty is created by the unrealistic approach to the question of postaccentual lengths. Our grammars and orthographies, following the tradition of Vuk and Daničić, consistently mark all postaccentual lengths that Vuk had in his speech, but nowhere mention the fact that those lengths are realized only partially in many parts of the country. For that reason the existing textbooks in nearly the whole of Serbia are unsuitable guides in this matter. With the lengths indicated in such manner we are not able to appeal to the linguistic intuition of the student, not even in Mačva or Tršić, and even less in the case of a student from central Šumadija or Vojvodina. This situation can definitely frighten off even the best student, even in otherwise optimal conditions. Even with the most serious effort and the most intelligent linking of his language intuition to the accent marks in the textbook, the student will find that they (his intuition and the accent marks) do not correspond to one another. This way he will be convinced that the accents are either something impossible to master, or that his textbook presents the facts unrealistically. It is difficult to say which of the two convictions is more harmful. To prevent this, it is necessary to introduce into our grammars and orthographies the explicitly formulated statement that the postaccentual lengths are not pronounced consistently in all parts of our country and that the pronunciation of the literary language must be considered normal even without a considerable part of those postaccentual lengths. After all it wouldn't be bad even if we were to tell the student openly that the Vukovian system of lengths has not been preserved either in the pronunciation of Belgrade or Zagreb radio and TV-announcers, that is to say, it has not been preserved in those versions of the literary language which directly affect the most people and which they consider as an official model for correctness or pronunciation. All this would help our students so that they will not be perplexed by the lengths indicated in the textbooks. It is good to have those lengths represented but the student must know that their realization is optional and regional."

[13] Ivić, "Komunikaciona vrednost jezika i naša škola," *Problemi jedinstva nastave maternjeg jezika i književnosti*, Belgrade: Biblioteka Savremena nastava, 1966, p. 38.

Another deviation from the Vukovian norms is the appearance in the language of a number of words with falling accents on inner syllables and even, *horribile dictu,* accent on the last syllable. Mihailo Stevanović comments on this phenomenon, deriving some comfort that such words are usually loan words and may eventually accommodate themselves to the Vukovian system (*Savremeni,* pp. 158-159):

"Very often even people, who otherwise have an exemplary accent and who would never be heard putting an accent on the final syllable in their pronunciation of native words, pronounce: *diletȁnt, dirigȅnt, docȅnt, komandȁnt, konkurȅnt, laborȁnt, lingvȉst, maturȁnt, komunȉst, solȉst, studȅnt, fotogrȃf,* etc. Likewise one often hears in the same circles the pronunciation of words taken from foreign languages with a falling accent on one of the inner syllables: *audȋcija, agitȃtor, Austrȃlija, regulȃtor, laborȁntkinja* and *laborȁntica, inteligȅntan, interesȁntan, kompetȅntan,* etc., and even some native combinations such as *Jugoslȃvija* and *poljoprȉvreda* . . . are heard more and more frequently with this [falling] accent."

What really troubles Stevanović is the permissive attitude of certain linguists towards this aberration: "And what is most curious is that even some language specialists consider that such accents . . . must be viewed as correct, because they [those words] have become so widespread." Ljudevit Jonke, in commenting on the same phenomenon, reminds his readers that according to the Vukovian canons falling accents can occur only on the first syllable.[14]

"It was important to emphasize that fact because there is in the dialects and, as a consequence, in the literary pronunciation counter tendencies and phenomena. Such is, for example, the tendency to maintain a falling syllable even in the middle of a word, so that alongside the new štokavian accent: *asìstent, dirìgent, okùpātor, irìgātor, Jugòslāvija, Indònēzija,* the unshifted accents are also appearing in strength: *asistȅnt, dirigȅnt, okupȃtor, irigȃtor, ambasȃdor, Jugoslȃvija, Indonȇzija,* etc."

[14] Jonke, *Književni jezik u teoriji i praksi,* 1965, p. 233.

Jonke, unlike Stevanović, is willing to accept certain native compounds which have a falling accent on an internal syllable (the first syllable of the second element of the compound); some examples of these words in the 1960 *Pravopis* are *kupopròdaja,* "sale," *poljoprìvreda,* "agriculture," *primoprèdaja,* "transmission," *ranorànilac,* "early riser," and *samoùprava,* "self-management."

The late Miloš Moskovljević, famous for his short-lived dictionary, had also pointed with alarm to the phenomena of end-accentuation and internal falling accents in loan words, citing many of the words noted above but also *adutȁnt, ambulȁntnī, alarmȁntan, arogȁntan, briljȁntan, pedȁntan, riskȁntan.*[15] He also notes that *Jugoslavija* is pronounced "almost everywhere" as *Jugoslȃvija* instead of *Jugòslāvija* and that in Zagreb not only are foreign words pronounced with ˆ in the middle, e.g. *agitȃtor,* but even "our words," e.g. *neprȃvda, napȋšēm.*[16] He continues:[17]

"If we also add to the situation mentioned above the loss of lengths after the accent, then we have before ourselves the main, most severe dislocations of our literary accentual system. And those are dislocations which become more frequent and stronger day by day. Today in our principal cultural centers, Zagreb and Belgrade, not only do the average urban residents speak with such a [defective] accent but even the most educated, including even professors and doctors of science . . . these principal cities of ours, even though they are the cultural centers, cannot serve as models for correct pronunciation. They cannot because Belgrade is located on the periphery of the Šumadian-Srem dialects, and as the capital city of the country became a conglomerate of all possible pronunciations and other linguistic features. After the war, because of the influx of people from Bosnia and Hercegovina, Lika and Slavonia the Belgrade pronunciation improved significantly, but before 1918 Belgrade had filled up with people resettled from the southeastern areas with the old accentuation, and thus there was created in Belgrade either a pure stress accent or an unstable accent. . . ."

Milivoje Pavlović notes that these changes have been under way

---

[15] Moskovljević, "Neke nove akcenatske pojave u našem književnom izgovoru," *Pitanja savremenog književnog jezika,* sv. 5, Sarajevo: Veselin Masleša, 1957, p. 80.
[16] *Ibid.,* p. 83.
[17] *Ibid.,* p. 84.

for some time:[18]

". . . in Belgrade [two phenomena] started to take place already at the end of the last century and have been constantly more noticeable: a shortening of lengths, and a merging of both short accents. In the equally important cultural center of Zagreb accentual disturbances also took place under different conditions."

The most striking statement about the accentual situation in the large cities has been made by Pavle Ivić:[19]

"And it happened that most of our cultural centers were formed outside that [Vukovian] zone: Belgrade, Zagreb, Novi Sad, and also Split, Rijeka, Osijek, Niš, Kragujevac, Cetinje, Titograd. Not having in their language feeling a sense for the fine points of the prescribed accentuation, the people in these centers very frequently do not even have the chance to learn how to accent [properly], because they are not able to establish a connection between their own pronunciation and the accents which are called for in the normative manuals. The natural result is the ignoring of those [accent] rules which actually only the most dedicated in our country know, that is, those people who also determine them [accent rules]. The development of the accentuation of our literary language is proceeding without regard to the accents which are entombed in grammars and dictionaries. . . . Our present-day pronunciation of the literary language deviates on the average significantly—though not everywhere in the same measure—from the norm of Vukovian accentuation."

One can test part of Ivić's sweeping indictment by comparing another linguist's observations of radio speech. Stevović made a study of the speech of Belgrade radio announcers and noted their deviations from the Vukovian system.[20] Some of his examples are the following:[21]

---

[18]Pavlović, *Osnovi metodike nastave srpskohrvatskog jezika i književnosti*, Belgrade: Naučna knjiga, 1962, p. 41.
[19]Ivić, "O Vukovom Rječniku iz 1818. godine," Pogovor [Epilogue] in Vuk's *Srpski rječnik* (1818), p. 78.
[20]Stevović, "Akcenat na radiju: Akcenat u izgovoru nekih spikera Beogradskog radija," *Naš jezik* V, sv. 9-10 (1954), pp. 349-353.
[21]*Ibid.*, p. 350-353.

OBSERVATIONS OF SERBOCROATIANISTS

Pronunciation of Belgrade radio announcer	Accentuation prescribed in Vukovian system
svòj nàrod	svôj národ
vèka	vêka
nàcije	nâcijē
bez vòde	bez vòdē
ìmaš prȁvo	ȉmāš právo
òdbacim	òdbācīm
vrème	vréme
Jugòslàvije	Jugòslāvijē
večèras	večèras
emìsije	emìsijē
mládi lèkar	mlādī lèkār
Tùraka	Tùrākā
sa sùprugom	sa sùprugōm

His general conclusion about their speech is:[22]

"They do not adhere to the four-accent system of the literary language; they do not adhere to any other accentual system of our dialects. . . . But as a general and constant tendency one notices a shortening of postaccentual lengths [in their speech]. In addition, the shortening process affects even long accents, so that in their pronunciation a long fall (ˆ) and a long rise (´) are realized as short rises (`) or as some type of half-accent. . . ."

After reading the many caveats about the putative Vukovian accentual system one can appreciate the temerity of the educator (denounced in *Jezik*) who suggested that high-school students not be subjected to such artificial rules:[23]

---

[22] *Ibid.* [Stevović], p. 353.
[23] *Pedagoški rad* (br. 2, 1954) quoted in *Jezik* 3 (1954-1955), p. 91.

"I do not think that it is necessary to lead high-school students into the labyrinth of the classical, Daničić accentuation. We cannot do that because it is too difficult and we will not do it because it is not necessary. I would almost dare to say that in actual usage there is even no Daničić accentuation, and that in no region do they talk in the way described in "Srpski akcenti".... It is a good idea to keep the classical accent for tragedies and in epic poetry, because it gives the language something unusual and solemn...."

In the foregoing quotations there are repeated references to the accentual phenomena of the urban areas, particularly Belgrade and Zagreb. Are the characteristics of these two cities really important if the standard language uses a Hercegovinian accentual model? After all, standard American English does not necessarily reflect the peculiarities of the speech of New York and Chicago. The difference in the two language situations lies in the central role Belgrade and Zagreb play in the cultural development of Yugoslavia and, of course, in the Serbo-Croatian speech area. As the Croatian and Serbian representatives concluded in their famous Novi Sad language agreement of 1954:*

"The national language of the Serbs, Croats and Montenegrins is one language. Consequently the literary language, which developed on the basis [of the national language] around *the two main centers, Belgrade and Zagreb,* is uniform, with two pronunciations, ijekavian and ekavian. [italics—T.F.M., L.M.]

---

*1960 Pravopis, p. 7.

CHAPTER FIVE

TESTING OF PROSODIC DISTINCTIONS

To be linguistically relevant, however, the pair must be used as an identification test; that is, pairs of sentences, containing different items suspected of being identifiable by their pronunciation, must be presented to a jury.
Archibald A. Hill

The ability of speakers and hearers to use sounds of their language for systematic distinctions in communication constitutes the very basis of every theory of phonology whether it uses the concept of phonemes or that of distinctive features or both. Most linguists would probably agree that the distinctiveness of two utterances cannot be proved instrumentally because there is no machine capable of establishing the phonological (phonemic/systematic phonetic) relevance of phonetic differences. It is, therefore, widely accepted (although not always fully admitted) that systematic distinctiveness, which constitutes the fundamental problem in phonology, can be established only and exclusively by a "jury" involving the speaking community, that is to say, the actual users of the linguistic system including not only speakers and their introspection, but also hearers. Nevertheless, most of the studies of Standard Serbo-Croatian accent are characterized by a striking absence of any such attempts to test the validity of the prosodic distinctions which were codified in the last century and which are still prescribed by contemporary normative grammars. One of the rare exceptions is the experimental study by Lehiste and Ivić (*Accent*) which reports briefly on a series of listening tests connected with their investigation; the tests were administered to two informants who were asked to identify *"minimally contrastive dissyllabic words with short rising and short falling accent,"* (p. 135). Unfortunately, the authors do not describe the method of testing in detail, though it seems that key words were tested within the frame sentence

Forma . . . data je kao primer.
(The form . . . is given as an example.)

In 1970 Lehiste revealed that this instrumental study of Serbo-Croatian accent was actually preceded by a test comprising *"300 minimally contrastive words, in random order,"* which were submitted for identification to Pavle Ivić; he functioned both as a speaker and a hearer and was able to identify all 300 words *"with 100% accuracy."*[1]

Peter Rehder's instrumental study of Serbo-Croatian accent (*Beiträge*) also used an identification test which was administered to twelve persons mostly from Belgrade; they were asked to produce and identify several word pairs, the individual members of which were embedded in real or imagined sentences and subsequently edited for analytic purposes.

Since the time of Ferdinand de Saussure and Baudouin de Courtenay word pairs or "minimally contrastive words" have been used as one of the most essential devices to establish what de Saussure called "a clearly delimited gamut of phonemes"[2] in accordance with his assumption that "each language operates on a fixed number of well-differentiated phonemes."[3] "Minimal pairs" have also been used in those phonological studies which reject the notion of the irreducibility of phonemes and consider distinctive

---

[1] Lehiste's review of P. Rehder's *Beiträge zur Erforschung der serbokroatischen Prosodie, Slavic and East European Journal,* 4, 1970, p. 410.
[2] Ferdinand de Saussure, *Course in General Linguistics,* New York: Philosophical Library, 1959, p. 221.
[3] *Ibid.,* p. 34.

features to be the minimal units of systematic differentiation. In the discussion of distinctiveness in verbal communication word pairs occur throughout the *Preliminaries to Speech Analysis* by Jakobson-Fant-Halle[4] and are repeatedly used in Jakobson-Halle's *Fundamentals of Language*[5] to illustrate the notion of "minimal distinctions." Chomsky and Halle, who explicitly avoid the concept of phoneme and/or morphophoneme, find sets of word pairs to be a handy device to illustrate, for example, the systematic differentiation between verbs and nouns in English by means of stress and its degrees, e.g.[6]

$$\overset{1}{torment} \qquad \overset{13}{torment}$$

$$\overset{1}{convict} \qquad \overset{13}{convict}$$

$$\overset{1}{export} \qquad \overset{13}{export}$$

$$\overset{1}{progress} \qquad \overset{13}{progress}$$

In our investigation word pairs were used primarily to verify, if possible, the prosodic distinctiveness claimed by grammarians of Standard Serbo-Croatian. Since virtually all of them have been using word pairs to prove their claims, our test was designed to verify especially those word pairs which have become famous as illustrations of Standard Serbo-Croatian prosodic differentiation.

If it is claimed, for example, that the verbal form *òrao*, "plowed," can be distinguished merely by its accent from the noun *òrao*, "eagle," the verification of such a claim cannot be without interest. It can be shown, of course, that the verbal form *orao* is a product of different derivational processes than the nominal form *orao*. In the speaker's mind there can be hardly any confusion between the meaningful usage of the verbal form *orao* and

---

[4] R. Jakobson, G. Fant, M. Halle, *Preliminaries to Speech Analysis*, Cambridge: M.I.T., 1952.
[5] R. Jakobson and M. Halle, *Fundamentals of Language*, 's-Gravenhage: Mouton, 1956.
[6] N. Chomsky and M. Halle, *The Sound Pattern of English*, New York: Harper and Row, 1968, p. 36.

the noun *orao*. But only an empirical test can really prove whether it is the prescribed accentual differentiation that makes it possible for the hearers to distinguish systematically between

    1. *Da li je òrao na tom brežuljku?*   "Has he been plowing on that hill?"

and

    2. *Da li je òrao na tom brežuljku?*   "Is that an eagle on that hill?"

If certain prosodic distinctions, prescribed by the normative grammars of Serbo-Croatian, are systematically identified only by some people born in Hercegovina or Bosnia but hopelessly confused by the majority of speakers in the major Yugoslav cities, the finding itself is, we believe, meaningful not only practically but also theoretically. Such a finding, of course, can be hardly established by any other means than by a test on a large scale. It is precisely for this reason that we decided to test prosodic distinctiveness in both rural and urban areas in Yugoslavia. By sheer coincidence the test was undertaken just a little more than one hundred years after the death of Vuk Karadžić, the founding father of Standard Serbo-Croatian accentuation. Implicitly, therefore, it tested what happened to a linguistic system after one century of evolution, a period of possible change ignored by contemporary normative grammarians.

1. METHOD OF TESTING

The classical method of investigating Serbo-Croatian accents, from Masing to Lehiste and Ivić, is to gather a number of speakers together, have them read texts or utter isolated forms and then analyze the prosodic features either by means of personal linguistic techniques (Masing) or with the aid of sophisticated machines (Lehiste and Ivić). Whatever the virtues of such an approach are, it is essentially an analysis of individual speech production and does not tell us anything about the essential other half of the communication act, that is, the reception of the speech by other members of the language community. Prosodic minutiae may be convoluted to a marvelous degree but, if they have no meaningful impact on the receiver, they are only so much "static." An attempt to approach the matter of Serbo-Croatian accentuation from the point of view of the receiver was made by the authors in 1966 when they carried out a large-scale investigation in the speech area of Yugoslavia: some 1600 people (mostly high school students) were tested on their ability to discriminate forms according to the Vukovian accentual norms.

After consultation with Yugoslav linguists and after some experimental testing, a set of 100 sentences was devised. Each investigated distinction was tested by two sentences at least; some distinctions were tested by means of 3 or 4 sentences. The individual sentences were so mixed that no direct comparison was possible. Thus, the distinction between *pâra*, "steam," and *pàra*, "money," occurred in the following order:

Sentence no. 50 - *I danas pàra igra ulogu.*
Sentence no. 95 - *I danas pâra igra ulogu.*

The distinction between the genitive forms of *Lûka*, "Luke," and *lúka*, "port," was presented in these three sentences:

No. 11   *Evo Lûkē u daljini.*
No. 44   *Evo lúkē u daljini.*
No. 78   *Evo lúkē u daljini.*

The distinction between the genitive forms of *učitelj*, "teacher," was represented in these 4 sentences:

No. 1   *Tu nema ùčitelja danas.*
No. 28   *Tu nema ùčitēljā danas.*
No. 57   *Tu nema ùčitēljā danas.*
No. 85   *Tu nema ùčitelja danas.*

All 100 sentences were recorded in a studio at the University of Zagreb by Mr. Danijel Alerić, an assistant in the University's

Institute of Linguistics, born and raised in Hercegovina. In all, the 100 sentences, each with the number identification and interspersed pauses, took 20 minutes in play-back time. After recording the 100 sentences, Alerić was immediately given a test form and tested on his own sentences; one week later, he was again tested. In both tests he succeeded without a single error.

A test form with 100 sets of choices was printed on both sides of a single sheet of paper. The test form also called for the respondent's name, his place and date of birth, the place where he attended elementary school, the place of his *gimnazija* (high school), and the name of his university; this latter item was useful only in the few situations where university students were tested. Here are the first twelve sets of choices which the respondents would see on his test form.

1. a) *učitelja* _____ .
   b) *učiteljâ* _____ .
2. a) *pitaju (/hrane)* _____ .
   b) *pitaju (/zapitkuju)* _____ .
3. a) *padeža* _____ .
   b) *padežâ* _____ .
4. a) *lukom (luk/svod)* _____ .
   b) *lukom (luk/česnjak)* _____ .
   c) *lukom (luka)* _____ .
   d) *Lukom (Luka)* _____ .
5. a) *konduktera* _____ .
   b) *kondukterâ* _____ .
6. a) *Jela* _____ .
   b) *jela (hranila se)* _____ .
7. a) *pas (životinja)* _____ .
   b) *pas (pojas)* _____ .
8. a) *Hrvata* _____ .
   b) *Hrvatâ* _____ .
9. a) *grad (geogr. pojam)* _____
   b) *grad (tuča)* _____ .
10. a) *konja* _____ .
    b) *konjâ* _____ .
11. a) *Luke (Luka)* _____ .
    b) *luke (luka)* _____ .
12. a) *sat kao* _____ .
    b) *satkao* _____ .
    c) *sad kao* _____ .

As can be seen from the above, no accent marks occur on the forms. The genitive singular is distinguished from the genitive plural by the orthographic sign ˆ on the plural form, a sign which is known to all Serbo-Croatian readers, whether school children or adults. In some cases, a word or so of explanation in parentheses would specify the homographs, e.g. *grad* (*tuča*, "hail"), *grad* (*geo. pojam*, "geographic concept"); for oblique forms, identical in writing, the nominative form was used to differentiate, e.g.

24. a. *vodom (voda)* _____.
 b. *vodom (vod)* _____.

In its entirety Test I comprised the following sentences (the numbers in parentheses indicate their order; two numbers in parentheses specify that the same sentence was used twice in the order indicated by each number):

(1/85)	*Tu nema ùčitelja danas.*	"There is no teacher here today."
(28/57)	*Tu nema ùčitēljā danas.*	"There are no teachers here today."
(2)	*Pȉtajū ga još sada.*	"They're still feeding him."
(45)	*Pítajū ga još sada.*	"They're still asking him questions."
(3/76)	*Izbor pádēžā obično muči stranca.*	"Selection of the cases usually troubles a foreigner."
(47)	*Izbor pádeža obično muči stranca.*	"Selection of a case usually troubles a foreigner."
(4/56)	*U vezi s lûkom ja mogu nešto reći.*	"About the arch I have something to say."
(27)	*U vezi s lȕkom ja mogu nešto reći.*	"About the onion I have something to say."
(88)	*U vezi s lȕkōm ja mogu nešto reći.*	"About the port I have something to say."

(5/33)   Broj konduktéra nije   "The number [badge] of
         poznat.   the conductor isn't
                                       known."
(80)   Broj konduktérā nije   "The number of conductors
         poznat.   isn't known."

(6)   Jesi li ti Jéla?   "Are you Jela [a girl]?"
(49)   Jesi li ti jȅla?   "Have you eaten?"

(7/43)   Čiji je to pȁs tamo?   "Whose dog is that there?"
(77)   Čiji je to pâs tamo?   "Whose belt is that there?"

(8)   Dužnost Hrváta je jasna.   "The duty of a Croat is
                                       clear."
(51/87) Dužnost Hrvátā je jasna.   "The duty of Croats is clear."

(9/90)   Na ovaj grȁd tuže se   "Drivers are complaining
         vozači.   about this city."
(52)   Na ovaj grȁd tuže se   "Drivers are complaining
         vozači.   about this hail."

(10/53) Zar nema kónjā za   "Don't you have riding
         jahanje?"   horses?"
(84)   Zar nema kònja za   "Don't you have a riding
         jahanje?   horse?"

(11)   Evo Lûkē u daljini.   "There's Luke in the dis-
                                       tance."
(44/78) Evo lúkē u daljini.   "There's the port in the dis-
                                       tance."

(12)   To je sȁt kao stroj.   "That watch is like a ma-
                                       chine."
(73)   To je sȁd kao stroj.   "Now that's like a machine."
(41/96) To je sàt kao stroj.   "A machine wove that."

(13)	Osim seljákā tko/ko tako govori?	"Outside of peasants who talks that way?"
(48/89)	Osim seljáka tko/ko tako govori?	"Outside of a peasant who talks that way?"
(14)	Òko vrāta je još prljavo.	"It's still dirty around the neck."
(75)	Oko vrátā je još prljavo.	"It's still dirty around the door."
(15)	Vera je pozvala Sašu sa sùprugōm na večeru.	"Vera invited Sasha [a man] and his wife to dinner."
(54)	Vera je pozvala Sašu sa sùprugom na večeru.	"Vera invited Sasha [a woman] and her husband to dinner."
(16/37)	Bibliotekar je kùpio knjige i redao ih na policu.	"The librarian gathered the books and arranged them on the shelf."
(59/97)	Bibliotekar je kúpio knjige i redao ih na policu.	"The librarian bought the books and arranged them on the shelf."
(17/81)	Prešli smo preko grȅbēnā u Dalmaciji.	"We crossed mountain ridges in Dalmatia."
(58)	Prešli smo preko grȅbena u Dalmaciji.	"We crossed a mountain ridge in Dalmatia."
(18)	Stȁra žena sporo radi.	"An old woman works slowly."
(70)	Stârā žena sporo radi.	"The old woman works slowly."
(19)	Bârom se ponosio taj gradić.	"That town is proud of its bar."
(61)	Bȁrōm se ponosio taj gradić.	"That town is proud of its pool."

(20/91) Òd kosti se pravi juha. "Soup is made from a bone."
(55) Od kòstī se pravi juha. "Soup is made from bones."

(21/86) Do ìzbora sve je bilo "Before the election every-
 mirno u gradu. thing was quiet in the
 city."
(60) Do ìzbōrā sve je bilo "Before the elections every-
 mirno u gradu. thing was quiet in the
 city."

(22) Cr̀venā ruža je krasna. "The red rose is beautiful."
(72) Crvèna ruža je krasna. "A red rose is beautiful."

(23) Milicajac pògledā "The policeman took a look
 naokolo. around."
(74) Milicajac pòglēdā "The policeman looks
 naokolo. around."

(24) Vojnik je stajao pred "The soldier stood in front
 vòdōm i gledao u of the water and gazed
 daljinu. into the distance."
(66) Vojnik je stajao pred "The soldier stood in front
 vòdom i gledao u of the squad and gazed
 daljinu. into the distance."

(25) To zavisi od okólnostī "That depends on the cir-
 i nam(j)ere. cumstances and the in-
 tent."
(63) To zavisi od okólnosti "That depends on the cir-
 i nam(j)ere. cumstance and the in-
 tent."

(26/71) Nepoznavanje jèzīkā "Ignorance of languages hin-
 smeta ovo naučno ders this scientific
 istraživanje. study."
(98) Nepoznavanje jèzika "Ignorance of language hin-
 smeta ovo naučno ders this scientific
 istraživanje. study."

TESTING OF PROSODIC DISTINCTIONS

(29) Vèsela d(j)evojka nas raduje. "A cheerful girl makes us happy."
(64) Vèselā d(j)evojka nas raduje. "The cheerful girl makes us happy."

(65) Svako je dužan da se pridržava zákona naše zemlje. "Every one is obliged to uphold the law of our country."
(30/93) Svako je dužan da se pridržava zákōnā naše zemlje. "Every one is obliged to uphold the laws of our country."

(31) Čuvaj se bádēmā ove vrste. "Avoid almonds of this type."
(62/94) Čuvaj se bádema ove vrste. "Avoid an almond of this type."

(32) Od dúžnosti ne možemo b(j)ežati. "We cannot flee from duty."
(69) Od dúžnostī ne možemo b(j)ežati. "We cannot flee from duties."

(34) Zòra je došla. "Dawn came."
(83) Zóra je došla. "Zora [a girl] came."

(35) Govorili su o položaju kombinátā u našoj republici. "They talked about the position of the business trusts in our republic."
(67) Govorili su o položaju kombináta u našoj republici. "They talked about the position of the business trust in our republic."

(36) Péro je tamo. "Pero is there."
(68) Pèro je tamo. "The pen is there."

(38)	Što se tiče oficíra nautike, to nije toliko velik problem.	"As far as the navigation officer is concerned, that's not such a great problem."
(79)	Što se tiče oficīrā nautike, to nije velik problem.	"As far as the navigation officers are concerned, that's not such a great problem."
(39)	Podržavamo borbu národā za slobodu.	"Let us support the struggle of nations for freedom."
(99)	Podržavamo borbu národa za slobodu.	"Let us support the struggle of the nation for freedom."
(40)	Što ćemo učiniti s Mârkom iz Amerike?	"What'll we do with Marc from America?"
(92)	Što ćemo učiniti s mȁrkōm iz Amerike?	"What'll we do with the stamp from America?"
(42)	Kokoš krade òd patkē svako jutro.	"The chicken steals from the duck every morning."
(100)	Kokoš krade òtpatke svako jutro.	"The chicken steals scraps every morning."
(46)	Zašto se bojiš ùčenīkā osnovne škole?	"Why are you afraid of elementary school students?"
(82)	Zašto se bojiš ùčenīka osnovne škole?	"Why are you afraid of an elementary school student?"
(50)	I danas pàra igra ulogu.	"Even today money plays a role."
(95)	I danas pȁra igra ulogu.	"Even today steam plays a role."

After using Test I in a number of cities, a shorter test of 50 sentences, Test II, was devised. Test II was recorded by Mr. Alerić and also by the renowned Yugoslav linguist, Dalibor Brozović of the Zadar Extension of the University of Zagreb. Professor Brozović is a native-born Bosnian and has devoted much of his scholarly activities to problems of dialectology and accentology. Subsequently, Brozović was asked to identify not only his own sentences but also all sentences read by Alerić and he succeeded perfectly. The same applies to Alerić who correctly identified without any hesitation all Brozović's as well as his own sentences.

In its entirety Test II comprised the following sentences:

(1/50)   *Dobro se sećam/sjećam pròfesora romanskih jezika.*   "I well remember the professor of Romance languages."

(10/32) *Dobro se sećam/sjećam pròfesōrā romanskih jezika.*   "I well remember the professors of Romance languages."

(2/41)   *Nestalo je rȉbāra za vreme/vrijeme te bure.*   "The sailor disappeared during that storm."

(21)   *Nestalo je rȉbārā za vreme/vrijeme te bure.*   "The sailors disappeared during that storm."

(3/15)   *Što se tiče sèla u ovo doba, to je velik problem.*   "Concerning the village at this time, that's a big problem."

(34)   *Što se tiče sêlā u ovo doba, to je velik problem.*   "Concerning the villages at this time, that's a big problem."

(4/39)   *Da li je to glàsilo dobro?*   "Is that publication a good one?"

(25)   *Da li je to glȁsilo dobro?*   "Did that sound alright?"

(5/23)	Sećam/Sjećam se prijatéljā svog oca.	"I remember the friends of my father."
(45)	Sećam/Sjećam se prȉjatelja svog oca.	"I remember the friend of my father."

(6)	Folklorni se referat tiče kòla šumadijskog tipa.	"The folklore paper treats a folkdance of the Shumadian type."
(27/36)	Folklorni se referat tiče kôlā šumadijskog tipa.	"The folklore paper treats folkdances of the Shumadian type."

(7/37)	Roditelji se boje stvárī te vrste.	"Parents fear things of that nature."
(29)	Roditelji se boje stvȃri te vrste.	"Parents fear a thing of that nature."

(8)	Moj će pomoćnik kùpiti te stvari.	"My assistant will gather up those things."
(22)	Moj će pomoćnik kúpiti te stvari.	"My assistant will buy those things."

(9)	Evo ȍstrva u daljini.	"There's an island in the distance."
(24/42)	Evo ȍstȓvā u daljini.	"There are islands in the distance."

(11/28)	Zar nema Gȓka u ovoj grupi?	"Isn't there a Greek in this group?"
(46)	Zar nema Gȓkā u ovoj grupi?"	"Aren't there any Greeks in this group?"

(12/31)	Što je râdio u našem društvu?	"What is radio in our society?"
(48)	Što je rádio u našem društvu?	"What has he been doing in our society?"

TESTING OF PROSODIC DISTINCTIONS 89

(13/47) *Da li je òrao na tom brežuljku?* "Is that an eagle on that hill?"
(20/30) *Da li je òrao na tom brežuljku?* "Has he been plowing on that hill?"

(14) *Ovo se tiče konduktéra na toj relaciji.* "This concerns the conductor on that line."
(38) *Ovo se tiče konduktérā na toj relaciji.* "This concerns the conductors on that line."

(16/33) *Evo kȍsti za vašu čorbu/juhu.* "Here's a bone for your soup."
(49) *Evo kȍstī za vašu čorbu/juhu.* "Here are some bones for your soup."

(17) *Tu nema kónjā za jahanje.* "There aren't any riding horses here."
(43) *Tu nema kònja za jahanje.* "There isn't a riding horse here."

(18) *Čini se da je moj pâs bolji nego tvoj.* "It seems that my belt is better than yours."
(40) *Čini se da je moj pàs bolji nego tvoj.* "It seems that my dog is better than yours."

(19) *Što se tiče ȉmena na vratima, ne mogu vam pomoći.* "I can't help you with the name on the door."
(35) *Što se tiče iménā na vratima, ne mogu vam pomoći.* "I can't help you with the names on the door."

(26) *I danas pȁra igra ulogu.* "Even today steam plays a role."
(44) *I danas pàra igra ulogu.* "Even today money plays a role."

During the months of March through July of 1966, both tests were used on a large scale in Yugoslavia. Test I was first administered in Banja Luka, Zagreb, Sisak, Belgrade, Loznica, and Niš. Test II was then developed and administered in Zagreb, Belgrade, Subotica, Novi Sad, Osijek, Rijeka, Split, Dubrovnik, Gacko, Stolac, Trebinje, Titograd, Nikšić, Mostar, Travnik, and Banja Luka; in order to compare the results on both tests Test I was used in different classes of the same schools in Gacko, Stolac, Dubrovnik, Travnik, Mostar, Banja Luka.* In sum, the testing situation was as follows:

Place	TEST I No. Tested	TEST II No. Tested	Total
Gacko	31	31	62
Stolac	27	27	54
Trebinje	–	29	29
Mostar	37	37	74
Titograd	26	27	53
Nikšić	–	19	19
Dubrovnik	30	30	60
Split	–	51	51
Rijeka	–	66	66
Sarajevo	91	–	91
Travnik	28	50	78
Banja Luka	50	45	95
Sisak	55	–	55
Zagreb	94	108	202
Osijek	–	33	33
Novi Sad	–	68	68
Subotica	–	32	32
Belgrade	61	96	157
Loznica	116	–	116
Niš	43	–	43
Others*	140	60	200
Total	829	809	1,638

*Special classes, groups of specialists, etc.

*The distribution of cities and towns by republic is the following: Serbia (Belgrade [capital], Novi Sad, Subotica, Loznica, Niš); Croatia (Zagreb [capital], Sisak, Osijek, Rijeka, Split, Dubrovnik); Bosnia-Hercegovina (Sarajevo [capital], Banja Luka, Travnik, Mostar, Gacko, Trebinje, Stolac); Montenegro (Titograd [capital], Nikšić).

The selection of the cities for testing was done largely on the basis of their population, it being the major purpose of the investigators to investigate the accentual situation in the major cities of Yugoslavia. Thus, on the basis of the 1961 census the following major cities were selected for testing: Belgrade (587,899), Zagreb (427,319), Sarajevo (142,423), Novi Sad (102,385), Rijeka (100,339), Split (99,426), Niš (81,706), Subotica (74,433), Osijek (71,843); these are, in fact, all the cities of Yugoslavia with a population of 70,000 or over. Students were tested in Sisak (26,466) simply because one of the investigators happened to be in that area working on kajkavian dialects and took advantage of the opportunity to test in the local *gimnazija*. The authors visited Tršić, the home of the great Vuk Karadžić, and made recordings of the children in the elementary school; the nearest *gimnazija* was a few kilometers away in Loznica (10,611) and here a very large number (116) of students was tested. For validation of the test and the testing methods students were also tested in smaller cities of Bosnia and Hercegovina where, it is said, the Vukovian system is still in full flower. Thus, testing was carried on in Banja Luka (50,463), Mostar (35,242), Travnik (9,984), Stolac (under 5,000), Trebinje (under 5,000). Testing was also conducted in the small but famous city of Dubrovnik (22,961) and in Titograd (29,100), a small city but the capital of its republic. A small group of high school students was tested in Nikšić (20,165), also a small city but, more importantly, the one nearest the Montenegrin (formerly Hercegovinian) village of Petnica, the home of Vuk's ancestors. A visit was paid to Petnica itself where the authors talked to and recorded members of the families all bearing the name of Karadžić.

In Sarajevo Professor Jovan Vuković, a well-known Yugoslav language scholar, allowed his class in accentology to be tested. In Zagreb Professor Bratoljub Klaić, an authority on the Vukovian system, invited the authors to test his diction class in the School of Drama. The Zagreb Linguistics Circle was tested at one of its meetings. Specialists were tested in the Language Institute of the Yugoslav Academy in Zagreb and in the Institute for Serbo-Croatian in Belgrade. All of these specialized testings were helpful in evaluating the test for strong and weak items and in assessing the ability of accentual specialists to perceive the Vukovian distinctions. Individual professors at Zagreb University, its Zadar extension, and at the universities of Belgrade and Sarajevo were also tested.

The overwhelming majority of those who took the test, however, were students in Yugoslav high schools. The high school or *gimnazija* was, in fact, the ideal place for conducting such tests: the students were usually from the city or town in which the school was located or from the neighboring region, they were young enough to be interested in this type of test, and yet they were old enough to understand the directions for the test. Our usual procedure was to approach the *direktor* of the *gimnazija*, introduce ourselves and show a letter of explanation by a professor of linguistics at a Yugoslav university, perhaps demonstrate our test, and request permission to test various classes, preferably third and fourth-year classes. On most occasions the directors were quite cordial and some became so interested in the test that they wanted to take it themselves. The next step was our introduction to the teacher of Serbo-Croatian who would escort us to the various classes to be tested. On a few occasions, a director would become rather suspicious and would follow us around on our activities; on one occasion a director of a Belgrade high school refused permission to test in his school without papers from the Belgrade municipality; in that situation, rather than getting papers (a time-consuming process in Yugoslavia) we simply moved on to another Belgrade high school where the director turned out to be exceptionally cordial. In most cases, though, the authors received friendly and hospitable treatment in their visits to high schools throughout Yugoslavia.

The test and the testing aroused a variety of emotions among the students. Like all students, they were ready for something new and different and the novelty of this test (two American professors, a portable tape recorder, printed forms) made them quite enthusiastic. In giving Test I one of us would explain to the teacher what we planned to do and he would explain to his students; this was not always satisfactory, since we might have to add instructions which the teacher forgot. We remedied this when we prepared Test II by having the instructions recorded by Dr. Damir Kalogjera of the University of Zagreb. Thereafter, in giving either test, we would first play the instructions; these instructions were delivered in a friendly, informal way and directed the students, step by step, in filling out the data for the form and then in explaining the test. During this explanation the students had the forms in front of them and completed the personal data as Dr. Kalogjera instructed them; while he explained the test, they could look at the test form and see what was involved. The last part of the recorded instructions directed the students to ask questions if they did not understand any part; such questions as came up were answered by us or the teacher. The test began with the tape recorder either placed on the teacher's desk or held by one of us; the other investigator would stand in the back of the classroom to make sure that the volume was sufficient. A problem in some schools was to keep the teachers from announcing his solution for a particular sentence; in many situations we were able to persuade the teacher himself to take the test.

We made a useful innovation with Test II, the shorter of the two tests. As we had the sentences read both by Alerić and Brozović, we often gave this test two times, once with each voice. We would first play the Alerić reading, collect all the forms, issue new response forms and play the Brozović reading; the students had been warned that the sentences would be the same but that they might not be in the same order; actually they were in the same order but it is doubtful that a student could remember his choices, even if he wished to. On the back of the second form the students were asked for their reactions to the test or to the voices. The remarks of students throughout Yugoslavia were remarkably uniform in their identification of Brozović's voice as the more natural one, the one whose pronunciation was closer to that of their own regions. Both Serbs and Croats considered him as "one of them" (*naš čovek/čovjek*) regardless of whether the local speech was ekavian or jekavian.

Also in connection with this short test, Test II, we tested the students on a third rendition of the 50 sentences, one read by one of their classmates. We would ask the teacher to identify one of the students who had been born in the city and one whose parents had also been born locally. This student was then given a copy of the 50 sentences; there were no accent marks on this copy but the homographic forms were distinguished by the orthographic sign for the genitive plural (e.g. *profesorà*) or by explanatory words in brackets, e.g. *para* (*novac*). The students in the class then filled out a third set of forms responding to their classmate's reading. During the reading the student's voice was being recorded on the tape-recorder; he was subsequently taken to another room to fill out a response form while listening to his own recording.

The analysis of the student's responses to their own classmate provides extremely interesting information about local situations and will be discussed in the following chapters. All of the local voices, which had been recorded, were then played and often many times replayed for Dr. Alerić who added the graphic accentuation of the complete sentences, a long and often strenuous process which took many days of concentrated effort. Some of the local voices were subjected to an equally painstaking scrutiny by Dalibor Brozović who, in some instances, found it necessary to replay a single sentence or its parts fifty times, if not more. Some of these renditions are reproduced in the Appendix.

As far as the actual testing is concerned, most of the students liked to play our language 'game' and to show the visiting foreigners how well they could identify forms in their own language. Tension seemed to be minimal; when they were faced with a choice involving a distinction which was not in their speech, the usual student reaction was a chuckle or a rueful smile. The only real tension we witnessed was in the testing of some Yugoslav specialists who obviously felt that their reputations were at stake. In the last analysis the "proof of the pudding is in the eating" and the proof of the testing process is in the results.

CHAPTER SIX

EVALUATING TEST PERFORMANCE

"Razvoj akcentuacije našeg književnog jezika odmiče ne obazirući se na akcente koji stoje mrtvi po gramatikama i rečnicima. . . . Naš današnji izgovor književnog jezika u proseku odstupa znatno—iako ne svuda podjednako—od norme vukovske akcentuacije."

Pavle Ivić

There are various ways of assessing test performance and each has special advantages and disadvantages. For example, if 50 students in a locality are tested on two sentences which present the contrast *päs* vs. *pâs*, the results could be the following:

Place A	item *päs*	item *pâs*	interpretation
50 students tested	48 correct identifications or 96% correct	42 correct identifications or 84% correct	average correctness: 45 or 90%

Or we could simply take the lower percentage, 84%, and say that not more than 84% identified the basic prosodic difference as presented in the two items. A more exact method would be to check the scores, student by student, in which case the following situation might result:

Place A	item *pàs*	item *pâs*	interpretation
50 student tested	students 1 through 48 correct, students 49 and 50 incorrect	students 9 through 50 correct, students 1 through 8 incorrect	80% correctness

In this latter situation only students numbered 9 through 48 (or 40 out of 50 students) got both items right and thus we can say that only 80% of the students tested in Place A actually succeeded while 20% failed. This counting procedure does not give credit for partial correctness and does not excuse any error, whether psychological, biological or technical; it simply assumes that the functionality of the distinction tested is revealed by correct identification while errors show deficiency of the prosodic system in the case tested. In our evaluation of test performance we did not use the first method of rough averages but rather the latter method, that of totalling the errors of each individual, student by student.

Let us take the difference between *učitelja* vs. *ùčitēljā* in Test I to illustrate the details. These forms were presented four times in the following sequence:

Sentence 1:

Tu nema ùčitelja danas.   There is no teacher here today.

Sentence 28:

Tu nema ùčitēljā danas.   There are no teachers here today.

Sentence 57:

Tu nema ùčitēljā danas.   There are no teachers here today.

Sentence 85:

Tu nema ùčitelja danas.   There is no teacher here today.

In Gacko all thirty-one students correctly identified the first occurrence of the singular (sentence 1) as well as the first occurrence of the plural (sentence 28); one of the thirty-one students, however, identified the second occurrence of the plural (sentence 57) as a singular and one student expresses his doubts by a double mark, e.g.

    57. a. *učitelja*   √

        b. *učiteljâ*   √

Since we counted the double marks and the absence of any mark as a failure, sentence 57 was thus correctly identified in Gacko by 29 students. As one student identified the second occurrence of the singular (sentence 85) as a plural, altogether 28 individual students in Gacko correctly responded to all four occurrences, while three students failed. Thus, in our evaluation the performance in Gacko amounted to 90% of correctness (or 10% of errors).

In Stolac, one of the 27 students tested identified the first occurrence of the singular as a plural; the same student was one of the two who identified the first occurrence of the plural as a singular. Since there were no errors in connection with the second occurrences of the plural and the singular, we can say that 25 students in Stolac succeeded and two erred. In other words, two errors of the same student were counted as a single failure so that Stolac achieved 93% of correctness (or 7% of errors).

On the other hand, of 61 students in Belgrade 12 incorrectly identified the first occurrence of the singular (sentence 1); the first occurrence of the plural (sentence 28) was incorrectly identified by 21 students; for 6 students, however, this was a second error, i.e. $15(+6)_2$. The second occurrence of the plural (sentence 57) in Belgrade was incorrectly identified by 29 students; for 9 students, however, this was a second error and for 5 students a third error, i.e. $15(+9)_2(+5)_3$. The second occurrence of the plural (sentence 85) in Belgrade was incorrectly identified by 10 out of 61 students; five of them, however, erred for the second time, three for the third time and one for the fourth time, i.e. $1(+5)_2(+3)_3(+1)_4$.

98   WORD ACCENT

Thus, in Belgrade 43 out of 61 students failed by making altogether 72 errors, while only 18 students succeeded in identifying all four occurrences correctly. Consequently, the performance in Belgrade amounts to 30% of correctness (or 70% of errors). In terms of averages, of course, the total of 72 errors in response to four occurrences would represent 31% of errors per occurrence.

The following table shows the performance of all students in Yugoslav gimnazije whose identification of *ùčitelja* vs. *ùčitēljā* was tested by means of Test I:

	1a *ùčitelja*	28b *ùčitēljā*	57b *ùčitēljā*	85a *ùčitelja*	Total of Students who Failed/	Succeeded
Gacko 31	0	0	2	1	3(10%)	28(90%)
Stolac 27	1	1(+1)$_2$	0	0	2(7%)	25(93%)
Travnik 28	2	2	(+1)$_2$	(+1)$_2$	4(14%)	24(86%)
Dubrovnik 30	0	2	3(+1)$_2$	0	5(17%)	25(83%)
Mostar 37	3	2	1(+3)$_2$	1	7(19%)	30(81%)
Sarajevo 91	6	8(+2)$_2$	8(+3)$_2$	1(+2)$_2$(+2)$_3$	23(25%)	68(75%)
Banja Luka 50	3	1(+2)$_2$	4(+2)$_3$	1(+2)$_4$	9(18%)	41(82%)
Titograd 26	5	1	1(+2)$_2$	1(+2)$_2$	8(30%)	18(70%)
Sisak 55	4	9(+1)$_2$	9(+4)$_2$	3(+1)$_2$	25(45%)	30(55%)
Zagreb 36	1	10(+1)$_2$	13(+7)$_2$(+1)$_3$	1(+1)$_2$	25(77%)	11(23%)
Belgrade 61	12	15(+6)$_2$	15(+9)$_2$(+5)$_3$	1(+5)$_2$(+3)$_3$(+1)$_4$	43(70%)	18(30%)
Loznica 116	31	12(+5)$_2$	21(+10)$_2$(+5)$_3$	4(+11)$_2$(+1)$_3$	68(59%)	48(41%)
Niš 43	24	7(+14)	4(+9)$_2$(+13)$_3$	1(+7)$_2$(+4)$_3$(+1)$_4$	36(84%)	7(16%)

Since slight variations in percentages can blur the overall picture, it is more feasible to put the results of the testing into the broader framework of letter grades based on the percentage of students who made no errors in identification:

A = 90%-100%*   D = 60%-69%
B = 80%-89%   E = 50%-59%
C = 70%-79%   F = 49%-0%

*A perfect score is indicated as A(100) or by a footnote.

EVALUATING 99

This means of evaluation can best reveal the relationship of score to place. Thus, the test of ùčitelja vs. ùčitēljā yields the following grouping:

    A: Gacko, Stolac
    B: Travnik, Dubrovnik, Banja Luka, Mostar
    C: Sarajevo, Titograd
    D: - -
    E: Sisak
    F: Zagreb, Loznica, Belgrade, Niš

1. TEST OF POSTACCENTUAL QUANTITY

If our evaluation had used only the four occurrences of *učitelja* (*ùčitelja–ùčitēljā–ùčitēljā–ùčitelja*) in Test I, the results alone would be sufficient proof that there is something basically wrong with the normative description of postaccentual quantity as compared with its usage in the two largest cultural centers of contemporary Yugoslavia. Let us take, for example, the results from Gacko and Stolac, where altogether 58 students were tested, and compare their performance with a group almost equal in size, the 61 students in Belgrade:

NUMBER OF ERRORS

	1a ùčitelja	28b ùčitēljā	57b ùčitēljā	85a ùčitelja
Gacko-Stolac 58	1(2%)	2(4%)	2(4%)	1(2%)
Belgrade 61	12(20%)	21(44%)	29(48%)	10(17%)

NUMBER OF THOSE WHO FAILED

					Total Failed	Succeeded
Gacko-Stolac	1	$1(+1)_2$	2	1	5(9%)	53(91%=A)
Belgrade	12	$15(+6)_2$	$15(+9)_2(+5)_3$	$1(+5)_2(+3)_3(+1)_4$	43(70%)	18(30%=F)

The difference in performance becomes even more significant if we use for comparison the 116 students from Loznica, a small town (about 10,000) located near the village of Tršić, the birthplace of Vuk Karadžić. In fact, the *gimnazija* where we tested was named in his honor. In this school, because of the unusual hospitality on the part of the director and the interest displayed in our investigation, we tested 116 students, the largest number tested in any one school. Now, let us compare Loznica's results with those obtained in Gacko, Stolac, Travnik and Dubrovnik, which altogether constitute a group of 116 students.

NUMBER OF ERRORS

		1a ùčitelja	28b ùčitēljā	57b ùčitēljā	85a ùčitelja
Gacko	31				
Stolac	27				
Travnik	28	3(3%)	6(5%)	7(6%)	2(2%)
Dubrovnik	30				
TOTAL	116				

vs.

| Loznica | 116 | 31(37%) | 17(15%) | 38(33%) | 16(14%) |

NUMBER OF THOSE WHO FAILED

	1a	28b	57b	85a	Failed	Total Succeeded
Gacko Stolac Travnik Dubrovnik 116	3	5(+1)$_2$	5(+2)$_2$	1(+1)$_2$	14(12%)	102(88%=B)

vs.

| Loznica 116 | 31 | 12(+5)$_2$ | 21(+10)$_2$(+5)$_3$ | 4(+11)$_2$(+1)$_3$ | 68(59%) | 48(41%=F) |

These comparisons make it perfectly clear that neither the students in Belgrade nor those in Vuk's Loznica can readily distinguish *Tu nema ùčitelja danas* ("There is no teacher here today") from *Tu nema ùčitēljā danas* ("There are no teachers here today"). On the other hand, students of the same age in Gacko, Stolac, Travnik and Dubrovnik have few problems with such identification.

One could perhaps argue that the sentence frame logically favored usage of the singular because, after all, during the testing there was at least one teacher present in the classroom. Such a logical inference, however, would have validity only in Belgrade or Loznica but not in Gacko, Stolac, Travnik, and Dubrovnik. It is evident that in Gacko, Travnik, Stolac and Dubrovnik the semantic bias or logic of the sentence was not capable of overpowering the signals furnished by the prosodic system. Therefore, it is possible to conclude that logic or the semantic plausibility of a sentence dominated the identification process only in those areas where postaccentual quantity does not properly function as a system. Thus, in this test Belgrade and Loznica appeared in conspicuous opposition to Gacko, Stolac, Travnik and Dubrovnik, indicating that the norms of postaccentual quantity failed to expand into those areas where the majority of contemporary speakers live.

In this connection it is interesting to look at the situation in Sarajevo, the cultural center of Bosnia-Hercegovina where 91 students were tested. In its size the Sarajevo group more or less corresponded to the total number of students tested in Gacko, Stolac and Travnik:

NUMBER OF ERRORS

	1a *ùčitelja*	28b *ùčitēljā*	57b *ùčitēljā*	85a *ùčitelja*
Gacko 31				
Stolac 27	3(3%)	4(5%)	3(3%)	2(2%)
Travnik 28				
TOTAL 86				
vs.				
Sarajevo 91	6(7%)	10(11%)	11(12%)	5(6%)

WORD ACCENT

NUMBER OF THOSE WHO FAILED

	1a *ùčitelja*	28b *ùčitēljā*	57b *ùčitēljā*	85a *ùčitelja*	Failed	Total Succeeded
Gacko Stolac Travnik 86	3	$3(+1)_2$	$2(+1)_2$	$1(+1)_2$	9(10%)	77(90%=A)
vs.						
Sarajevo 91	6	$8(+2)_2$	$8(+3)_2$	$1(+2)_2(+2)_3$	23(25%)	68(75%=C)

The comparison shows that Sarajevo, in terms of postaccentual quantity, differs from Belgrade and Loznica on the one hand and from Gacko, Stolac and Travnik on the other. It appears that in Sarajevo, as in all bigger cities, postaccentual quantity is unstable as a system.

The precarious status of postaccentual quantity in the large cities was decisively confirmed by other test sentences in both Test I and II. In Zagreb, where Test II was administered to 108 students, more than half of them failed to distinguish *pròfesora* from *pròfesōrā,* used four times in the sentence frame:

Dobro se s(j)ećam pròfesora   I well remember the professor
romanskih jezika.   of Romance languages.

Dobro se s(j)ećam pròfesōrā   I well remember the professors
romanskih jezika.   of Romance languages.

Test I and II included several types of postaccentual differentiation normatively assigned either to the last two vowels (A) or to the penultimate vowel (B) or to the very last vowel only (C):

A.

(A1) ùčitelja vs. ùčitēljā
pròfesora vs. pròfesōrā
grȅbena vs. grȅbēnā
ȍstrva vs. ȍstŕvā

(A2) pádeža vs. pádēžā
zákona vs. zákōnā
bádema vs. bádēmā
národa vs. nárōdā

B.

pògledā vs. pòglēdā

C.

(C1) kombináta vs. kombinátā
Hrváta vs. Hrvátā
oficíra vs. oficírā
seljáka vs. seljákā
konduktéra vs. konduktérā

(C2) ùčenīka vs. ùčenīkā
r̂ibāra vs. r̂ibārā
(C3) okólnosti vs. okólnostī
dúžnosti vs. dúžnostī
(C4) sùprugom vs. sùprugōm
(C5) vȅsela vs. vȅselā

While Belgrade and Zagreb scored E or F (i.e. 50% or worse of accuracy) in the majority of the cases tested, the rural areas were generally much more successful. In connection with type C, however, even the most successful places in the classical region of the Vukovian prosodic system were in trouble. As a matter of fact, the test of

Vȅsela d(j)evojka nas raduje.   "A cheerful girl makes us happy."

Vȅselā d(j)evojka nas raduje.   "The cheerful girl makes us happy."

turned out to be a complete disaster virtually everywhere. There was not a single location which scored better than F. Almost the same applies to the test of *konduktéra* vs. *konduktérā* used in Test I as well as in Test II. In Test I, the sentence frame, *Broj konduktera nije poznat*, clearly favored plurality (i.e. "The number of the conductors isn't known") rather than singularity ("The number [badge] of the conductor isn't known."). In Test II, however, the sentence frame was much more neutral with regard to the choice between singular and plural (i.e. *Ovo se tiče konduktera na toj relaciji*, "This concerns the conductor / conductors on that line."). In Test I the identification of *konduktéra* in distinction from *konduktérā* failed everywhere, whereas in Test II Gacko and Trebinje scored A, Stolac, Mostar, and Travnik scored B and Nikšić, in the region of Vuk Karadžić's ancestors, scored D. Belgrade scored F (out of 96 students tested, only 47 succeeded).

In the rural areas the best results in general were obtained in connection with postaccentual quantity displayed by the last two vowels or by the penultimate vowel. In Gacko, Stolac, Travnik, Trebinje, Dubrovnik, Osijek, Subotica and Novi Sad most of the items of that type were identified with an average of B in accuracy. Many items of that type were also successfully identified in Sarajevo, Banja Luka, Split and Titograd. In Belgrade and Zagreb, however, the test of postaccentual quantity in its entirety disclosed that postaccentual quantity as a system is failing or has failed in every respect. There were, of course, several students in both Zagreb and Belgrade who were more successful than their fellow students. Some of these students tested in Zagreb and Belgrade were born elsewhere, or their parents migrated from the classical areas of Vuk's prosodic system and the families apparently managed to retain, at least partially, the regional prosodic characteristics. None of the students in Zagreb and Belgrade, however, was capable of identifying all instances of postaccentual quantity in the test. This is illustrated by the following survey which tabulates the incorrect identifications of postaccentual quantity by 10 Zagreb students who otherwise successfully identified all four occurrences of *ùčitelja / ùčitēljā* in Test I:

EVALUATING 105

Zagreb*

ITEMS	A	B	C	D	E	F	G	H	I	J	K	L	M	N	O	P	Total of Errors
Errors Possible	3	3	3	3	2	2	2	3	2	3	3	2	2	2	2	2	39
Tatjana Š. (Belgrade)						1			2		2	1	1	1		2	10
Jelica C. (Zagreb)			1					1	2		2			1	2	1	10
Zvezdana Š. (Belgrade)		1		1				2	1		2			1	1		9
Jadranka P. (Banja Luka)	1			2	1		1	2	2	1	2			1	2	1	16
Ljerka B. (Zagreb)	1	1						3		1	1	1	1		2		11
Kaća I. (Osijek)	2	1	2	1				2	1	1	2		1	2	1	1	17
Ankica Ž. (Zagreb)	2	1	3	1	1	1	2		2	2			1	1	1	1	19
Jadranka V. (Zagreb)	1	1	1	1	1	1		1	1	1	2		1	1	1	1	15
Alka K. (Zagreb)		1	1	1	1	1	1	1		3	3	1	1		1	1	17
Ivanka K. (Zagreb)	1	1	1			1		3		1	2		1		2		13

A: grȅbena - grȅbēnā
B: pȁdeža - pȁdēžā
C: zȁkona - zȁkōnā
D: bȁdema - bȁdēmā
E: nȁroda - nȁrōdā
F: pȍgleda - pȍglēdā
G: kombinȁta - kombinȁtā
H: Hrvȁta - Hrvȁtā
I: ofícira - ofícīrā
J: seljáka - seljákā
K: konduktéra - konduktérā
L: ùčenika - ùčenīkā
M: sùprugom - sùprugōm
N: okólnosti - okólnostī
O: dúžnosti - dúžnostī
P: vȅsela - vȅselā

*Birthplace is shown in parentheses after the student's name; 6 out of the 10 were born in Zagreb.

A comparable situation was found in Belgrade, as illustrated by the following survey which tabulates the incorrect identifications of postaccentual quantity by 18 Belgrade students who otherwise successfully identified all four occurrences of ùčitelja/ùčitēljā in Test I (the letters are specified underneath the previous figure):

WORD ACCENT

Belgrade*

ITEMS	A	B	C	D	E	F	G	H	I	J	K	L	M	N	O	P	Total of Errors
Errors Possible	3	3	3	3	2	2	2	3	2	3	3	2	2	2	2	2	39
Slobodanka S. (Sarajevo)								1		2	1	1					5
Ljiljana Č. (Belgrade)		1							1	1				1	2		6
Rajka M. (Herceg-Novi)	2			1	1	1			1	1	1		1		2	1	12
Nadira B. (Sarajevo)				1	1			1	1		3	2			1		10
Ljiljana P. (Titograd)	1		1	1	1		1	1	2	1	2	1	1		1	1	15
Milenko T. (Belgrade)		1		2	1			1	1		2	1	1	1		1	12
Danica S. (Belgrade)								1	1	2	2	1	2				9
Ljiljana K. (Virovitica)	1	1		2	1		1	2	1	1	1	1	2	1	2	2	19
Ljubinka C. (Belgrade)		1	1	1	1			2	2		3		2	2		1	16
Ivan G. (Bakionica)			1	1	1			1	2	1	2	1	1	1			12
Tatjana T. (Šabac)		1		1	1		1	1	2		3		1	2	2		15
Dušanka M. (Belgrade)				2	1		1		2	1	2		1	1	1	2	14
Loja N. (Mostar)	1	1	2		1			1	2	2	2			1	1	1	15
Radenka B. (Belgrade)		2	1	1	1		1	2		1	3	1		1		1	15
Slobodan M. (Niš)	1	1	1	2	1	1	1		1	2	2	1	1	2	1	1	19
Melanija B. (Belgrade)	1	1	2	2	1	1	1		2	1	3			1	2		18
Venera T. (Ohrid)	1	3	2		1	1	1		1		1	1	1	2	1	1	17
Olga V. (Belgrade)	1	1	1	1	2		1		1	3	2	1	1			1	16

*Of these 18 students only 8 were born in Belgrade.

2. TEST OF ACCENTUAL QUANTITY

The striking failure of postaccentual quantity in Belgrade, Zagreb, and other cities appears in remarkable contrast to the test of accentual quantity which yielded positive results everywhere with one exception only: Niš, the third largest city in Serbia. The following table shows the performance of all the Yugoslav high school students whose powers of identification were tested in Test I by means of

    Sentence 7: *Čiji je to pȁs tamo?* Whose dog is that there?
    Sentence 43: *Čiji je to pȁs tamo?* Whose dog is that there?
    Sentence 77: *Čiji je to pâs tamo?* Whose belt is that there?

TEST I

	7a *pȁs*	43a *pȁs*	77b *pâs*	Total of Students who Failed	Succeeded
Gacko 31	3	2	0	5(16%)	26(84%=B)
Stolac 27	1	1	1	3(12%)	24(88%=B)
Travnik 28	1	0	2	3(11%)	25(89%=B)
Dubrovnik 30	0	1	0	1(3%)	29(97%=A)
Mostar 37	2	3(+2)$_2$	0	5(12%)	32(88%=B)
Sarajevo 91	9	6	(+1)$_2$	15(16%)	76(84%=B)
Banja Luka 50	1	5	2	8(16%)	42(84%=B)
Titograd 26	2	1	1	4(16%)	22(84%=B)
Sisak 55	2	3	(+1)$_2$	5(9%)	50(91%=A)
Zagreb 36	1	6	(+1)$_2$	7(19%)	29(81%=B)
Belgrade 61	5	8(+1)$_2$	3(+1)$_2$(+1)$_3$	16(26%)	45(74%=C)
Loznica 116	11	16(+2)$_2$	10(+3)$_2$(+1)$_3$	37(32%)	79(68%=D)
Niš 43	6	9(+1)$_2$	15(+10)$_2$(+1)$_2$	30(70%)	13(30%=F)

The contrast between pȁs - pâs was also used in Test II and the results are complementary to the conclusions indicated by the results of Test I, e.g.,

TEST II

	18b	40a		Total of Students
	pâs	pȁs	Failed	who Succeeded
Trebinje 29	0	0	0	29(100%=A)
Nikšić 19	1	(+1)$_2$	1(5%)	18(95%=A)
Split 51	1	0	1(2%)	50(98%=A)
Rijeka 66	9	2(+1)$_2$	11(17%)	55(83%=B)
Osijek 33	1	0	1(3%)	32(97%=A)
Subotica 32	0	0	0	32(100%=A)
Novi Sad 68	2	0	2(3%)	66(97%=A)

The quantitative difference between short rising and long rising accent was also identified equally well everywhere, Niš again excepted. The following table compares Niš with Loznica, Belgrade and Zagreb with respect to their identification of

Sentence 36: Péro je tamo.   Pero is there.
Sentence 68: Pèro je tamo.   The pen is there.

	36a	68b		Total of Students
	Péro	pèro	Failed	who Succeeded
Niš 43	5	25(+4)$_2$	30(70%)	13(30%=F)
Loznica 116	6	14(+1)$_2$	20(17%)	96(83%=B)
Belgrade 61	1	8	9(15%)	52(85%=B)
Zagreb 36	0	9	9(25%)	27(75%=C)

In spite of the disastrous failure in the identification of accentual quantity in Niš, there were thirteen students there who identified Péro - pèro without any error. None of them, however, succeeded in identifying correctly all the other cases involving accentual quantity. This is illustrated by the following survey which tabulates performance of those thirteen on other items involving accentual quantity.

ITEMS	grȁd grâd	pȁs pâs	zòra Zóra	lȕkom lȗkom (lȗkōm)	sȁd kao sât kao (sàtkao)	Total of Errors
Errors Possible	3	3	2	4	4	16
Vlastimir L. (Knjaževac)	0	0	0	0	1	1
Mario B. (Trebinje)	0	0	0	1	1	2
Radisav I. (Radosinj)	2	2	0	0	1	5
Marija T. (Split)	2	0	1	1	0	4
Verica S. (Taskovići)	0	0	0	1	1	2
Jelena M. (Titovo Užice)	0	0	2	1	0	3
Miroslav C. (Miljkovac)	2	0	0	0	0	2
Miroslav B. (Niš)	2	1	1	1	0	5
Novica S. (Odžaci)	2	2	1	1	1	7
Filip T. (Niš)	2	2	2	1	1	8
Slobodan K. (Kragujevac)	2	1	0	2	0	5
Slavoljub H. (Leskovac)	2	0	0	1	0	3
Živojin M. (Niš)	2	0	2	2	1	7

As a group Niš scored F in all instances involving accentual quantity. For that reason it offers a unique contrast with all other places in Yugoslavia where the test was administered. It is now apparent that accentual quantity has different isoglosses than postaccentual quantity and, implicitly, a different status in the hierarchy of prosodic features in contemporary Serbo-Croatian.

The overall success in the identification of accentual quantity in Zagreb and Belgrade, where the identification of postaccentual quantity failed, indicates that accentual quantity served as a basis for the positive identification of those items which involved both accentual and postaccentual quantity; such items are mȁrkōm - Mârkom, bȁrōm - bârom in Test I, kȍla - kôlā, Gȑka - Gȓkā in Test II and kònja - kónjā in both Test I and II.

This general success in the identification of accentual quantity, however, does not apply to all tested items in all areas. In particular, sentences involving the differences between a common noun and a proper name disclosed certain vacillations which could be perhaps explained by the frequency of occurrence of the proper names in specific regions. For example, Dubrovnik was 100% successful in the identification of *pèro - Péro* but failed to identify *zòra - Zóra*. Zagreb also had difficulties with *zòra - Zóra* although it scored B in connection with *màrkōm - Mârkom* and C in connection with *pèro - Péro*. Gacko scored A in connection with *zòra - Zóra* and *pèro - Péro* but C in connection with *màrkōm - Mârkom*. Here the problem may have been in the accentuation of the noun *marka*, "stamp"; the 1960 *Pravopis* has *màrka* or *màrka* but the *Hrvatskosrpsko-francuski rječnik* of Dayre-Deanović-Maixner (2nd. ed., Zagreb, 1960) has *mârka*. If Gacko uses this latter accent, then the students there were being tested on postaccentual quantity in this item, e.g. *Mârkom - mârkōm*.

In some cases the weakness in identification results from local lexical anomalies. This seems to be the case with *grȁd - grâd* ("hail" - "city") which Gacko identified with D accuracy although Dubrovnik in that case scored A and Zagreb C; subject to verification, it could be assumed that in Gacko the word for "hail" is *tùča* or *krúpa* rather than *grȁd*.

The fragility of the system using accentual quantity for semantic differentiation was also convincingly demonstrated by the test involving multiple contrasts such as *sȁd kao - sât kao - sàtkao* or *lȕkom - lûkom - Lûkōm - lúkōm*. The multiple choice turned out to be a confusing factor even in those places where both accentual and postaccentual quantity was found to be functional in the majority of the other cases tested.

Also the distinction between indefinite and definite adjective forms in the attributive function appeared to be confusing everywhere in spite of the normative requirement. There was not a single group which was capable of using accentual quantity combined with postaccentual quantity for meaningful distinction between

Sentence 18 *Stȁra žena sporo radi* An old woman works slowly

and
Sentence 70 *Stârā žena sporo radi*   The old woman
works slowly

In this case the test clearly showed that the system of quantitative differentiation is bound to fail when the expected semantic differentiation has become obsolete or, simply, is absent or weak for whatever reasons. It is reasonable to assume that many students recognized the shortness in *stàra* and the lengths in *stârā* but they could not utilize the phonetic difference for the expected semantic differentiation between indefiniteness and definiteness of the given adjective. It is, of course, also tempting to speculate that the lack of semantic differentiation interferred with the adequate recognition of phonetic duration. At any rate, there was not a single group which scored better than F.

3. TEST OF TONE

Of all the prosodic features tone generally caused the greatest confusion in both Test I and Test II. In particular, performance on discrimination between short falling and short rising accent failed virtually everywhere. Even the results of testing the difference between long falling and long rising accent reflect a conspicuous uncertainty in many places including those which excelled in the identification of accentual and postaccentual quantity. For example, half of the students in Stolac and almost half of those in Travnik failed to identify the difference between

Što je râdio u našem društvu?   What is radio in our society?
Što je rádio u našem društvu?   What has he been doing in
our society?

It is noteworthy, however, that of the 33 students in Osijek only 3 failed in this discrimination while in Novi Sad it was only 12 out of 68 and in Split only 10 out of 51 students. The following table shows the number of students who failed in each location and the number of errors in connection with each occurrence of the sentence:

TEST II.

	12 *râdio*	31 *râdio*	48 *rádio*	Failed	Total of Students who Succeeded
Gacko 31	4	3	3(+1)$_2$*	10(32%)	21(68%=D)
Trebinje 29	3	2	3	8(28%)	21(72%=C)
Stolac 27	10	3(+5)$_2$	1(+2)$_2$(+1)$_3$	14(52%)	13(48%=F)
Mostar 37	7	11(+3)$_2$	6(+3)$_2$(+1)$_3$	24(65%)	13(35%=F)
Travnik 50	11	4(+6)$_2$	6(+2)$_2$(+2)$_3$	20(40%)	30(60%=D)
Banja Luka 45	9	8(+2)$_2$	4(+3)$_2$	21(47%)	24(53%=E)
Titograd 27	12	5(+8)$_2$	4(+1)$_2$(+2)$_3$	21(78%)	6(22%=F)
Nikšić 19	3	3(+1)$_2$	1	7(37%)	12(63%=D)
Dubrovnik 30	12	6(+4)$_2$	4	22(73%)	8(27%=F)
Split 51	4	5	1	10(20%)	41(80%=B)
Rijeka 66	17	11(+4)$_2$	5(+6)(+2)$_3$	44(67%)	22(33%=F)
Zagreb 108	27	29(+13)$_2$	10(+10)$_2$(+2)$_3$	66(61%)	42(39%=F)
Osijek 33	1	0	2	3(10%)	30(90%=A)
Subotica 32	5	6(+2)$_2$	1(+5)$_2$(+2)$_3$	12(37%)	20(63%=D)
Novi Sad 68	1	5	6	12(18%)	56(82%=B)
Belgrade 96	16	11(+10)$_2$	5(+2)$_2$(+4)$_3$	32(33%)	64(67%=D)

*The figures in parentheses indicate the number of students who failed twice, (n)$_2$, or three times, (n)$_3$.

The instability of tonal differentiation becomes even more apparent if Dubrovnik's failure in connection with *râdio - rádio* (Test II) is compared with its spectacular success in connection with *Lûkē - lúkē* (Test I). In the latter case, of the 28 Dubrovnik students only 2 failed while in Stolac it was only 5 out of 27 and in Travnik only 4 out of 28. In other words, the students in Dubrovnik, Stolac and Travnik failed as a group to identify Brozović's difference between *râdio - rádio* but they succeeded in identifying *Lûkē - lúkē* in Alerić's realization of

EVALUATING 113

Evo Lûkē u daljini. There's Luke in the distance
Evo lúkē u daljini. There's the port in the distance.

The following table presents the number of students who failed and the number of errors in each instance:

TEST I	11 *Lûkē*	44 *lúkē*	78 *lúkē*	Total of Students who Failed	Succeeded
Gacko 31	5	4(+2)₂	1(+1)₃	10(32%)	21(68%=D)
Stolac 27	3	2(+1)₂	(+1)₂	5(19%)	22(81%=B)
Mostar 37	5	5(+2)₂	6(+3)₂(+1)₃	16(43%)	21(57%=E)
Sarajevo 91	9	9(+1)₂	11(+2)₂	29(32%)	62(68%=D)
Travnik 28	3	1	0	4(14%)	24(86%=B)
Banja Luka 50	14	4(+1)₂	3(+4)₂	21(42%)	29(58%=E)
Titograd 26	10	1(+3)₂	4(+1)₂(+2)₃	15(58%)	11(42%=F)
Dubrovnik 30	2	(+1)₂	0	2(7%)	28(93%=A)
Zagreb 36	12	4(+1)₂	2(+3)₂	18(50%)	18(50%=E)
Sisak 55	6	8(+3)₂	2(+5)₂(+1)₃	16(29%)	39(71%=C)
Belgrade 61	13	13(+7)₂	10(+10)₂(+4)₃	36(59%)	25(41%=F)
Loznica 116	30	23(+9)₂	5(+11)₂(+3)₃	58(50%)	58(50%=E)
Niš 43	20	8(+9)₂	3(+10)₂(+4)₃	31(72%)	12(28%=F)

The variability in the degree of exactness seems to indicate that tone constitutes a system which is even more fragile than quantity. Its autonomy in semantic differentiation can be easily affected by various factors whether linguistic or extra-linguistic. Indeed, it is reasonable to speculate that Dubrovnik succeeded in distinguishing *Lûkē* from *lúkē* because the tonal system was corroborated by the maritime tradition as well as by the frequent occurrence of the name Luka in that region. On the other hand, these factors were not sufficient to dispel confusion caused in Dubrovnik by the multiple contrast *Lûkōm** - *lúkōm* - *lûkom* - *lükom* where tonal differences appeared in combination with quantity, e.g.

U vezi s lúkōm ja mogu nešto reći	About the port I have something to say
U vezi s lûkom ja mogu nešto reći	About the arch I have something to say
U vezi s lükom ja mogu nešto reći	About the onion I have something to say

In this case 6 out of 30 students in Dubrovnik failed to identify *lúkōm* as "harbor"; 3 of them took it to be *Lûkōm* (Luke), 2 identified it as *lûkom* (arch) and one vacillated between "arch" and "Luke." Nevertheless, Dubrovnik was much more successful than, for example, Belgrade, where 25 out of 61 students took *lúkōm* (harbor) for *Lûkōm* (Luke), or Zagreb, where 9 out of 36 students identified *lúkōm* as *Lûkōm*, while 8 students felt so insecure that they refrained from indicating any choice at all.

While discrimination of the difference between long falling and long rising accent was quite successful at least in certain items and in some locations, the situation with short rising and short falling accent, as represented in Test I and II, was a thoroughgoing failure. Within the framework of the test the identification failure of the short tonal distinction contrasts uniquely with all other types of prosodic differentiation tested and suggests that it is precisely the difference between short falling and short rising accent which is the most unstable as a system. The following table shows the number of students who failed to distinguish *örao* from *òrao* in the sentence frame

Da li je örao na tom brežuljku?	Has he been plowing on that hill?
Da li je òrao na tom brežuljku?	Is that an eagle on that hill?

---

*Lûkōm was presented to the students as a possible choice on the answer sheet (i.e. Luka _____) but did not occur in the sentences read.

EVALUATING

TEST II	òrao	ȍrao	ȍrao	òrao	Failed	Succeeded
Gacko 31	7	8(+3)₂	11(+10)₂(+3)₃	1(+6)₂(+3)₃(+2)₄	27(87%)	4(13%)
Trebinje 29	11	3	5(+2)₂	6(+5)₂(+1)₃	25(86%)	4(14%)
Stolac 27	17	4(+10)₂	3(+6)₂(+4)₃	3(+6)₂(+5)₃(+3)₄	27(100%)	0
Mostar 37	25	5(+7)₂	1(+12)₂(+5)₃	5(+5)₂(+11)₃(+3)₄	36(97%)	1(3%)
Travnik 50	23	5(+4)₂	9(+7)₂(+1)₃	4(+12)₂(+6)₃	41(82%)	9(18%)
Banja Luka 45	22	7(+6)₂	5(+11)₂(+2)₃	9(+13)₂(+6)₃(+2)₄	43(96%)	2(4%)
Titograd 27	7	13(+2)₂	4(+11)₂(+1)₃	3(+7)₂(+2)₃	27(100%)	0
Nikšić 19	7	4(+3)₂	5(+6)₂(+3)₃	(+2)₂(+4)₃(+3)₄	16(84%)	3(16%)
Dubrovnik 30	15	9(+10)₂	3(+9)₂(+3)₃	1(+3)₂(+5)₃(+2)₄	28(93%)	2(7%)
Split 51	23	10(+10)₂	4(+11)₂(+6)₃	7(+7)₂(+6)₃(+3)₄	44(86%)	7(14%)
Rijeka 66	29	23(+24)₂	8(+21)₂(+15)₃	3(+10)₂(+12)₃(+8)₄	63(95%)	3(5%)
Zagreb 108	58	17(+40)₂	12(+12)₂(+15)₃	7(+21)(+19)(+7)₄	94(87%)	14(13%)
Osijek 33	9	5(+2)₂	3(+4)₂(+1)₃	8(+1)₂(+2)₃(+1)₄	25(76%)	8(24%)
Subotica 32	18	1(+1)₂	4(+6)₂(+1)₃	6(+12)₂(+3)₃(+1)₄	29(91%)	3(9%)
Novi Sad 68	36	4(+6)₂	5(+6)₂(+1)₃	11(+22)₂(+2)₃	56(83%)	12(17%)
Belgrade 96	44	13(+13)₂	15(+16)(+8)	13(+24)₂(+8)₃(+6)₄	85(89%)	11(11%)

Total of Students who Failed / Succeeded

The degree of failure in the identification of Brozović's and Alerić's difference between short falling and short rising accent was confirmed by all items in both tests. Thus, within the framework of the tests the short accents turned out to be the least autonomous as a tool of semantic differentiation and, consequently, the most subordinated in the hierarchy of the tested prosodic means. In fact, the tonal differentiation in general appeared in the tests as less successful than the differentiation by quantity whether accentual or postaccentual. It is therefore feasible to conclude that, in the combinations of tone and quantity tested, it was the quantity which primarily carried the differentiating role. This applies to the sentences with *jèla - Jéla, kùpio - kúpio, pïtajū - pítajū, vòdōm - vòdom, izbora - ȉzbōrā, jèzika - jȅzīkā, kùpiti - kúpiti, sèla - sêlā, kòsti - kòstī*. The identification of these combinations essentially correspond to the results obtained in connection with accentual quantity on the one hand and postaccentual quantity on the other.

4. TEST OF ACCENTUAL POSITION

In normative descriptions of Standard Serbo-Croatian the place of the accent is sometimes expected to distinguish two forms which would be otherwise identical. For example.

gùščetina "goose meat" vs. *guščètina* "big goose"
zèlenīh G pl. def. "green" vs. *zelènīh* G. pl. indef. "green"

In setting up a test for this feature one soon discovers that pairs involving just place of accent are extraordinarily difficult to find. Usually the average speaker knows one member of a pair, but not the other. Thus, place of accent has to be tested along with other prosodic features. In Test I we had the sentences:

Crvèna ruža je krasna.   "A red rose is beautiful."
Cr̀venā ruža je krasna.   "The red rose is beautiful."

in which definiteness and indefiniteness of adjective is to be distinguished by the place of accent and the postaccentual length. This pair would furnish a good contrast in regions where postaccentual length was not functional. However, as mentioned in a preceding section, testing involving selection of an indefinite and definite form failed because the usage of the students tested was not in accord with textbook prescriptions and the test form did not have space for lengthy explanations. As a matter of fact, the identification *crvèna-cr̂venā* produced essentially the same pattern of results as the identification of *vèsela-vȅselā* and *stȁra-stârā*. Thus, with regard to the examples tested, neither tone nor quantity nor place of accent in any combination was effective enough to signal definiteness vs. indefiniteness of adjectives.

A difference in place of accent, established by the normative shift onto the proclitic, also resulted in problems of identification. Alerić's sentences

20/91 *Ȍd kosti se pravi juha.*   Soup is made from a bone.
55   *Od kòstī se pravi juha.*   Soup is made from bones.

were incorrectly identified by half of the students tested in Belgrade and Zagreb. On the other hand, all the students in Travnik identified the distinction correctly. Since the distinction involves postaccentual quantity, it could well be that in Travnik and other places in Bosnia and Hercegovina the basis for identification was postaccentual quantity (ineffective in Belgrade and Zagreb) and not the shift of the accent onto the proclitic (ineffective virtually everywhere). The results of the test, however, strongly suggest that cases such as *ȍd kosti - od kòstī* have to be kept apart from cases such as *òd patkē - òtpatke* where the shift onto the proclitic in a prepositional phrase appears in distinction from a single lexical word. Alerić's sentences

Kokoš krade òd patkē svako jutro.   The chicken steals from the duck every morning.
Kokoš krade òtpatke svako jutro.   The chicken steals scraps every morning.

caused confusion everywhere. In Travnik, where all 28 students tested correctly identified *òd kosti* vs. *od kòstī*, only 5 succeeded in distinguishing *òd patkē* from *òtpatke*. Of the 31 students in Gacko 26 correctly distinguished *òd kosti* from *od kòstī* but only 6 students succeeded in distinguishing *òd patkē* from *òtpatke*. Of the 27 students in Stolac 23 correctly identified the difference between *òd kosti* and *od kòstī* but only 5 students distinguished *òd patkē* from *òtpatke*. Of the 30 students in Dubrovnik 25 correctly identified the contrast between *òd kosti* and *od kòstī* but only 2 were able to discriminate between *òd patkē* and *òtpatke*.

Another contrast involving *skakanje* was presented in the following sentences of Test I:

Òko vrāta je još prljavo.   "It is still dirty around the neck."
Oko vrátā je još prljavo.   "It is still dirty around the door."

The results were very poor though it is noteworthy that the form with the normatively shifted accent, i.e. *òko vrata* (so also *òd kosti*), generally caused more errors than the form retaining accent. For example, attempts to identify *òko vrāta* produced more than three times the number of errors recorded for *oko vrátā*. It appears, therefore, that the phonological distinctiveness of the place of accent does not generally apply to the cases involving the shift on the proclitics. Although such a shift may result in a clear-cut phonetic contrast, the majority of the tested students were not capable of using it phonologically for the expected semantic differentiation. It seems, therefore, that the studies of Serbo-Croatian which treat the shift of accent onto the proclitics as a principal phonological rule may generate forms which are found obscure by the majority of contemporary speakers of Serbo-Croatian. In this case, the fulfillment of the norms, codified more than a century ago, produce phonetic contrasts which are not only atypical for contemporary usage but may appear strange and, for many, even ridiculous.

The difference in the place of accent connected with *skakanje* obviously produces artificial contrasts which have little relevance to the prosodic situation of Modern Serbo-Croatian. But when we examine contrasts not involving *skakanje*, we see that the place of accent is actually the most successful prosodic element; in the successful operation of place of accent there is really no significant difference in the results obtained in the large cities and those from Bosnia-Hercegovina. In response to the sentences

> 5. *S(j)ećam se prijatéljā svog oca.*   I remember the friends of my father.
> 23. *S(j)ećam se prijatéljā svog oca.*   I remember the friends of my father.
> 45. *S(j)ećam se prȉjatelja svog oca.*   I remember the friend of my father.

not only Gacko and Travnik but also Zagreb and Belgrade did well. Since postaccentual quantity carried by the last vowel caused a general failure of identification in both Zagreb and Belgrade, it appears that the successful identification of *prȉjatelja - prijatéljā* was based on the place of accent. Equally good identification was recorded in connection with

> 19. *Što se tiče ȉmena na vratima, ne mogu vam pomoći.*   I can't help you with the name on the door.
> 35. *Što se tiče iménā na vratima, ne mogu vam pomoći.*   I can't help you with the names on the door.

In this case all 50 students in Travnik, all 30 students in Dubrovnik and all 33 students in Osijek succeeded without *any* error.

Thus, in spite of certain types of exceptions, the differentiation by the place of accent turned out to be the most successful among all the cases testing the phonological usage of prosody. Within the framework of the test the place of accent clearly dominates the hierarchy of prosodic differentiation. It appears to be the most autonomous, the most resistant to the impact of the context, whether linguistic or extra-linguistic, and regionally the most generalized. From the point of view of the test (which, of course, represents only a sampling of the universe of prosodic possibilities) the place of accent as a tool of differentiation appears to be more generalized than accentual quantity which in turn appears to be more generalized than postaccentual quantity while tone appears to be the most fragile prosodic element, the one most vulnerable to contextual skewing and, in the larger cities, the one most questionable as a system.

CHAPTER SEVEN

CUMULATIVE TEST SCORES

> *"Što se tiče postakcenatskih duljina, tu je test opet u punom pravu: one se u gradovima o kojima je riječ: Beogradu, Zagrebu, Rijeci i Nišu, donekle i u Splitu, i u nizu manjih gradova veoma često reduciraju, pa čak i iščezavaju kao fonematska vrijednost."*
>
> Miroslav Kravar

In testing a word pair, say *jȅla-Jéla*, two sentences are obviously needed and indeed in Test I two sentences occurred, one with *jȅla* and the other one with *Jéla*. However, for some word pairs three and even four sentences were used; thus, Test I had three sentences which presented not only the basic contrast *kònja-kónjā* but an additional *kónjā* as well, while the same test used four sentences to present *ùčitelja-ùčitēljā* as well as an extra *ùčitēljā* and *ùčitelja*. It would of course have been desirable to use the same number of sentences for each contrast but limitations of testing time prevented it. It is possible, however, to refine the test scores so that better comparison can be made between the different items tested. In Chapter Six the scores are cumulative for each item in all its sentences so that Sarajevo receives a C rating because 75% of the 91 students tested correctly identified the four forms *ùčitelja-ùčitēljā-ùčitēljā-ùčitelja*. In the same test the Sarajevo students received a B for their performance on the three forms *kònja-kónjā-kónjā* and an A for their identification of the two forms *jȅla-Jéla*.

But if we limit our scoring to the basic contrast of *ùčitelja-ùčitēljā* and *kònja-kónjā*, taking those two sentences which present the contrast and on which the group performed most successfully, then the scores would be different, that is, in addition to its A rating on *jȅla-Jéla* Sarajevo would also earn an A on *kònja-kónjā* and a B on *ùčitelja-ùčitēljā*. In this last case we can add a third sentence, the one with the next best performance for the group, and we will find that Sarajevo earns another B; a fourth sentence will yield a cumulative score of C. The scores would then be recorded for Sarajevo as A for *jȅla-Jéla*, A-B for *kònja-kónjā* (and *kónjā*), and B-B-C for *ùčitelja-ùčitēljā* (and *ùčitēljā*, and *ùčitelja*). To summarize, the one letter grade indicates the score on the basic contrast presented in two sentences, a second letter indicates the cumulative score in three sentences, and a third letter the cumulative score in four sentences.

It might be useful at this point to discuss the meaning of the scores earned by student groups in this testing process. As explained in the previous chapter, letter grades are felt to be more useful than the number grades since small differences in the number grades might convey a false impression of great accuracy. Letter grades (see page 98) indicate the range of achievement and make for easier comparison. What do the letter grades actually tell us about the powers of prosodic discrimination in a particular classroom? An A obviously indicates good to excellent achievement since it tells us that from 9/10ths to 10/10ths of the students identified the prosodic difference presented in two sentences. The grade B would seem to indicate solid performance while the grade C indicates a lower level of achievement, perhaps signifying adequate performance. But to be fair to the Yugoslav students tested and to compensate for any minor faults of the testing process, let us assume that C is a good grade, indicating good performance in prosodic discrimination; B, then, is a better grade with A the best. D covers a range of uncertain achievement since such a score may indicate that 1/3 or more of the class failed a particular item. E and F must be regarded as "failing" grades.

Cumulative grades are very helpful in assessing achievement. As pointed out above, the 91 students of Sarajevo earned an A for their discrimination of *jëla-Jéla* and an A-B for *kònja-kónjā* (and *kónjā*). If an additional *jëla* or *Jéla* had been added, Sarajevo might have earned another A or might have gone down to B. If a group earns not only one A but two A's as in the case of Dubrovnik's performance on *lúkē–Lûkē* (and *lúkē*), its overall competence on this item is without question; triple A's, i.e. A-A-A, for Gacko and Stolac on *ùčitelja-ùčitēljā* (and *ùčitēljā* and *ùčitelja*) provide impressive and redundant evidence of the discrimination ability of students in these towns. The B-B-C for Sarajevo on *ùčitelja-ùčitēljā* (and repetitions) must be considered a "strong" score since a good level of competence is attested to over four test sentences.

The following pages present in tabular form the results of the testing in the major cities; only those items which were successfully identified in one or more places are included. Where there are not many A's in the scores for a particular item, a footnote will indicate the small towns which had A or A-B results; the absence of references to the small towns for other items does not mean that they were unsuccessful but rather that one or more of the major cities provides sufficient evidence of successful performance. The students tested in Niš were consistently unsuccessful and so Niš is not included in the table. The first table contains items, places and results from Test I, while the second table has the same information from Test II.

In most of the towns and cities the students tested were native to the respective town or city or its immediate environs. In the three largest cities (Belgrade, Zagreb, and Sarajevo) we checked the students' backgrounds to see if they might affect the test scores. Of the 91 students tested in a Sarajevo *gimnazija* 64 had been born and brought up in Sarajevo, while 27 had been born in Bosnian towns and gone to elementary schools in those towns. There was no appreciable difference in the scores of the Sarajevo-born and the later arrivals. A similar situation obtained in Belgrade where of the 61 tested 40 had been born and raised in Belgrade while 21 had been born outside of Belgrade. But Zagreb was quite different; here we tested a *gimnazija* class of 36 students and a university freshman group of 58. Of the total of 94 students in these two groups 50 had been born and raised in Zagreb while 44 (mostly university students) had come from other regions.

WORD ACCENT

Test I

Place	Sarajevo	Belgrade	Zagreb	Sisak	Loznica	Mostar	Banja Luka	Dubrovnik	Travnik
(Number Tested)	(91)	(61)	(36)	(55)	(116)	(37)	(50)	(30)	(28)
Item									
pȁs-pâs	A-B	B-C	A-B	A-A	B-D	A-B	A-B	A(100)-A	A-B
grȁd-grâd	B-C	C-D	B-C	C-D	C-E	B-D	B-D	A-A	B-C
zòra-Zóra[1]	B	B	E	D	C	B	B	F	A
pèro-Péro	A	B	C	A	B	B	B	A(100)	A(100)
jȅla-Jéla	A	B	B	A	A	B	A	A	B
pȉtajū-pítajū	D	F	F	E	F	B	C	A	B
lȕkē-Lûkē	B-D	E-F	E-E	C-C	C-E	C-E	D-E	A-A	B-B
kònja-kónjā	A-B	B-C	B-B	B-C	B-B	A-B	A-A	A-A(100)	A-A
mȁrkōm-Mârkom	B	B	C	B	C	E	B	B	A
bȁrōm-bârom	B	C	C	B	D	D	B	C	B
grȅbena-grȅbēnā[2]	C-D	D-E	D-E	D-F	D-E	B-D	B-C	A-C	A(100)-A
pádeža-pádēžā[3]	E-F	F-F	F-F	F-F	F-F	D-D	E-E	F-F	B-B
zákona-zákōnā[4]	B-C	F-F	F-F	F-F	F-F	F-F	B-C	B-B	B-B
jèzika-jèzīkā[5]	B-C	D-E	D-F	C-E	C-D	B-C	B-B	B-C	A-B
ìzbora-ȉzbōrā[6]	B-E	F-F	F-F	D-F	C-F	B-D	B-E	D-E	B-C
ùčitelja-ùčitēljā[7]	B-B-C	D-E-F	D-D-F	C-C-E	D-E-F	A-B-B	A-A-B	A-A-B	A-A-B
pògledā-pògledā	B	C	E	E	F	D	D	C	B

[1] A: Gacko, Stolac, Titograd; [2] A-A: Stolac; [3] A-C: Gacko; B-C: Stolac; [4] B-B: Gacko; [5] A-B: Gacko; [6] B-C: Stolac; [7] A-A-A: Gacko, Stolac.

CUMULATIVE SCORES

Test II

Place	Subotica	Novi Sad	Osijek	Belgrade	Zagreb	Rijeka	Split	Dubrovnik	Travnik
(Number Tested)	(32)	(68)	(33)	(96)	(108)	(66)	(51)	(30)	(50)
Item									
pȁs-pȁs	A(100)	A	A	B	B	B	A	A	B
kȕpiti-kúpiti	A	B	A	D	E	E	C	E	C
kònja-kónjā	B	A	A	B	B	C	A	B	A
sèla-sȇlā[1]	B-B	A-B	A-A	C-D	C-D	C-D	A-B	B-D	B-C
kȍla-kȏlā[2]	B-B	B-B	A-B	B-C	C-D	D-D	A-B	B-B	B-B
Gȑka-Gȓkā[3]	B-D	B-D	A-B	C-D	F-F	D-F	B-C	C-E	B-C
rádio-rȁdio	C-D	A-B	A-A	C-D	E-F	E-F	A-B	E-F	D-D
stvȃri-stvárī[4]	D-F	C-E	B-C	D-E	F-F	F-F	B-C	A-B	C-D
konduktéra-konduktérā[5]	E	D	F	F	F	F	E	D	B
ȍstrva-ȍstȓvā[6]	B-C	C-D	B-C	D-F	F-F	F-F	C-F	C-F	B-E
pròfesora-pròfesōrā	A-B-D	C-D-D	A-A-D	F-F-F	F-F-F	D-D-F	A-C-E	A-B-C	A-B-D
rȉbāra-rȉbārā[7]	C-F	E-F	B-F	D-F	E-F	E-F	C-F	D-F	D-F
ȉmena-iménā	A	A	A(100)	B	B	B	A	A(100)	A(100)
prȕjatelja-prijatéljā	A-B	A-A	A-A	A-B	A-B	B-B	A-A	C-C	A-B

[1] A-A: Gacko, Trebinje, Nikšić; [2] A-A: Trebinje, Nikšić; [3] A-A: Trebinje; A-B: Gacko, Stolac;
[4] A-B: Trebinje; [5] A: Gacko, Trebinje; B: Stolac, Mostar; [6] A-A: Nikšić; A-B: Gacko;
[7] B-C: Gacko, Trebinje.

In Zagreb, the test results show striking differences between the native-born and the later arrivals, the latter performing more successfully on the test. The following table compares the scores of the university and the *gimnazija* groups without regard to birthplace as well as the scores of Zagreb natives (born in Zagreb) and the non-native Zagreb residents regardless of *gimnazija* or university status.

ZAGREB

	Natives (50 tested)	Non-natives (44 tested)	*Gimnazija* (36 tested)	University (58 tested)
pȁs-pȃs	B-B	A-A	A-B	A-A
grȁd-grȃd	C-D	B-B	B-C	C-D
zòra-Zóra	F	E	E	F
pèro-Péro	D	B	C	D
jȅla-Jéla	C	A	B	B
pȉtajū-pítajū	F	D	F	E
kònja-kónjā	B-C	A-B	B-B	B-B
lûkē-Lûkē	F-F	B-C	E-E	D-E
mȁrkōm-Mȃrkom	B	B	C	B
bȁrōm-bȃrom	D	A	C	B
grȅbena-grȅbēnā	D-D	C-D	D-E	B-D
pádeža-pádēžā	F-F	F-F	F-F	F-F
zákona-zákōnā	F-F	D-E	F-F	E-F
jèzika-jȅzīkā	E-F	D-F	D-F	D-F
ìzbora-ȉzbōrā	E-F	D-F	F-F	D-F
ùčitelja-ùčitēljā	D-E-F	A-B-D	D-D-F	B-C-F
pògledā-pòglēdā	F	B	E	C

1. POSTACCENTUAL QUANTITY

In Chapter Six a preliminary analysis of the test scores showed quite clearly the strengths and weaknesses of the various prosodic features of Serbo-Croatian. In the remaining part of this chapter we shall consider the same features, adding new material but, more importantly, utilizing the cumulative test scores.

One of the most striking results of the two tests was the poor performance of students in reacting to postaccentual quantity. The most successful contrast in the small towns of Bosnia and Hercegovina was *ùčitelja-ùčitēljā,* a contrast involving no change of accent but a difference in vowel quantity: four short vowels in the genitive singular *ùčitelja,* two short vowels followed by two long vowels in the genitive plural *ùčitēljā.* The results range from excellent (A-A-A in Gacko, Stolac; A-A-B in Dubrovnik, Travnik, Banja Luka) to the expected low in the case of Niš (F-F-F). The results shown below are creditable in Sarajevo (B-B-C) but poor in the other two major cities, Belgrade and Zagreb.

ùčitelja-ùčitēljā-ùčitēljā-ùčitelja

A-A-A:	Gacko, Stolac
A-A-B:	Dubrovnik, Travnik, Banja Luka
A-B-B:	Mostar
A-C-C:	Titograd
B-B-C:	Sarajevo
C-C-E:	Sisak
D-D-F:	Zagreb
D-E-F:	Belgrade, Loznica
F-F-F:	Niš

Let us now look at all three items on Test I involving postaccentual quantity in three major cities; contrasts where the accent difference involves only the putative distinction between short rise and short fall are also included. These items, then, are those which were reacted to successfully in at least some towns (see preceding charts for results in all places).

	Sarajevo	Belgrade	Zagreb
ùčitelja-ùčitēljā	B-B-C	D-E-F	D-D-F
zákona-zákōnā	B-C	F-F	F-F
grȅbena-grȅbēnā	C-D	D-E	D-E
jèzika-jèzīkā	B-C	D-E	D-F
ìzbora-ȉzbōrā	B-E	F-F	F-F
pádeža-pádēžā	E-F	F-F	F-F

In Test II the results were poorer even in the towns which scored well on the Test I postaccentual items. One item which was planned to be analogous to *ùčitelja* of Test I was the contrast involving *profesora*, viz. *pròfesora-pròfesōrā*. Though creditable results for this item were obtained in Dubrovnik (A-B-C) and Gacko (B-B-C), still the results for this term were surprisingly weak or showed strange patterns (A-D-D in Osijek, A-B-D in Travnik, etc.). One reason may have been the accentual instability of the forms (G pl. *profesórā* in the local voices of several places); another may have been the sentence itself, *(S(j)ecám se pròfesora/pròfesōrā romanskih jezika* ("I remember the professor/professors of Romance languages.") which may have been semantically skewed toward the genitive singular.* Perhaps, a better sentence might have been *Bojim se pròfesora/pròfesōrā na fakultetu* ("I'm afraid of the professor/professors at the university"). At any rate the results for this item were dismal in Belgrade and Zagreb (F-F-F in both places). Results were equally bad for the contrast *òstrva-òstȓvā;* here we were interested in seeing the effect of postaccentual length on the

---

*Results in Niš, Zagreb, and Belgrade were helpful in showing the semantic bias of particular sentences since students in these three places seem impervious to postaccentual quantity and so use criteria of contextual probability in making their selection.

r-vowel as far as perception was concerned. Though the sentence was quite neutral as to the form tested, an objection might be made that Croats are more used to the word *otok* for "island" rather than *ostrvo*. This contrast which has results of A-A in Nikšić and A-B in Gacko failed in Zagreb and Belgrade. (F-F and D-F respectively). The contrast of *r̀bāra-r̀bārā* was selected for Test II because it presents an exact test of the discrimination of postaccentual quantity; the genitive singular already has one long vowel, viz. *r̀bāra*, and so the genitive plural can be identified only by the second long vowel, viz. *r̀bārā*. Except for Gacko and Trebinje (B-C in both places) the results for this item indicated a widespread lack of discrimination. A similar failure attended the testing of the contrast *konduktéra-konduktérā*.

The difficulty facing Yugoslavs in identifying postaccentual quantity is quite general, particularly in the large cities. If it is difficult for them to discriminate between forms such as *ùčitelja* and *ùčitēljā*, it is well-nigh impossible for them to distinguish singular from plural in the genitive forms of a word such as *kondùktēr*, "conductor." Only students in the small towns of Bosnia and Hercegovina had any success in making this latter discrimination; to most of the other students these forms (G sg. *konduktéra* - G pl. *konduktérā*) appear as homophonous. That this failure was not due to the particular word involved became clear when similar results appeared with other examples of this type of contrast: *seljáka-seljákā* (*sèljāk*, "peasant"), *Hrváta-Hrvátā* (*Hr̀vāt*, "Croat"), *ofìcíra-ofìcírā* (*ofìcīr*, "officer"), *kombináta-kombinátā* (*kombìnāt*, "business trust"). What predictably makes for difficulty in such a contrast is the fact that the genitive plural signal of two added lengths (e.g. *ùčitelja-ùčitēljā*) is reduced to one in these nouns since the first length of the plural signal coincides with the existing length in the singular form, thus G sg. *aása* vs. G pl. *aáā*.

Even if speakers of Serbo-Croatian had no difficulty in discriminating genitive forms of the type *ùčitelja-ùčitēljā*, their failure in identifying the distinction of the *konduktera* type would mean that number discrimination in the genitive would be lost for a large body of nouns, since this accentual pattern (N sg. *àā*, G sg. *aása*, G pl. *aáā*) is very common, embracing several noun types, e.g.

bìrāč, "voter," jùnāk, "hero," mòrnār, "sailor," Ènglēz, "Englishman," etc.

A similar theoretical contrast which met with failure of identification throughout the country is that between the genitive forms of účenīk, "pupil." Here as in the case of konduktéra-konduktérā the genitive plural signal of two added lengths is vitiated since the genitive singular already has length on the penultimate syllable (G sg. účenīka - G pl. účenīkā), the more important syllable since, as the literature tells us, final vowels tend to be shortened. As mentioned above, a similar situation exists with the contrasts between the genitive forms of rȉbār, "fisherman," viz. rȉbāra-rȉbārā. Only in small towns like Gacko and Trebinje was this distinction identified; for the rest of the country the distinction is either weak or nonexistent. As one can quickly learn from glancing at Matešić's dictionary* there are about 1,500 nouns with the suffix -nīk; there is also a sizeable number of nouns with suffixes such as -āk (prȍsjāk, "beggar"), -ār (kùhār/kùvār, "cook"), -ānje (pítānje, "question"), -ēnje (mùćēnje, "torture"). Such nouns have, in effect, homophonous genitive forms in Yugoslav cities.

As difficult as it is for the students to identify unaccented length in a final syllable when the vowel a is concerned, it is apparently even more difficult to distinguish between long and short i in final syllables. This length distinction supposedly differentiates the genitive forms of the i-nouns. However, sentences involving such contrasts as G sg. okólnosti - G pl. okólnostī (okólnōst, "circumstance") dúžnosti-dúžnostī (dúžnōst, "obligation"), and kȍsti-kȍstī (kȍst, "bone") had no success except in small places (e.g. Travnik).

Let us consider two contrasts involving postaccentual quantity, účitelja vs. účitēljā and jèzika vs. jèzīkā, since these two seem to have tested well. To simplify the scores we shall take only the first letter score, that is, the grade earned on the two items which gave the basic contrast. Limiting ourselves to the cities, we see the following results:

---

*Josip Matešić, Rückläufiges Wörterbuch des Serbokroatischen, Wiesbaden: Harrassowitz, 1965.

CUMULATIVE SCORES

Test I

	ùčitelja vs. ùčitēljā	jèzika vs. jèzīkā
Travnik	A	A
Dubrovnik	A	B
Banja Luka	A	B
Mostar	A	B
Sarajevo	B	B
Sisak	C	C
Loznica	D	C
Belgrade	D	D
Zagreb	D	D

Test II

	pròfesora vs. pròfesōrā	òstrva vs. òstȓvā
Travnik	A	B
Osijek	A	B
Subotica	A	B
Dubrovnik	A	C
Split	A	C
Novi Sad	C	C
Rijeka	D	F
Belgrade	F	D
Zagreb	F	F

The preceding tables contain those items which were discriminated without difficulty in Bosnian and Hercegovinian towns. By eliminating the results of the cumulative score, this partial report (biased in favor of the students) makes it clear that postaccentual quantity in Belgrade, Zagreb, Rijeka, and, of course, in Niš hardly fulfils expectations of the normative grammarians. In this respect the language planning, devoted to the Vukovian ideal, clearly failed.

2. ACCENTUAL QUANTITY

Test I had eight contrasts involving accentual quantity. Test II had three such contrasts. Thus,

Test I	Test II
pȁs vs. pâs	pȁs vs. pâs
grȁd vs. grâd	glàsilo vs. glásilo
zòra vs. Zóra	kùpiti vs. kúpiti
pèro vs. Péro	
jȅla vs. Jéla	
pȉtajū vs. pítajū	
kùpio vs. kúpio	
sàtkao vs. sȁd kao vs. sât kao	

Both tests had additional contrasts involving accentual quantity and also postaccentual quantity. In view of our findings in the preceding section about postaccentual quantity in certain cities, these contrasts can then be judged for what they tell us about accentual quantity. Such contrasts are:

CUMULATIVE SCORES

Test I	Test II
kònja vs. kónjā	kònja vs. kónjā
mȁrkōm vs. Mârkom	sèla vs. sêlā
bȁrōm vs. bârom	kȍla vs. kôlā
lȕkom vs. lûkom vs. lúkōm	Gȑka vs. Gȓkā
stȁra vs. stȃrā	

A "classical" pair which turned out to be a problematic test item is kȕpiti (/kȕpio), "to gather," kúpiti (/kúpio), "to buy"; the contrast yielded poor results on Test I but slightly better results on Test II in a few places (A in Trebinje, Nikšić, Osijek, Subotica; B in Novi Sad). Judging by the fact that one member of the pair, namely, kȕpiti, "to gather," causes twice as many mistakes as kúpiti, "to buy," one would conclude that the verb is losing out in usage to the forms such as sakupljati/skupljati, "to gather." The sàtkao-sȁd kao-sȃt kao items were evidently too tricky for the students tested though their choices confirmed their identification of quantity as indicated by other items; if they could distinguish between pàs and pâs, they could also recognize the difference between sȃt kao and the two short items: sàtkao and sȁd kao, though they usually could not distinguish between the latter two.

A similar situation obtained for the lȕkom-lûkom-lúkōm contrast; whatever their success in distinguishing tonal differences under the accent or postaccentual quantity (e.g. lûkom-lúkōm), they could distinguish the short lȕkom from the two long items (lûkom-lúkōm) as well or as poorly as they could distinguish pàs from pâs. The theoretical contrast glàsilo-glásilo had poor results throughout the country; evidently glàsilo, "publication," is a bookish word to most students. The contrast pȋtajū-pítajū was obviously artificial for most of the students since it tested poorly except in a few places like Dubrovnik (A) and Travnik (B=89%). With all this in mind let us see how well the three largest cities made out on Test I with successful items involving accentual quantity.

	Sarajevo	Belgrade	Zagreb
pȁs-pâs	A-B	B-C	A-B
grȁd-grâd	B-C	C-D	B-C
zòra-Zóra	B	B	E
jȅla-Jéla	A	B	B
pèro-Péro	A	B	C
mȁrkōm-Mârkom	B	B	C
kònja-kónjā	A-B	B-C	B-B

Sarajevo was not tested with Test II but for the sake of comparison perhaps Travnik can be used in its stead. Thus, the items involving accentual quantity on Test II had the following results for Travnik, Belgrade and Zagreb.

	Travnik	Belgrade	Zagreb
pȁs-pâs	B	B	B
kònja-kónjā	A	B	B
sèla-sêla	B-C	C-D	C-D
kȍla-kôla	B-B	B-C	C-D
Gȑka-Gȓkā	B-C	C-D	F-F

On the basis of the foregoing results it seems clear that the *pȁs-pâs* contrast and the *kònja-kónjā* contrast are identified successfully, though not perfectly, in the major cities (except Niš); in cities where postaccentual quantity still plays a role, *kònja-kónjā* obviously offers a more pronounced distinction than *pȁs-pâs*. Assuming that the distinction is similar (i.e. just involving accentual quantity) for Belgrade and Zagreb, let us now see the cities divide on the basis of these two contrasts from both tests. We will just consider the first letter of any score since that will tell us how the students performed on the basic contrast for any item.

	pȁs vs. pâs		kònja vs. kónjā	
	Test I	Test II	Test I	Test II
Sarajevo	A		A	
Mostar	A		A	
Travnik	A	B	A	A
Novi Sad		A		A
Osijek		A		A
Split		A		A
Dubrovnik	A(100)	A	A(100)	B
Banja Luka	A		A	
Sisak	A		B	
Subotica		A(100)		B
Belgrade	B	B	B	B
Zagreb	A	B	B	B
Loznica	B		B	
Rijeka		B		C
Niš	F		F	

The table clearly indicates that speakers of Serbo-Croatian in all the cities except Niš can identify the difference between an accented short vowel and an accented long vowel; it is, therefore, possible to conclude that in their speech accentual quantity is meaningfully utilized and appears as a functional prosodic system.

3. TONE

Both Test I and Test II contained the contrast *pàra-pàra* in the sentences: *I danas pȁra igra ulogu,* "Even today steam plays a role," and *I danas pàra igra ulogu,* "Even today money plays a role." In no locality was there any significant success in the discrimination of these forms. Moreover, in Test II, the sentences

Evo kȍsti za vašu juhu/čorbu.   Here's a bone for your soup.
Evo kòstī za vašu juhu/čorbu.   Here are some bones for your soup.

caused an obvious confusion.

Contrast: *kȍsti* vs. *kòstī*

B-D: Travnik
C-D: Gacko, Stolac, Split, Mostar
C-E: Trebinje
C-F: Dubrovnik
E-F: Osijek, Novi Sad, Subotica, Banja Luka, Rijeka
F-F: Nikšić, Zagreb, Belgrade, Titograd

Test I had another contrast which involved the short accents and a postaccentual length in the sentences:

Vojnik je stajao pred vȍdom i gledao u daljinu.   The soldier stood in front of the squad and gazed into the distance.

Vojnik je stajao pred vȍdōm i gledao u daljinu.   The soldier stood in front of the water and gazed into the distance.

Again the results are so bad that it is useless to speculate as to the nature of the contrast:

Contrast: vòdom vs. vòdōm

C: Sarajevo, Gacko, Dubrovnik

D: Stolac, Travnik

E: Banja Luka

F: Mostar, Titograd, Sisak, Belgrade, Zagreb, Niš, Loznica

That the short accents can be distinguished in certain places by certain people is without question; the authors themselves tested educated individuals from Sarajevo and other Bosnian and Hercegovinian towns who could identify the distinction.* But the testing clearly shows that certain forms which, according to the voluminous literature on accents, are distinguished only by the short accents, are by and large homophonous to speakers of Serbo-Croatian. Accentologists will no doubt continue to find " and ' accents in the speech of informants but there is no proof that, for the mass of urban speakers, such accents are as functional as it is expected by the normative grammarians.

A contrast between the long accents occurred on Test I in the sentences *Evo lúkē u daljini,* "There's the port in the distance." and *Evo Lûkē u daljini,* "There's Luke in the distance." Since these forms occur over and over in the literature of accents and are claimed to provide a tonal contrast, one could assume that they would be a fair test of the putative contrast. The results indicate either that the tonal contrast between the long accents is artificial or that the tones in the two forms used are not, in many localities, those of the normalizing dictionaries, i.e. *lúka, Lûka.* The performance was not very good with the exception of Dubrovnik (A for the basic contrast in 2 sentences, A also for the cumulative 3 sentences) or Travnik (B-B).

Test II had the sentences *Što je rádio u našem društvu,* "What has he been doing in our society?", *Što je râdio u našem društvu?,* "What is radio in our society?" The two cities, Dubrovnik and

---

*E.g. Dr. Ranko Bugarski and Dr. M. Ridjanović, both of Sarajevo.

Travnik, which did well on *luka-Luka,* showed a disastrous performance on *radio-radio,* suggesting perhaps that the noun *radio* might have a different accentual realization in these places. Yet some cities did quite well on this item with scores such as the following: Osijek: A-A; Novi Sad: A-B; Split: A-B. Here are the results for the two contrasts involving tone on an accented long syllable.

Test I

Contrast: *lúkē* vs. *Lûkē*

A-A: Dubrovnik
B-B: Travnik, Stolac
B-D: Gacko, Sarajevo
C-C: Sisak
C-E: Loznica, Mostar
D-E: Banja Luka, Titograd
E-E: Zagreb
E-F: Belgrade
F-F: Niš

Test II

Contrast: *rádio* vs. *râdio*

A-A: Osijek
A-B: Novi Sad, Split
B-C: Trebinje
C-D: Belgrade, Subotica, Gacko, Nikšić
D-D: Travnik
D-F: Stolac
E-F: Zagreb, Mostar, Dubrovnik, Rijeka
F-F: Titograd

4. PLACE OF ACCENT

Test II had two contrasts which involved, among other features, a difference in the place of accent. Thus,

Što se tiče ȉmena na vratima, ne mogu vam pomoći.	"I can't help you with the name on the door."
Što se tiče iménā na vratima, ne mogu vam pomoći.	"I can't help you with the names on the door."
S(j)ećam se prȉjatelja svog oca.	"I remember the friend of my father."
S(j)ećam se prijatéljā svog oca.	"I remember the friends of my father."

Of all the contrasts on Test II these two drew the most accurate responses regardless of area. The results were:

	ȉmena vs. iménā	prȉjatelja vs. prijatéljā
Osijek	A (100)	A-A
Novi Sad	A	A-A
Split	A	A-A
Trabinje	A	A-A
Nikšić	A	A-A
Travnik	A (100)	A-B
Subotica	A	A-B
Stolac	A	B-C
Dubrovnik	A (100)	C-C
Mostar	A	C-D
Belgrade	B	A-B
Zagreb	B	A-B
Rijeka	B	A-B
Gacko	B	B-B
Titograd	C	C-D

These two pairs make maximum use of prosodic features since they show contrasts in place of accent, in tone, in accentual quantity and in postaccentual quantity. Yet the astounding success of these pairs across the whole Serbo-Croatian speech territory compels us to conclude that the difference in place of accent played a major role in the differentiation of *ȉmena* from *iménā*, of *prȉjatelja* from *prijatéljā*, since the other features (tone, accentual quantity, postaccentual quantity) both alone and in combination did not enjoy such testing success. It seems therefore, that precisely the difference in place of accent is most distinctly used for semantic differentiation and appears as the most generalized prosodic device in contemporary Serbo-Croatian.

CHAPTER EIGHT

LOCAL VOICES

"Mnogi na žalost misle da je poznavanje naših akcenata sasvim teoretska stvar, pa se zbog toga i ne zanimaju za njih."

Ljudevit Jonke

The response of the students tested to the readings of Alerić and Brozović are, of course, relevant only to the recognitory aspects of prosodic distinctions. Since there is no good reason to assume that the ability to identify various prosodic distinctions necessarily implies the ability to produce them, the second part of the test was designed to investigate the local production of prosodic differentiation and the local responses to it. For this purpose, each group tested was represented by one of the participants who was born and raised in the community and preferably one whose parents were born there as well.

The role of the local representatives consisted in reading aloud the fifty sentences of Test II, thus making it possible for us to test the responses of the rest of the group to the local usage without the mediation of the tape-recorder. This aspect of the test was rather close to the local communication, although reading, of course, cannot fully represent spontaneous speech. Nevertheless, the data provided an interesting basis for comparison with the responses to the two main speakers (i.e. Alerić and Brozović).

Each local reading was recorded (during the reading in front of the class) to enable a subsequent test of the local speaker on the basis of his or her own voice. Alerić, moreover, submitted each recording of the local production to a careful analysis by means of repeated playback and detailed phonetic evaluation of the sentences in their entirety. Thus, more than one thousand sentences were turned into a corpus of phonetic data reflecting the responses of a trained linguist with a Hercegovinian dialectal background to the variability of local usage in the urban areas of Yugoslavia. The results implicitly represent a contrastive analysis of the prosodic variants viewed strictly from a Hercegovinian standpoint.

1. ACCENTUATION OF THE LOCAL VOICES

The local voices, that is, the voices of selected *gimnazija* students in all locales tested, were recorded reading the 50 sentences of Test II. These recordings were then transcribed for accentuation by Danijel Alerić; he also accented the sentences as read by some special readers (e.g. Dalibor Brozović, Pavle Ivić). The normative accentuation of these 50 sentences is presented in the Appendix; it agrees exactly with that noted by Alerić as he listened to Brozović's reading of the sentences. This latter fact indicates the existence of some accentual standards, at least for the specialists.

In providing accent marks for the students' renditions, Alerić exployed the usual notation, i.e. four marks (" ˋ ˆ ´) plus the macron (-) for length. In addition, he added observations about the accents he was hearing, observations which sometimes question the value of a standard notation for that particular rendition (see his remarks for Milenko P. of Belgrade, Nevenka Ž. from Zagreb). He also used another sign (′′) for an accent called *tromi* ("heavy, sluggish"); in the transcriptions following we use a simple tick mark (') for his *tromi* accent. The *tromi* accent seems to be very indefinite and Alerić uses it as an all-purpose mark for uncertain cases. Quoting Ivšić, Alerić defines it being "somewhat rising; the quantity differs in various dialects, but can reach a full length, especially on the *a* vowel." To this Alerić adds: "it is a fact that of all the Serbo-Croatian accents the *tromi* is the least musical." When he makes the accentual notation for the Zagreb voices, he uses the *tromi* sign extensively. Of its value in Zagreb he says that it is *upravo ekspiratoran naglasak, veoma sličan naglasku u njemačkom jeziku,* "precisely a stress accent, very similar to the accent in the German language."

As a check on Alerić's accentuation, we asked Professor Brozović to add the accentual notation for the local voices of Belgrade and Zagreb. Brozović's accentuation of the Belgrade voices agreed in general with that of Alerić but there were some interesting differences. First of all, Brozović did not use the *tromi* but tried to encompass the accentual variations by means of the four accent marks. Thus, for Miroslava P.:

Alerić's notation	Brozović's notation
Gŕka	Gr̃ka
kónja	kònja
prȋjatelja	prȉjatelja
sȇla	sȅla
búrē	búrē

In the last case, that of *bure,* Alerić had added a note that here the *tromi* was lengthened so as to make it almost a long rise. From these and other examples Alerić's *tromi* in Belgrade voices can be interpreted by Brozović as ` ` ` or ` " ` or ` ' `. Particular problems come with the short rise ( ` ` `). Though Brozović agrees with Alerić in the marking of such forms as *dòbro, vèlik, òca,* etc., with the short rise accent, he adds the note *spori prekratak, gotovo brzi,* "short rise [is] too short, almost a short fall." What Alerić identifies as a short rise strikes Brozović, depending on the form, either as a short rise, a short fall, or a long rise. This last interpretation is particularly interesting because it affects the minimality of a contrast in the Belgrade voice of Milica V. In the four sentences which tested the distinction *òrao - ȍrao,* Miroslava P. produced the same accent for the *orao* form in all four sentences. Alerić hears the accent as a short rise (` ` ` ), Brozović as a long rise ( ` ' `).

	Alerić's interpretation	Brozović's interpretation
20	Dȁ li je òrao na tôm brežúljku?	Dȁ li je órao na tôm brežúljku?
30	Dȁ li je òrao na tôm brežúljku?	Dȁ li je órao na tôm brežúljku?
13	Dȁ li je òrao na tôm brežúljku?	Dȁ li je órao na tôm brežúljku?
47	Dȁ li je òrao na tôm brežúljku?	Dȁ li je órao na tôm brežúljku?

This difference in interpretation also shows up in the same sentences in the reading of Milica V. In Alerić's notation Milica produced the contrast *(òrao-ȍrao)* in the manner hoped for; in addition, Milica made the correct selections when she was later tested on her own voice. The performance of her fellow students on this elusive short rise–short fall contrast was, if not perfect, still rather impressive (C-C-C = 4 sentences). On the surface it would seem that Milica and her fellow students are able to produce and distinguish the short accents. But Brozović hears the contrast as ȍrao - órao and so for him the contrast is simply short fall vs. long rise or a short syllabic vs. a long one.

	Alerić's interpretation	Brozović's interpretation
20	Dȁ li je ȍrao na tôm brežúljku?	Dȁ li je ȍrao na tôm brežúljku?
30	Dȁ li je ȍrao na tôm brežúljku?	Dȁ li je ȍrao na tôm brežúljku?
13	Dȁ li je òrao na tôm brežúljku?	Dȁ li je órao na tôm brežúljku?
47	Dȁ li je òrao na tôm brežúljku?	Dȁ li je órao na tôm brežúljku?

Asking a Yugoslav specialist in accents to add the accentual notation to a text by a native of Zagreb is to offer him a mild form of torture. Typically such a specialist operates with the premise (or the hope) that the Vukovian system is inherently in the speech of young Yugoslavs (in the Serbo-Croatian speech area) and that the accentual features of Zagreb speech can somehow be noted in relation to the Vukovian standards. To an outsider the prosodic character of Zagreb speech seems to consist only of a stress accent. In this situation Alerić makes constant use of his "crutch," the *tromi* accent, while Brozović discovers new accent designations to describe the Zagreb accentual exotica. Consider their accentuation of a few sentences in the reading of Marina Š. First the sentence will be given in the notation of the Vukovian ideal (V.i.), as it would, in fact, be read by both Alerić and Brozović; then Alerić's (A.) transcription, then Brozović's (B.) transcription.

1. V.i. Dòbro se sjẽćām pròfesora ròmānskīh jȅzīkā.
   A. Dóbro se sjéćam prófesora rómanskih jézika. *
   B. Dȍbro se sjêćam prȍfesora rȍmanskih jêzika. *

In his notation B. defines his ˇ accent as a "kajkavian ˋ," and the ˜ as "a kajkavian ˆ."

2. V.i. Nèstalo je rȉbāra za vrijȅme tê bȗrē.
   A. Néstalo je rībara za vrjéme te búre.
   B. Nèstalo je rȉbara za vrjême te bȕrẽ.

3. V.i. Štȍ se tȋčē sèla u òvō dôba, tô je vèlik pròblēm.
   A. Štó se tíče séla u óvo doba, tó je vélik próblēm.
   B. Štȍ se tȋče sȅla u ȍvo dôba, tô je vȅlik prȍblẽm.

Here B. uses the sign ˜ which usually indicates the neoacute or čakavian acute, a long rising accent, but B. labels it "˜ kratak" or a short neoacute.

13. V.i. Dȁ li je ȍrao nà tom brežùljku?
    A. Dá li je órao na tóm brežúljku?
    B. Dȁ li je ȍrao na tȍm brežȕljku?

In other sentences B. also uses the signs for a short rise and a long rise (ˋ, ˊ) but specifies that each is *jednosložan*, "one syllable."

Brozović was also tested on the Zagreb voices in that he completed test forms for the 3 voices from Zagreb. As he himself said while taking the test, "It's a pure lottery," and indeed he scored no better than Zagreb students who, listening to their fellow

---

*The accentologists did not indicate local pronunciation features unless they affected the accent; thus *sjećam* in Zagreb comes out *sjećam*. But see *vrjeme* in sentence 2.

student's voice, tried in vain to interpret it with a test form set up for Vukovian distinctions.

2. POSTACCENTUAL QUANTITY IN THE LOCAL VOICES

The majority of the local speakers disclosed either consistent deviations in the usage of postaccentual quantity or various types of vacillation. The recordings of all four local speakers from Zagreb and of two from Belgrade were found to lack postaccentual quantity almost completely. It was, therefore, only natural that the test in Zagreb and Belgrade, based on local voices, resulted in total confusion.

As a matter of fact, the local voices, as compared with Brozović's implementation, caused more errors in many places, including the homeland of Vuk's ancestors. For example, in Nikšić, 19 students made altogether 11 errors in response to Brozović's four sentences with *pròfesora/pròfesōrā* but they made 14 errors in response to the local voice of Bogoljub Č. In Trebinje, where 29 students were tested, Brozović's four sentences caused altogether 16 errors while the local production of Dragica M. caused 33 errors. Alerić's analysis of Dragica's voice revealed that she pronounced the penultimate vowel with length in both singular and plural so that her contrast appeared as *pròfesōra* vs. *pròfesōrā;* it is quite possible that precisely this deviation lowered the accuracy. Exactly the same type of deviation was found in the local voice of Stolac (Muharem D.) and in Travnik (Emil L.). The local voice in Banja Luka was found vacillating in the plural between *pròfesōra* and *pròfesōrā*. On the other hand, in Titograd on the Albanian border, and in Subotica on the Hungarian border, the local voices changed postaccentual quantity into a long rising accent so that the difference between genitive singular and plural appeared as *pròfesora* vs. *profesóra*. The same transformation, combined with length of the last vowel, was found in the local voices in Rijeka, Osijek and in one of the local voices in Belgrade (Milica V.). The response to this irregular plural in Belgrade and Osijek was surprisingly accurate. Among the 32 students in Belgrade responding to Milica's voice, only one erred while 7 students took Brozović's standard pròfesōrā for singular. In Osijek, 9 out of 33 students incorrectly identified Brozović's pròfesōrā but only 3 students took the local profesóra for singular.

In Osijek the contrast rȉbāra vs. rȉbārā was reinterpreted by the local speaker into rȉbara vs. rȉbārā and caused fewer errors than Brozović's standard pronounciation. The irregular contrast rȉbara vs. rȉbārā with two short vowels in the singular and two long vowels in the plural was also found in the local voice in Banja Luka. On the other hand, the local voice in Rijeka and two local voices in Belgrade (Milenko's and Milica's) used the irregular contrast rȉbara vs. rȉbāra (instead of rȉbāra vs. rȉbārā) so that the standard singular form rȉbāra appeared as a plural in opposition to the irregular singular rȉbara. In Rijeka the irregular singular was properly identified by 27 out of 31 students whereas the regular singular in Brozović's production caused 15 errors (i.e. 50%). In Belgrade Milenko's irregular plural rȉbāra caused 8 errors in the group of 30 students, whereas Brozović's regular plural rȉbārā caused 11 errors. Milica's irregular singular, used in the Belgrade group of 32 students, caused 9 errors, while Brozović's regular singular caused 25 errors.

In Zagreb Pavlin D. and Marina Š. replaced in their pronounciation the standard contrast rȉbāra vs. rȉbārā by rȋbara vs. ribára, that is to say, by the difference between short prominent first syllable vs. long prominent second syllable. Alerić in his analysis denoted the irregular contrast in two Zagreb voices as rȉbara vs. ribára with the provision that the sign ´ in that case should not be taken for Hercegovinian long rising accent but rather for an accent which is neither rising nor falling but long. The major characteristic of such an accent, which Alerić calls tromi, consists in the prominence of the carrying syllable without tonal distinction (i.e. ᷉ = short prominent or "stressed" syllable; ᷊ = long prominent, "stressed" syllable). It is noteworthy that the Zagreb students, responding to Pavlin's and Marina's voices, more accurately identified the non-standard distinction in the place of accent than the standard usage of postaccentual quantity in Brozović's voice. The difference in accuracy provides, of course, a significant illustration of a conflict between two prosodic systems: one using quantitative distinction without any change in accent, the other making the distinction by changing the place of accent and adding accentual quantity.

A replacement of postaccentual quantity by a difference in the place of accent was also found in the local voice in Nikšić, where the speaker used the irregular contrast *kònduktera* vs. *konduktérā* (i.e. short rising on the first syllable vs. long rising on the third syllable) instead of the standard *konduktéra* vs. *konduktérā*. Among 19 students in Nikšić, eleven took Brozović's standard singular *konduktéra* for a plural but all of them correctly identified the irregular *kònduktera* as singular. For that particular contrast, Marina Š. in Zagreb used *konduktěra* vs. *konduktéra* (i.e. short prominent vs. long prominent on the penultimate syllable.) Among 27 students responding to her voice nine wrongly identified the irregular singular and ten Brozović's regular singular, while 6 students misunderstood the irregular plural and eight students Brozović's regular plural

Rather consistent deviation in postaccentual quantity was found in the local production of the genitive plural of *ostrvo:* in Stolac, Banja Luka, Dubrovnik and Sarajevo, the local speakers used *òstrvā* instead of *òstrvā*. Even more general was the shortening of the last vowels in the majority of verbal forms used in the test sentences, e.g., *tiče* instead of *tičē*, *boje* instead of *bojē*, *igra* instead of *igrā*, *čini* instead of *činī*, *nema* instead of *nemā*, *s(j)ećam se* instead of *s(j)ećām se*. In Mostar and Stolac the local voices were found pronouncing *nêmā* as *némā* but preserving the expected postaccentual length in all other verbal forms.

The shortening of the last vowel of the nominal forms was found in the speech of many local speakers, particularly in Belgrade. In Zagreb, moreover, the local speakers shortened the last two vowels or postaccentual length in general. It is noteworthy, however, that almost all local speakers, including those in Zagreb and Belgrade, clearly expressed postaccentual quantity in the noun *problem* used in the sentence *Što se tiče sela u ovo doba, to je velik problem* (which occurred three times in the test). In that case, perhaps postaccentual quantity was reinforced by sentence intonation (i.e. final pitch). It is possible, however, that length in the form *pròblēm* was maintained because of its foreign background. Actually, the only exceptions were found in the local voices in Gacko and Nikšić which had *próblem* instead of standard *pròblēm*.

3. ACCENTUAL QUANTITY IN THE LOCAL VOICES

In the matter of accentual quantity the local voices displayed considerably fewer deviations from the standard than in postaccentual quantity. Nevertheless, in certain areas, particularly in Zagreb and Belgrade, the expected distinctions between length and shortness in the accented position were often non-existent. Moreover, Alerić's analysis of the local voices in Zagreb as well as in Belgrade showed a lack of distinction in terms of accentual quantity, combined in some instances with lack of distinction in tone. In Belgrade's Milenko P., for example, the expected sentences

16a	*Ȅvo kȍsti zà vašu júhu*
33a	*Ȅvo kȍsti zà vašu júhu*
49b	*Ȅvo kȍstī zà vašu júhu*

appeared as

16a	*Ėvo kosti za vašu juhu*
33a	*Ėvo kosti za vašu juhu*
49b	*Ėvo kosti za vašu juhu*

It is apparent that Milenko's voice did not permit analysis in terms of tone (i.e. rising/falling) or quantity (long/short), whether accentual or postaccentual. Only the prominence (or "stress") of the accented positions was left and was clearly detectable. This reduction of prosodic distinctions to the binary contrast of accented and unaccented positions also characterized all five local voices recorded in Zagreb. For example, the expected sentences:

| 40a | *Čìnī se da je môj pȁs bȍljī nego tvôj* |
| 18b | *Čìnī se da je môj pȁs bȍljī nego tvôj* |

were found in all five local voices in Zagreb as

40a   Čȉni se da je mȏj pȁs bȍlji nego tvȏj.
18b   Čȉni se da je mȏj pȃs bȍlji nego tvȏj.

Needless to say the reduction of prosodic contrasts necessarily affected the accuracy of identification. The crucial distinction between *pȁs,* "dog," and *pȃs,* "belt," was lost and caused, of course, the loss of semantic distinction. In response to Alerić's *pȁs* (40a) and *pȃs* (18b), a Zagreb class of 25 students made 6 errors. The same group, however, made 26 errors in response to the same sentences produced by their own colleague, Mirjana Š., or almost perfect statistical chance. A Belgrade group of 30 students made totally 7 errors in response to Alerić's *pȁs* (40a) and *pȃs* (18b) but made 29 errors (i.e. 50%) in response to *pȁs* (40a) and *pȃs* (18b) produced by their own colleague, Milenko P.

In Alerić's phonetic analysis, the production of Milenko in Belgrade appeared as

40a   Čȉni se da je mȏj pȁs bȍlji nego tvȏj.
18b   Čȉni se da je mȏj pȃs bȍlji nego tvȏj.

In this case, the difference between the local voice in Belgrade and the local voices in Zagreb consists only in the amount of remnants of accentual quantity (and tone) remaining in a system which basically utilizes only the difference between accented (i.e. prominent or "stressed") positions and non-accented positions in the sentence.

Deviations from the expected implementation of accentual quantity were also found in the local voices in Bosnia and Hercegovina. In Gacko, for example, the local speaker Milan B. vacillated between the expected *jȕhu* and the irregular *jȕhu*. The local speakers in Mostar, Travnik and Sarajevo consistently pronounced *vȑstē* instead of the expected *vȑstē*.

Several variants were also found in the local voices in Slavonia and Vojvodina. The local speaker in Osijek, for example, used *vȑstē* for *vȑstē, vrijéme* for *vrijème* and *relàciji* for *relàciji*. The local speaker in Subotica consistently used *relàciji* for *reláciji* and *jùhu* for *júhu*. Also one local speaker in Novi Sad used *jùhu* for *júhu*, *vr̀stē* for *vŕstē* and *bùrē* for *bȕrē*.

On the whole, however, the deviations in accentual quantity in the local voices were less striking than the numerous variants deviating from the expected usage of postaccentual quantity. It seems, therefore, that the fate of accentual and postaccentual quantity is not identical and should be studied as two systems with their own autonomous history in spite of many common denominators.

4. TONE IN THE LOCAL VOICES

The analysis of the local voices from the Hercegovinian point of view (as interpreted by Alerić) revealed two types of deviations: in some instances in certain areas rising accent was replaced by falling accent or vice versa. On the other hand, in some areas, particularly in Belgrade and Zagreb, the Hercegovinian distinction between rising and falling accent was not applicable. In his analysis of the local voice of Nevenka Ž. in Zagreb, Alerić found it necessary to provide a comment to clarify the difficulties in evaluating one system from the point of view of another system:

> "In her pronunciation there is absolutely no difference between " and ', but one always hears ' (the *tromi*). The difference between ˝ and ′ is weak; these accents are often so short that they approximate the *tromi*. Unaccented lengths are heard somewhat better at the end of the sentences. Therefore, one must not take the accents ˝ and ′ and the length mark ¯ in the Hercegovinian sense."

In accordance with this approach, the expected distinction

26a *I dànas pàra ȋgrā ȕlogu.*
44b *I dànas pàra ȋgrā ȕlogu.*

appeared as

26a *I dànas pâra ȉgra ùlogu.*
44b *I dànas pâra ȉgra ùlogu.*

The *"tromi"* accent was also found by Alerić in the local voices in Belgrade. Commenting on the production of Belgrade's Milenko P., Alerić writes:

"In his pronunciation there is practically no difference between ˝ and ˋ ; his ˆ is like ˈ (the *tromi*) and his ˊ is not well expressed. His lengths are also unexpressed. Thus, the marking of his accents by means of the signs used for the literary accents cannot really be justified."

These comments reflect the difficulties of a phonetician who was asked to adhere as strictly as possible to his concept of Hercegovinian prosody and thus to the Standard Serbo-Croatian accentuation. Implicitly, the problem illustrates the dialectal clash which takes place in the two largest cities in contemporary Yugoslavia. More generally, it also illustrates the dilemma of any linguist who is evaluating the prosodical characteristics of a dialect which is not his own, a dilemma which in the past was certainly common to all accentologists who could not use recording equipment for verification of their subjective findings.

Alerić's observation about the lack of tonal distinctions in the Hercegovinian (and *eo ipso* standard) sense was fully confirmed by the responses of the groups tested to the local voices. In Belgrade and Zagreb the sentences designed to test tonal distinctions resulted in total chaos.

The substitution of rising accent for falling accent or falling for rising was found in some instances in the "classical" areas. For example, the local speakers in Travnik, Mostar, Nikšić, Sarajevo, and also in Dubrovnik and Osijek consistently used *sélā* for the expected *sêlā*. The local speaker in Stolac was found to use *némā* for the expected *nêmā* while the local speakers in Mostar and Sarajevo vacillated between *némā* and *nêmā*. The local speaker in Novi Sad consistently used *órao* for the expected *òrao* so that the difference between "he plowed" and "the eagle" appeared as *òrao* vs. *órao* instead of the expected ȍrao vs. ȍrao. In four occurrences of these forms the group of 36 students made only two errors in response to the local ȍrao vs. órao while they made 44 errors in response to Alerić's pronounciation and 54 errors in response to that of Brozović. In other words they failed to identify the distinction in the standard version although they were almost perfect in identifying the local version. It follows that the promotion of the standard system of prosody can cause not only difficulties but direct confusion in communication, at least in certain cases in which the tonal difference plays a crucial role.

5. PLACE OF ACCENT IN THE LOCAL VOICES

Cases such as the local contrast kònduktera vs. konduktérā instead of konduktéra vs. konduktérā or the local rȉbara vs. ribára instead of rȉbāra vs. rȉbārā were discussed in connection with post-accentual quantity as efficient local substitutes enhancing the accuracy of identification. The analysis of the local voices made it very clear that the place of accent may become the only distinct prosodic characteristic if tonal and quantitative differences are non-existent or appear only as phonetic features without any clear-cut phonological role on the word level. This was particularly true of the local voices in Belgrade and even more so in Zagreb. In Zagreb Pavlin D., for example, was found to distinguish prȉjatelja from prijatélja instead of the expected prȉjatelja vs. prijatéljā so that the difference between short falling and long rising accent combined with postaccentual quantity was replaced merely by the distinction in place of accent without any difference in tone or accentual and postaccentual quantity.

Thus, the expected sentences

    45a   Sjȅćām se prȉjatelja svôg òca.
    5b   Sjȅćām se prijatéljā svôg òca.

appeared as

    45a   Sjećam se prijatelja svog oca.
    5b   Sjećam se prijatelja svog oca.

The group of 39 students in Zagreb, responding to Pavlin D., their own colleague, made 2 errors in connection with *prȉjatelja* and 4 errors in connection with *prijatélja* but the same group made 12 errors in response to Brozovic's *prijatéljā*.

In one class in Belgrade Milica, the local voice, produced the form *profesórā* for the expected plural *pròfesōrā;* her fellow-students overwhelmingly interpreted this form as a plural. Compare the response of the students to the voice of Brozović and that of Milica.

	Brozović's voice		Milica's voice	
	sg.	pl.	sg.	pl.
pròfesora	10	22	*pròfesora*	29	3
pròfesora	22	10	*pròfesora*	31	1
pròfesōrā	13	19	*pròfesōrā*	21	11
pròfesōrā	7	25	*profesórā*	1	31

One might think that the final length in *profesórā* plays a part in the discrimination. However, it is clear that the students in this (and other) schools cannot perceive such final length when it follows a long rising accent; they cannot, for example, hear the difference between the G sg. *konduktéra* and the G pl. *konduktérā*. It is interesting that Brozović, tested on Milica's voices three years later, also interpreted *profesórā* as a plural; in addition, he perceived *pròfesōra* as a plural. One can see the importance in the change of position of stress by looking at the reaction to the forms of *prijatelja* in the same Belgrade classroom.

	Brozović's voice		Milica's voice	
	sg.	pl.	sg.	pl.
prȉjatelja	31	1	*prȉjatelja*	32	0
prijatéljā	1	31	*prijatéljă*	0	32
prijatéljā	0	32	*prijatéljă*	0	32

In these items 94% of the students perceived the Brozović distinction, while 100% perceived it in the voice of their fellow student even though she did not produce the final length.

The shifting of the accent seems to be a more effective discriminator of number than the mere addition of posttonic length. Compare, for example, the responses of a class of 27 Zagreb students to the *ribara* forms as articulated by Brozović and by Marina who indicates the plural by shifting the accent.

	Brozović's voice			Marina's voice	
	sg.	pl.		sg.	pl.
rȉbāra	11	16	rȋbara	23	4
rȉbára	12	15	ribára	2	25
rȉbārā	3	24	ribára	2	25

The two sentences, expected to be pronounced as

19a Štȍ se tȋčē ȉmena na vrátima, ne mògu vam pòmoći.
35b Štȍ se tȋčē iménā na vrátima, ne mògu vam pòmoći.

were found in Belgrade in the local pronounciation by Milenko P. as

19a Štȍ se tȉče ȉmena na vrátima, ne mògu vam pȍmoći.
35b Štȍ se tȉče iména na vrátima, ne mògu vam pȍmoći.

In other words, the expected difference between short falling and long rising accent combined with postaccentual quantity was implemented as a difference in the place of accent combined with the difference in the accentual quantity. The group of 30 students, responding to Milenko's voice, make 2 errors in connection with ȉmena but 6 errors in connection with Brozović's ȉmena; they made 5 errors in response to Milenko's iména but 7 errors in response to Brozović's iménā. Thus, in terms of the average, the responses to Brozović represent 20% of errors while the responses to Milenko amount to 10% of errors. In both cases, the degree of accuracy is relatively high but, in this instance, it is higher in response to the local production.

The place of accent in the local voices, however, presents a strikingly different picture in connection with the expected shift of accent onto the proclitic where the difference in the place of accent may actually involve a contrast between a word and a phrase. In accordance with normative grammar both Alerić and Brozović used the shift to the proclitic, e.g., *nà tom brežùljku; ù našem drùštvu; nà tōj relāciji; zà vȁšu jùhu*. Most of the local speakers, however, totally disregarded the rules of the shift. Milan B. in Gacko shifted the accent only once: in the phrase *nà tom brežùljku;* in three other occurrences of the same phrase he articulated *na tôm brežùljku*. Some of his other phrases were:

*u nȁšēm drùštvu
na tôj relāciji
za vȁšu jùhu*

The local speakers in Stolac, Nikšić, Trebinje, Travnik, Banja Luka, Dubrovnik, Split, Titograd, Rijeka, Subotica, Novi Sad consistently used *na tôm, u nȁšem (/nȁšēm), na tôj, za vȁšu*. Likewise in Belgrade and Zagreb none of the speakers shifted the accent to the proclitic. Among all local speakers only one was found to follow the rules of the normative grammar (which, of course, in that case were identical with the local usage). This single exception was recorded in Mostar in the pronounciation of Slobodanka N. One of the local speakers in Sarajevo (Irfan H.) consistently used *nà tom brežùljku* but *u nȁšem drùštvu* and *za vȁšu jùhu (/jùhu)* while he vacillated between *nà tōj relāciji* and *na tôj relāciji* (the other local speaker in Sarajevo did not use the shift to the proclitic at all). Margita P. in Osijek consistently used *nà tōm brežùljku* and *nà tōj relāciji* but always *u nȁšem drùštvu (/drùštvu)* and *za vȁšu jùhu*. Thus, a clear majority of the local speakers did not follow the rules of normative grammar concerning the shift of accent to the proclitic and so the textbook rules of accent shift appear to contradict prevailing contemporary usage. This finding perhaps explains why the identification involving the shift to the preposition (e.g. òtpatke vs. òd patkē) in Test I ended in a total failure. It follows that prescriptive grammars which insist on the shift actually neglect an obvious trend in the language and represent a conservative effort which is apparently doomed to the failure. By the same token the tightly knitted sequences of rules in generative grammars, which use normative manuals as primary sources, are designed to produce forms which appear as well-formed only in a couple of regional enclaves in contemporary Yugoslavia.

6. A BELGRADE VOICE

In making their accentual notations, both Alerić and Brozović worked very slowly and carefully, listening to each sentence several times. With such attention a specialist can detect nuances which would escape the casual listener. This can be seen in the results obtained when we tested Brozović on some of the Belgrade voices, having him fill out the test form as he listened to the voice, just as the many students in Yugoslavia had done. In fact, on one voice, that of Milica V., we tested him twice within an interval of a few weeks. Here are the results with the responses indicated by an English translation of the test choice; responses not in agreement with the accentuation are underlined.

Milica's rendition as accented by Alerić	As accented by Brozović	As heard by Milica	As heard by Brozović on his first test	As heard by Brozović on his second test
pȁra	pȁra	steam/money*	steam	steam
pȁra	pȁra	steam/<u>money</u>	steam	<u>money</u>
ȍrao	ȍrao	plowing	plowing	plowing
ȍrao	ȍrao	plowing	plowing	plowing
òrao	órao	eagle	eagle	eagle
òrao	órao	eagle	eagle	eagle

*Here Milica checked both entries, indicating that she could not make a choice.

WORD ACCENT

Milica's rendition as accented by Alerić	As accented by Brozović	As heard by Milica	As heard by Brozović on his first test	As heard by Brozović on his second test
pȁs	pȁs	dog	dog	dog
pâs	pâs	belt	belt	belt
glàsilo	glàsilo	publication	sounded	sounded
glàsilo	glàsilo	publication	publication	publication
glàsilo	glàsilo	sounded	publication	publication
kȕpiti	kȕpiti	to gather	to gather	to gather
kȕpiti	kȕpiti	to gather	to buy	to buy
râdio	râdio	radio	radio	radio
râdio	râdio	radio	radio	radio
rádio	rádio	doing	doing	doing
stvári	stvári	thing	things	things
stvári	stvárĩ	things	things	things
stvárĩ	stvárĩ	things	things	things
kȍsti	kȍstĩ	bone	bones	bone
kȍsti	kȍsti	bone	bone	bone
kòsti	kòsti	bones	bones	bones
prȉjatelja	prȉjatelja	friend	friend	friend
prijatélja	prijatéljă	friends	friends	friends
prijatélja	prijatéljă	friends	friends	friends
ȉmena	ȉmena	name	name	name
iména	iménă	names	names	names
kònja	kònja	horse	horse	horse
kónja	kónjă	horses	horses	horses
konduktéra	konduktéra	conductor	conductors	conductor
konduktéra	konduktéră	conductors(?)	conductor	conductor

Milica's rendition as accented by Alerić	As accented by Brozović	As heard by Milica	As heard by Brozović on his first test	As heard by Brozović on his second test
pròfesora	pròfesora	professor	professors	professor
pròfesora	pròfesora	professor	professor	professor
prŏfesōra	prŏfesōra	professor	professors	professors
profesórā	profesórā	professors	professors	professors
rȉbara	rȉbăra	fisherman	fisherman	fisherman
rȉbāra	rȉbāra	fisherman	fisherman	fisherman
rȉbāra	rȉbāra	fishermen	fishermen	fishermen
sèla	sèla	village	village	village
sèla	sèla	village	village	village
sélā	sélā	villages	villages	villages
kȍla	kȍla	dance	dance	dance
kôla	kôlă	dances	dances	dances
kôlā	kôlā	dances	dances	dances
Gȑka	Gȑka	Greek	Greek	Greek
Gȑka	Gȑka	Greeks	Greeks	Greeks
Gȑka	Gȓkă	Greeks	Greeks	Greeks
ȍstrva	ȍstrva	island	islands	islands
ȍstȓva	ȍstȓva	islands	islands	islands
ȍstȓvā	ȍstȓvā	islands	islands	islands

Brozović's results and, in particular his "errors," underscore the very important point mentioned above: there is a big difference between carefully analyzing a person's articulation in order to provide it with a Vukovian prosodic notation and then quickly making a form selection based on prosodic features as the particular articulation is made and heard only once. Brozović and Alerić have no difficulty in both situations (i.e. prosodic transcriptions after many listenings, and form selection at one listening) when specialists such as themselves or local voices from small towns in

7. A ZAGREB VOICE

It is possible for us to look rather closely at the results obtained with local voices in Zagreb and Belgrade. We have not only the results of students tested on the local voice but we have the accentuation of the voices by two specialists; in addition, one of the specialists (Brozović), was tested twice on these voices. Here, for example, are the test items abstracted from the sentences of Test II as read by Marina Š., a high school girl in Zagreb. Alerić used his all-purpose *tromi* extensively in trying to cope with Marina's prosody; Brozović used a variety of accent marks but qualified them in different ways, e.g. a kajkavian ", a short ˉ, etc. Marina's responses to her own voice are given without comment; those of Brozović's are underlined when they do not agree with his own accentual evaluation. It is, however, interesting to note that on one of the few items where Alerić and Brozović agreed in their accentuation, namely, on the *radio* forms, Marina's interpretation was exactly opposite to the Vukovian values.

Marina's rendition as accented by Alerić	As accented by Brozović	As heard by Marina	As heard by Brozović on his first test	As heard by Brozović on his second test
pȁra	pȁra	steam	steam	steam
pȁra	pȁra	steam	money	money
ȍrao	ȍrao	eagle	eagle	plowed
ȍrao	órao	plowed	eagle	eagle
ȍrao	ȍrao	eagle	eagle	eagle
ȍrao	órao ('jednosložan)	plowed	eagle	eagle

Marina's rendition as accented by Alerić	As accented by Brozović	As heard by Marina	As heard by Brozović on his first test	As heard by Brozović on his second test
rádio	rádio	radio	doing	doing
rádio	rádio	radio	doing	doing
râdio	râdio	doing	radio	radio
pâs	pâs	dog	belt	dog
pâs	päs	dog	belt	belt
glàsilo	glä̀silo	publication	publication	publication
glàsilo	glä̀silo	publication	sounded	publication
glàsilo	glä̀silo	sounded	publication	publication
kúpiti	kúpiti	to gather	to buy	to buy
kúpiti	kǜpiti	to gather	to gather	to gather
konduktéra	konduktéra	conductor	conductors	conductors
konduktéra	konduktéra	conductors	conductors	conductors
Gȑka	Gȑka	Greek	Greeks	Greeks
Gȑka	Gȑka	Greeks	Greeks	Greek
Gȑka	Gȑka	Greeks	Greeks	Greeks
kòla	kö̀la	dances	dance	dance
kòla	kö̀la	dances	dances	dances
kòla	kôla	dances	dances	dances
kònja	kö̀nja	horse	horse	horse
kónja	kónja	horses	horses	horses
sèla	sèla	villages	villages	village
sèla	sèla	villages	village	villages
sèla	sèla	villages	villages	villages
kòsti	kõsti	bone	bones	bones
kòsti	kö̀sti	bone	bones	bones
kòsti	kö̀sti	bones	bones	bones

WORD ACCENT

Marina's rendition as accented by Alerić	As accented by Brozović	As heard by Marina	As heard by Brozović on his first test	As heard by Brozović on his second test
stvȃri	stvȃri	things	things	things
stvȃri	stvȃri	things	things	things
stvȃri	stvȃri	things	things	things
rȉbara	rȉbara	fisherman	fisherman	fisherman
ribára	ribára	fishermen	fishermen	fishermen
ribára	ribára	fishermen	fishermen	fishermen
ȍstrva	ȍstrva	islands	islands	island
ȍstrva	ȍstrva	islands	islands	islands
ȍstrva	ȍstrva	islands	islands	islands
prȍfesora	prȍfesora	professor	professor	professors
prȍfesora	prȍfesora	professor	professors	professor
prȍfesora	prȍfesora	professor	professors	professors
prȍfesor	prȍfesora	professors	professors	professors
imèna	iména	name	names	names
imèna	iména	name	names	names
prȉjatelja	prȉjatelja	friend	friend	friend
prȉjatelja	prȉjatelja	friend	friend	friend
prȉjatelja	prȉjatelja	friend	friends	friend

It is interesting that Brozović reacted to the change of place of accent in the *ribara* forms in exactly the same way as the Zagreb girl, Marina, namely he interpreted *rȉbara* as a genitive singular, but *ribára* (2 times) as a genitive plural. Thus, when the Vukovian pattern of *rȉbāra* (G sg.) - *rȋbārā* (G pl.) is replaced by one involving a simple change in the place of accent, there is no hesitation in identifying the singular and plural parts of the pattern, undoubtedly after the analogy of *ȉmena-iménā, prȉjatelja-prijatéljā;* typically, for Zagreb speakers, these forms are produced with a simple stress accent, viz. 'imena-im'ena, pr'ijatelja-prijat'elja.

8. COMMUNICATION WITHIN THE CLASSROOM

As mentioned earlier, teachers reacted in different ways to our testing: some tried to help the students, some very carefully avoided taking the tests themselves (though invited to), while some quite enthusiastically participated in the testing. A good example of the participating teachers is Mrs. Jelena M. of High School No. 6 in Belgrade; she took the test (No. II) with all three voices: Alerić, Brozović, and the local voice, that of the student she selected as being representative. According to the data on her test forms she was born in 1929 in Mokrin (Vojvodina), went to the elementary school there, to the high school in Kikinda (Vojvodina), and to the University of Belgrade. In the version of Test II using Alerić's voice she made 11 errors (out of 50 possible), while to the Brozović version she made only 3. In her written comments she said: *"Drugi glas je bliži mom izgovoru. Akcenat je bolje naglašen."* "The second voice [Brozović's] is closer to my pronunciation. (His) accent is better enunciated." Her three mistakes were with *para-para* which she interpreted as being the opposite to the manner intended (and read), and she mistook one of the four occurrences of the *orao-orao* item. Compared to other teachers tested, her performance was quite good.

Miroslava P., the student selected as being representative of Belgrade, had also made a good score on the Brozović reading, making only 4 errors: 1 on *orao,* 1 on *para,* and 2 on *stvari.* In her comments she has written: *Veoma interesantan test. Test sa bržim izgovorom je mnogo bliži našem svakodnevnom govoru. Čini mi se da je najteže razlikovati kod "stvari" da li je množina ili jednina.,* "A very interesting test. The test with the faster pronunciation [Brozović's] is much closer to our everyday speech. It seems to me that the most difficult thing is to distinguish between the plural and singular in [the item] *"stvari."*

Miroslava read the 50 sentences of Test II while her fellow-students and her teacher filled in their reactions to her sentences; later Miroslava completed a test form, listening to her own voice which had been recorded while she read. At a still later period Alerić listened to Miroslava's recorded voice and supplied the accentuation for her sentences. In the first column below we have Miroslava's test forms as accented by Alerić; in parentheses after each form we have put the English meaning of the accented form or an indication as to whether it is a singular or plural form; where Alerić's accentuation indicates some deviation from the expected accentuation a question mark is added. In the second column we have Miroslava's choices as indicated in English by meaning or grammatical number (sg., pl.), in the third column the teacher's choices, and in the fourth column the students' choices. Besides Miroslava, there were 33 students in the class; in addition to their specification we have added the percentage of correctness where that seems to be determinable; it should be remembered that the percentage is determined on a student by student basis and thus is often lower than the correctness for any particular item. For example, in the *konduktera-konduktera* item 24 (out of 33) students correctly identified the first occurrence as a sg.; that would indicate 73% correctness for that occurrence. On the second occurrence 26 students correctly identified the second occurrence as a pl.; that would be 78% of correctness. However, if we examine the responses, student by student, we will find that only 19 students were correct in making the basic discrimination in the two occurrences; that would yield a 58 percentage of correctness for the basic contrast.

As accented by Alerić	As identified by Miroslava	As identified by teacher	As identified by other (33) students
pȁs (dog)	dog	dog	dog - 33, belt - 0
pâs (belt)	belt	belt	dog - 3, belt - 30
			(91% correctness)
ȉmena (sg.)	sg.	sg.	sg. - 30, pl. - 3
iménā (pl.)	pl.	pl.	sg. - 2, pl. - 31
			(88% correctness)
prȉjatelja (sg.)	sg.	sg.	sg. - 28, pl. - 5
prijéljā (pl.)	pl.	pl.	sg. - 3, pl. - 30
prijéljā (pl.)	pl.	pl.	sg. - 1, pl. - 32
			(79% - 2, 79% - 3)

As accented by Alerić	As identified by Miroslava	As identified by teacher	As identified by other (33) students
konduktéra (sg.)	sg.	pl.	sg. - 24, pl. - 9
konduktérā (pl.)	pl.	pl.	pl. - 7, pl. - 26 (58%)
kôlā (pl.)	pl.	pl.	sg. - 4, pl. - 29
kȍla (sg.)	sg.	sg.	sg. - 30, pl. - 3
kȍla (sg.)	sg.	sg.	sg. - 29, pl. - 4 (82% - 2, 76% - 3)
kònja (sg.)	sg.	sg.	sg. - 31, pl. - 2
kónjā (pl.)	pl.	pl.	sg. - 8, pl. - 25 (73%)
kúpiti (to buy)	to buy	to buy	to buy - 23, to gather - 9
kúpiti (to buy)	to buy	to buy	to buy - 26, to gather - 6 (61%)
rȁdio (doing)	doing	doing	doing - 26, radio - 6
rȁdio (doing)	doing	doing	doing - 18, radio - 15
rȁdio (doing)	doing	doing	doing - 26, radio - 7 (70% - 2, 40% - 3)

In all the foregoing items Miroslav's choices have agreed with the answers indicated by Alerić's accentuation; the correctness of the other students has been judged by the agreement of their choices with Miroslava's. In the following items her choices do not completely agree with the accentuation; except for the first item (*sela*) the percentages of correctness (no matter how judged) of the students is around 50% or lower and so will not be listed.

sêlā (pl.)	pl.	pl.	sg. - 3, pl. - 30
sèla (sg.?)	sg.	sg.	sg. - 26, pl. - 7
sȅla (sg.)	pl.	sg.	sg. - 29, pl. - 4

(if we take the teacher's answers, pl.-sg.-sg., as correct here, the student percentage of agreement is 82% - 2, 70% - 3; if Miroslava's answers are used, the percentage for 3 occurrences would be much lower. It seems quite possible that her last choice of pl. was a *lapsus calami*.)

Gȓkā (pl.)	pl.	pl.	sg. - 10, pl. - 23
Gȓka (sg.?)	sg.	sg.	sg. - 21, pl. - 12
Gȓka (sg.)	sg.	pl.	sg. - 12, pl. - 19*
ȍstȓvā (pl.)	sg.	pl.	sg. - 10, pl. - 23
ȍstrva (sg.)	sg.	pl.	sg. - 22, pl. - 11
ȍstrva (sg.)	sg.	pl.	sg. - 25, pl. - 8
rȉbārā (pl.)	sg.	sg.	sg. - 18, pl. - 13
rȉbāra (sg.)	sg.	sg.	sg. - 27, pl. - 6
rȉbārā (pl.)	pl.	sg.	sg. - 11, pl. - 22
pròfesōrā (pl.)	sg.	sg.	sg. - 22, pl. - 10
pròfesōrā (pl.)	sg.	sg.	sg. - 17, pl. - 16
pròfesora (sg.)	sg.	sg.	sg. - 28, pl. - 5
pròfesōrā (pl.)	sg.	sg.	sg. - 26, pl. - 7
kòsti (sg.?)	sg. (?)	pl. (?)	sg. - 26, pl. - 7
kòsti (sg.)	sg.	pl.	sg. - 24, pl. - 7
kòstī (pl.)	sg.	pl.	sg. - 9, pl. - 22
stvȃrī (pl.)	pl.	pl.	sg. - 7, pl. - 25
stvȃrī (pl.)	sg.	pl.	sg. - 11, pl. - 20
stvȃrī (pl.	pl.	pl.	sg. - 4, pl. - 28

It is interesting to note that Brozović, whose accentuation of the *profesora* items agrees exactly with that of Alerić's, responded to these items in a way consistent with the accentuation but at variance with the classroom response; as mentioned before, he was tested on Miroslava's voice in 1969.

*On certain items some students will indicate both answers (sg. and pl.) or will indicate none; thus, here and elsewhere the total of single choices will be less than 33.

Miroslava's reading as accented by both Alerić and Brozović	Test forms as identified by Brozović
pròfesōrā	pl.
pròfesōrā	pl.
pròfesora	sg.
pròfesōrā	pl.

Let us compare the performance of Miroslava and her classmates for the two readings: that by Brozović and that by Miroslava. Here we shall list only those items which were perceived by the students with a score of at least 70% or higher. As you can see, the list is not very long.

	To Brozović	To Miroslava*
pȁs-pȃs	88%	91%
kònja-kónjā	88%	73%
kȍla-kôlā	82%	82%
kȍla-kôlā-kôlā**	71%	76%
sèla-sêlā	71%	79%
sèla-sèla-sêlā	62%	71%
ȉmena-iménā	94%	88%
prȉjatelja-prijatéljā	88%	79%
prȉjatelja-prijatéljā-prijatéljā	85%	79%

*Here Miroslava's own performance is calculated in with that of the other 33 students; this results in a slight difference of percentage only in the *sela* item.
**The test reading; Miroslava, however, read 2 singulars *(kȍla, kȍla)* and 1 plural *(kôlā)*.

Putting the same results into letter grades, we have these scores:

	To Brozović	To Miroslava
pȁs-pȃs	B	A
kònja-kónjā	B	C
kȍla-kȏlā-kȏlā	B-C	B-C
sèla-sêlā-sêlā	C-D	C-C
ȉmena-iménā	A	B
prȉjatelja-prijatéljā-prijatéljā	B-B	C-C

9. VARIATIONS IN ACCENTUATION OF LOCAL VOICES

Even in those areas where the Vukovian standard seems to be represented in the local voices, there are deviations from the orthodox accentuations.

Vukovian standard: G sg. pròfesora - G pl. pròfesōrā
- short fall instead of short rise, i.e. prȍfesora - prȍfesōrā, found in Gacko, Trebinje, Stolac, Mostar, Travnik, Banja Luka, Nikšić, Piva, Dubrovnik, Split, Sarajevo.
- accent shift in plural, i.e. pròfesora - profesórā, found in Titograd, Split (i.e. profesóra; also prȍfesōra in same voice), Rijeka, Osijek (also prȍfesōrā in same voice), Subotica, Belgrade (also pròfesōra in same voice).

Vukovian standard: G sg. prȉjatelja - G pl. prijatéljā
- no change in place of accent, i.e. prȉjatelja - prȉjatēljā, found in Gacko (also prijatéljā in same voice), Stolac, Trebinje (also prijatéljā in same voice), Travnik, Banja Luka, Sarajevo, Nikšić, Dubrovnik.

Vukovian standard: G sg. Gȑka - G pl. Gȑkā
- short fall in G pl., i.e. Gȑkā, in Dubrovnik, Sarajevo (in 3 out of 4 voices), Travnik, Subotica.
- long rise in G pl. form, i.e. Gŕkā, in Osijek.
- short rise in G pl., i.e. Gȑkā, in Banja Luka.

Vukovian standard: G sg. sèla - G pl. sêlā
- long rise in G pl., i.e. sélā, in Mostar, Travnik, Banja Luka, Sarajevo, Nikšić, Dubrovnik, Osijek, Belgrade (one voice)

Vukovian standard: G sg. rȉbāra - G pl. rȉbārā
- shift in accent, i.e. ribára, which seems to be sg. in Titograd, Rijeka, but pl. in Zagreb.

There were, of course, variations in many other items in the sentences but here only a few will be mentioned. Throughout the ijekavian area local readers consistently pronounced *vrjéme* for *vrijème*. Almost invariably the student readers rejected the word order of the printed sentences: *Moj će pomoćnik kupiti . . .* in favor of *Moj pomoćnik će kupiti. . . .* Also the suggested word order: *Folklorni se referat tiče . . .* was often changed to *Folklorni referat se tiče . . .* or *Folklorni referat tiče se. . . .*

10. TEST OF THE SPECIALISTS

In addition to the many hundreds of students who were tested in Yugoslav classrooms, several linguists, native speakers of Serbo-Croatian, agreed to take the verification test individually. Since all of them were chosen because of their interest or specialization in accentology, it was possible to assume that they had a more sophisticated approach to the testing than the majority of the seventeen-year-old participants in the classroom testing. Moreover, the classroom with its various types of environmental interference was replaced by a less distracting setting so that the test conditions were optimal. Undoubtedly, there was also a higher degree of concentration and more motivated attitude to the challenge on the part of the specialists tested. The outcome, therefore, is not directly comparable with the data from the collective testing although it is, in many respects, complementary to the findings about the phonological role of the Vukovian system and about its fate in contemporary Yugoslavia.

On the basis of the responses two groups became very clearly distinguishable. One group comprised those who were born and raised in Bosnia and Hercegovina, like Professor Brozović, Dr. Bugarski and Dr. Ridjanović. They responded with admirable accuracy and implicitly proved that the Vukovian system, as it was represented in the test, should be considered as being still operative in the usage of some speakers who were raised in those areas which served more than a century ago as a basis for Vukovian normalization.

On the other hand, the second group comprised those linguists who were born and raised outside of the classical area of Vukovian normalization, like Dr. Božidar Finka (born in the čakavian area in Sali, graduated from high school in Split), Dr. Bratoljob Klaić, (born in Bizovac in Slavonia, raised in Zagreb), Dr. Mitar Pešikan, (born in Cetinje in Montenegro, raised in Peć), and Professor Pavle Ivić (born in Belgrade, raised in Subotica in Vojvodina). In striking distinction to the first group, the members of the second group found certain parts of the test confusing to such a degree that all of them without exception failed the expected identification of various contrasts.

Dr. Finka in his response to the hundred sentences of Test I read by Alerić misunderstood 14 of them and doublemarked an additional four as ambiguous so that, in terms of a generalized percentage, he made altogether 18% of errors. Most of the errors were caused by wrong identification of postaccentual quantity: *konduktéra* was twice identified as *konduktérā*, *ùčenīka* was taken for *ùčenīkā*, *oficīrā* for *oficíra*, *zákōnā* for *zákona*, *Hrváta* for *Hrvátā*, *pògledā* for *pòglēdā*, *lûkom* for *Lûkōm*, *sùprugom* for *sùprugōm*. Moreover, four contrasts involving postaccentual quantity were doublemarked as ambiguous in his reactions to the following sentences:

Govorili su o položaju kombináta *u našoj republici*
(hesitation between *kombináta* and *kombinátā*)
Što se tiče oficíra *nautike, to nije toliko velik problem.*
(hesitation between *oficíra* and *oficírā*)
Podržavamo borbu národa *za slobodu.*
(hesitation between *národa* and *nárōdā*)
Dužnost Hrváta *je jasna.*
(hesitation between *Hrváta* and *Hrvátā*)

Also the expected differentiation by tone or by the combination of tone and postaccentual quantity caused a couple of wrong identifications: *lȕkē* was identified as *Lûkē* and *vȍdom* as *vòdōm*. In one case the difference in accentual quantity was misunderstood: *zòra* was identified as *Zóra*. Furthermore, the shift of accent caused two errors: *crvèna* was taken for *crvenā* and *ȍd kosti* for *od kòstī*. It is interesting, however, that with exception of *crvèna* vs. *crvenā* Finka properly identified all other instances involving the difference between indefinite and definite adjectives, i.e. *vȅsela* vs. *vȅselā* and *stȁra* vs. *stârā*. Moreover, he correctly recognized two occurrences of *kȕpio* and two occurrences of *kúpio*, *pàra* as well as *pàra*, *ȍko vráta* as well as *oko vrátā*, two occurrences of *sàtkao*, one occurrence of *sȁd kao* and one occurrence of *sât kao*, *òtpatke* as well as *òd patkē*, *jèzika* as well as *jȅzīkā*, *izbora* as well as *ȉzbōrā*, etc.

In response to the same one hundred sentences Professor Bratoljub Klaić made totally 13% of errors. Some of them were also caused by postaccentual quantity: *konduktéra* was twice identified as *konduktérā*, *oficíra* was taken for *oficírā*, *lûkom* for *Lûkōm*, *dúžnostī* for *dúžnosti*, *učenīka* for *ȕčenīkā*, *seljáka* for *seljákā*, *zákōnā* for *zákona*, and *vȅselā* for *vȅsela*. Moreover, Professor Klaić once took *òd patkē* for *òtpatke* and once *òtpatke* for *òd patkē*, once *pàra* for *pàra* and once *sàtkao* for *sȁd kao*.

Dr. M. Pešikan was twice confused by the sentence, *Broj konduktéra nije poznat*, and took *konduktéra* for *konduktérā*. He could not make any distinction between *pàra* and *pàra* and double-marked both occurrences. Moreover, he put a question mark in connection with *Crvèna ruža je krasna*, although he correctly identified *Crvenā ruža je krasna* as well as all other occurrences of indefinite and definite adjectives (i.e. *vèsela d(j)evojka nas raduje; vèselā d(j)evojka nas raduje; stàra žena sporo radi; stārā žena sporo radi).* Like Finka, he took *sùprugom* for *sùprugōm* and had doubts about the form *ùčenīka.* Although he identified it correctly, he added a question mark revealing his uncertainty. In a generalized percentage his results represent 9% of errors; they are comparable to the performance of some students in Bosnia and Hercegovina, although a few students responded to Alerić's hundred sentences even more accurately.

Among the four linguists Professor Pavle Ivić achieved the best results. Out of one hundred sentences read by Alerić he correctly identified 95, so that his test represents 5% of errors: once he took *pàra* for *pȁra,* once *Mârkom* for *mȁrkōm,* once *vèselā* for *vèsela,* once *sȁd kao* for *sàtkao* and once, vice versa, *sàtkao* for *sȁd kao.* His errors were connected with Alerić's difference between short rising and short falling accent, with the distinction between definite and indefinite adjectives and, in one instance, with the distinction between the proper name *Marko* and the common noun *marka.*

It is certainly noteworthy that the classical example *pàra* vs. *pȁra* was found confusing by three of the four specialists, although the contrast is often quoted in the literature as an illustration of the difference between short rising and short falling accent. It is also significant that all four specialists had difficulties with the difference between definite and indefinite adjectives and that three of them identified *sùprugom* as *sùprugōm* and *konduktéra* as *konduktérā.* This suggests that postaccentual quantity as well as tonal contrast (i.e. short rising vs. short falling) is a questionable source of phonological distinction even for the trained ear, particularly if the syntactic arrangement of the sentence or some other linguistic or non-linguistic peculiarities interfere. Most important, however, is the fact that all four linguists, who were not able to identify Alerić's one hundred sentences with absolute accuracy, were born and raised in the dialectal areas, the linguistic systems of which appear to be in conflict with Vukovian accentuation. It is precisely the conflict of various dialectal backgrounds which appears as a major and most probably unsurmountable obstacle to the expansion of the Vukovian accentual system from its narrow rural basis into the major cultural centers of contemporary Yugoslavia. Since the great majority of contemporary speakers of Serbo-Croatian do not have the native dialectal background, which is required for mastering Vukovian accents, the system has hardly any chance to become standardized in the true sense. Therefore, it can be predicted that the Vukovian normalization will be either abandoned by normative grammarians or it will continue to exist as a challenge which most native speakers of Serbo-Croatian will be unable to meet despite the best efforts of schools. This prediction implies that the natural process of standardization now taking place in the major cultural centers will validate another system or systems.

CHAPTER NINE

GENERAL CONCLUSIONS

"Daleko sam od zadovoljstva stanjem naše akcentologije."
Mitar Pešikan

Slavic accentology remains in the peculiar position of attempting to solve (in the spirit of XIX century linguistics) problems pertaining to Slavic prehistory without solving first the more immediate and verifiable questions of synchrony and historical change. . . .
Edward Stankiewicz

The results of our testing are quite startling, challenging as they do the Vukovian accentual canons, and so it is hardly surprising that questions have been raised about the validity of certain test items and test sentences. Since Serbo-Croatian word accent characterizes virtually all lexical words and all possible morphological permutations, a workable identification test can be based only on a restricted selection from such accentual riches. Our first selection was incorporated into a test of one hundred sentences and yielded good results, but in an effort to avoid possible test fatigue on the part of the students tested we developed our second test of only fifty sentences. In selecting items for such restricted tests we used as much as possible those word pairs which occur so often in the literature as pat illustrations of the differentiating role of the Serbo-Croatian accent that they can be termed accentual cliches. Such cliches are pairs like pȁra, "steam," pàra, "money"; Lûka, "Luke," lúka, "port"; pȁs, "dog," pâs, "belt"; grȁd, "hail," grâd, "city"; and many more. We felt that if generations of Yugoslav accentologists were basing their claims to the functionality of the Vukovian system on these examples, then we could hardly be criticized for using them in our tests.*

Some of the oft recurring pairs are, however, so patently artificial that we eliminated them from consideration. For example, Vuk in his 1818 grammar cites the minimal pair jȁrica, "goat," and jàrica, "wheat," and Stevanović is still citing them in his 1964 grammar, but our preliminary testing showed quite clearly that few speakers of Serbo-Croatian know both words and many do not know either one. For the same reason our tests avoided all pairs involving the bookish difference between aorist and imperfect forms, although all of the normative grammars make much of the "fact" that in some cases only the contrast between the short falling and long falling accents distinguishes an aorist form from an imperfect as in the following forms of the verb brȁti, "to pick."

---

*As this work was being prepared for the printer, the authors received copies of Josip Matešić, Der Wortakzent in der serbokroatischen Schriftsprache, Heidelberg: Carl Winter, 1970, 345 pp. To show that the traditional Vukovian system still has a strong supporter in Matešić, it is necessary only to quote this section from pages 37-38:

"Der Akzent besitzt in der skr. Schriftsprache distinktive Funktion sowohl auf phonologischer wie auch auf morphologischer Ebene, z.B. dȕga "Daube" : dúga "Regenbogen," lȕk "Zwiebel" : lûk "Bogen," Lûka "Lukas" : lúka "Hafen," pèro "Feder" : Péro "Peter." Ebenso wird die Verschiedenheit sonst gleichlautender Flexionsformen durch den Akzent signalisiert: pȍlja (Gen. sg.) : pòlja (Nom., Akk., Vok. pl.), sȅla (Gen. sg.) : sèla (Nom., Akk., Vok. pl.), mêdo (Nom. sg.) : médo (Vok. sg.). Merkmal für die semantische Differenzierung kann also sein:
   a) die Quantität der betonten Silbe, wie lȕk : lûk, slȁže "er lügt" : slâže "er setzt zusammen, er schichtet," pèro : Péro, malìna "eine kleine Anzahl," malína (~màlin, -ína) "Rufname für Pferde";
   b) die Qualität der betonten Silbe, wie pȁra "Dampf" : pàra "Geld," sȅla : sèla, Lûka : lúka, mêdo : médo.
   c) Quantität und Qualität der betonten Silbe, wie dȕga : dúga, pèro : Péro, Vok. sg."

	aorist		imperfect
1st sg.	brȁh	1st sg.	brâh
1st pl.	brȁsmo	1st pl.	brâsmo
2nd pl.	brȁste	2nd pl.	brâste
3rd pl.	brȁše	2nd/3rd sg.	brâše

Most normative grammars also like to dwell on the derivational patterns of indefinite and definite adjectives which in many instances are allegedly differentiated by prosodic features only, e.g. indef. fem. *vȅsela,* "gay," def. fem. *vȅselā;* indef. fem. *crvèna,* "red," def. fem. *cr̀venā.* In our longer test (Test I), however, all sentences involving such a distinction resulted in complete confusion and so in the shorter test (Test II) we refrained from testing for this elusive distinction. Likewise, the confusion caused by the shift of accent onto the proclitic and/or by the expected assimilation of word boundaries led to the elimination of pairs such as

1. *Ȍd kosti se pravi juha.* "Soup is made from a bone."
2. *Od kòstī se pravi juha.* "Soup is made from bones."

or

1. *Ȍko vrāta je još prljavo.* "It's still dirty around the neck."
2. *Oko vrátā je još prljavo.* "It's still dirty around the door."

or

1. *Kokoš krade òtpatke svako jutro.* "The chicken steals scraps every morning."
2. *Kokoš krade òd patkē svako jutro.* "The chicken steals from the duck every morning."

In other words we wanted to avoid, as much as possible, interference caused by the obsolescence of certain grammatical categories, by obvious bookishness, by regional peculiarities and, in general, by those non-prosodic factors which might obscure the role of the prosodic features under investigation.

GENERAL CONCLUSIONS

Of course, factors causing interference are not as easy to isolate as completely as one would like. Members of pairs, whether lexical or grammatical, may differ in frequency of occurrence and this fact may become an important aspect in the identification procedure. For example, *grâd,* meaning "city," has a predictably higher frequency of occurrence in contemporary Yugoslavia than *grȁd,* meaning "hail" or "sleet," so that the isolated sentence, *Na ovaj grad tuže se vozači* seems to favor the interpretation, "Drivers are complaining about this city," rather than "Drivers are complaining about this hail." Or interference may be caused by regional restriction of certain lexical items; for example, *ostrvo,* "island," has a Serbian or eastern flavor in distinction to the Croatian or western *otok.* In some cases the preference for one of the two possible interpretations may have been influenced by the syntactic arrangement of the entire sentence. For example, in contemporary Yugoslavia the sentence, *Podržavamo borbu naroda za slobodu* seems to favor the plurality of nations rather than one nation, i.e. "Let us support the struggle of nations for freedom," rather than "Let us support the struggle of the nation for freedom." The preference for the plural is even stronger in a sentence such as *"Broj konduktera nije poznat* where the plural (i.e. "The number of conductors isn't known") is favored by the fact that the singular (i.e. "The [badge] number of the conductor isn't known") could also be expressed by means of a possessive adjective, e.g., *Kondukterov broj nije poznat.* For that very reason we replaced this sentence in the shorter test by a much more neutral syntactic frame. *Ovo se tiče konduktera na toj relaciji* ("This concerns the conductor/the conductors on that line"). Significantly, however, this neutralization of the syntactic frame did not prevent total disaster in Belgrade, Zagreb and Rijeka, although it helped students in Gacko, Trebinje, Stolac, Mostar and Travnik. The striking difference between rural Bosnia-Hercegovina and the big cities is, in general, the most conspicuous result of the entire test. As a matter of fact, it can serve as a calibration of the soundness of the tested sentences on the one hand and the testing procedures on the other. As a rule, the potential interference of any kind, whether semantic, grammatical or extra-linguistic, appeared to play a much less important role in Gacko, Stolac or Travnik than in Sarajevo, Belgrade or Zagreb.

If the techniques of recording or reproduction had any impact on the naturalness of the communication, then the test rather convincingly disclosed that such potential interference was much less relevant in Gacko than in Belgrade. It seems, therefore, the technical aspects of the test can hardly explain the striking differences in identification displayed in the rural areas in contrast to the urban areas. The same reasoning applies to potential psychological problems connected with the testing itself. There is no reason to believe that the boys and girls in rural Gacko should be more sophisticated and confident in the testing process than the students in Belgrade or Zagreb. Nor would it be justifiable to claim that teenagers in the Hercegovinian mountains or in the bucolic valleys of Bosnia are on the average more intelligent than the youth in the Yugoslav cultural centers. *Mutatis mutandis,* the same applies to the teachers, professors and specialists in accentology who were tested and whose results reflect similar regional patterns. It follows, therefore, that the striking differences in the results have to be primarily interpreted in linguistic terms rather than in terms of technical or psychological obstacles or other extralinguistic factors. In our opinion it is precisely the conspicuous opposition between good and bad results which is the most revealing contribution of our test. In the most general sense, this opposition appears to reflect the differences between the rural and urban areas in contemporary Yugoslavia, or, more precisely, between the shrinking dialectal base of the Vukovian system and the city dialects.

1. CONCLUDING OBSERVATIONS ABOUT POSTACCENTUAL QUANTITY

The test of postaccentual quantity provided a revealing insight into the present status of the Vukovian system. In Gacko, for example, all thirty-one tested students without exception identified in Test I the first sentence, *Tu nema ùčitelja danas* as "There is no teacher here today." They identified equally well sentence 28, *Tu nema ùčitēljā danas* as "There are no teachers here today."

GENERAL CONCLUSIONS 179

When the sentence with the plural form re-appeared as item 57 in the test, two out of thirty-one students erred while one student erred when the sentence with the singular form re-appeared as item 85. In Stolac, where twenty-seven students were tested, one erred in connection with the first singular, two misinterpreted the first plural but all twenty-seven students correctly identified the third and fourth occurrence of the tested sentence. These results convincingly show that in Gacko and Stolac postaccentual quantity makes it possible to distinguish *učitelja* from *učitēljā* almost perfectly; the few errors in identification seem to be negligible and cannot seriously weaken the findings about the role of postaccentual quantity in the given four sentences. Moreover, the results provide clear evidence that Alerić's way of reading the sentences, the techniques of recording and production, the size and the trade-mark of the tape-recorder and student test fright could not really shake the Vukovian norm in Gacko and Stolac. On the other hand, the same four sentences caused total chaos in Belgrade and Zagreb as well as in Vuk's Loznica and in many other places. Since there was nothing wrong with the test in Gacko and Stolac, there is no reason to blame the test elsewhere. Rather, the remarkable failure of identification seems to indicate that there must be something wrong with postaccentual quantity in Belgrade, Zagreb, Loznica and in many other places. At least, one has the right to conclude that postaccentual quantity (as it was used by Alerić for the distinction *učitelja-učitēljā*) plays a different role in Gacko and Stolac than elsewhere. And this is precisely what we claim.

Now, the question is, of course, how the findings about the distinctiveness and non-distinctiveness of postaccentual quantity relate to the Vukovian system as a whole and, in particular, to the numerous functions assigned to postaccentual quantity by normative grammarians. In this respect the results of the test can only provide certain indications. It is, indeed, indicative that in Gacko, Stolac and other rural communities in Bosnia and Hercegovina the more successful identification of postaccentual quantity was obtained in connection with the pairs involving the quantitative distinction of the penultimate vowel as in *učitelja - učitēljā* as well as in *pògledā - pògledā*. On the other hand, identification was considerably less successful in connection with those pairs which involve only the very last syllable in a quantitative distinction such as *okólnosti - okólnostī, dúžnosti - dúžnostī, ùčenīka - ùčenīkā, ofícíra - ofícírā, sùprugom - sùprugōm*. This could mean that among those speakers, who are capable of using postaccentual quantity functionally, the penultimate syllable is more crucial as a carrier of quantitative distinction than the very last syllable. This is confirmed quite consistently by the results from various places and, in fact, also by the test of two accentologists from Zagreb, Finka and Klaić who made mistakes in the identification of pairs distinguished only by the quantity of the last syllable. Also the analysis of the local voices shows frequent omissions of the quantity prescribed for the last syllable (i.e., *tiče* for *tičē*, *boje* for *bojē*, *igra* for *igrā*, *čini* for *činī*, *nema* for *nemā*, *ovo* for *ovō*, etc.*

This observation, however, requires essential qualification. Even in those areas where postaccentual quantity resulted in successful identification of certain cases, the signal provided by the quantity of the penultimate syllable was often not significant enough to overcome the impact of a biased syntactic structure favoring one of the two interpretations. In other words the distinctive role of postaccentual quantity was found as being easily susceptible to skewing by semantic probability. This is best shown by the relatively poor identification of the plural form in the sentence *Dobro se s(j)ećam pròfesōrā romanskih jezika* ("I well remember the professors of Romance languages") or by the failure in identification of the singular form in the sentence *Podržavamo borbu národa za slobodu* ("Let us support the struggle of the nation for freedom"). This seems to indicate that postaccentual quantity among those speakers, who are still capable of using it meaningfully, is a delicate and rather unreliable system which can be easily neutralized by other sources of linguistic information. Moreover, it appears that a detailed investigation of this delicate

---

*Obvious deficiencies in articulating postaccentual quantity occur even in the speech of that celebrated authority, Univ. Prof. Dr. Ljudevit Jonke; Jonke was recorded giving a public speech in March, 1966.

system should consider not only word syllable structure but also the role of postaccentual quantity in various grammatical categories, in inflectional and derivational patterns and, finally, in the individual lexical items in order to determine where Vukovian postaccentual quantity has simply a graphic rather than a linguistic function. This has to be done, we believe, prior to any generative or typological treatment of Contemporary Standard Serbo-Croatian if such a treatment is to be more than a mere scholastic exercise.*

2. CONCLUDING OBSERVATIONS ABOUT ACCENTUAL QUANTITY

The testing results indicate clearly that accentual quantity (i.e. " vs. ˆ ; ' vs. ´ ; or short [" or '] vs. long [ˆ or ´]) has had a different fate in contemporary Yugoslavia than that of postaccentual quantity. In general, it is possible to say that the normative prescription of accentual quantity seems to be less artificial than the prescription of postaccentual quantity. The relatively successful identification of accentual quantity became particularly meaningful in those places where the test of postaccentual quantity turned out to be a failure. For example, the identification of the first two occurrences of the sentence frame, designed to test pȁs - pâs, kònja - kónjā, mȁrkōm - Mârkom, resulted in B in both Belgrade and Zagreb (native), where the corresponding test of ùčitelja - ùčitēljā resulted in D. The difference between B for accentual quantity and D for postaccentual quantity contrasts startingly with the results from Sarajevo where the corresponding test of ùčitelja - ùčitēljā gave B whereas pȁs - pâs and kònja - kónjā in the same test gave A. It is, however, noteworthy that even in Sarajevo, where cases of postaccentual quantity were identified considerably better than in Belgrade and Zagreb, the identification of accentual quantity yielded still better results. This could mean that even in Sarajevo accentual quantity is generally more distinctive than postaccentual quantity or, at least, it occupies a different position in the hierarchy of prosodic markers. Confirmation of our observations

*Cf. Moris Halle's reliance on Daničić's data in his "Remarks on Slavic Accentology," *Linguistic Inquiry,* II, 1 (1971), pp. 1-19.

would require, of course, much more extensive testing as well as a thorough investigation on both the lexical and grammatical levels. In fact, the test clearly revealed that differentiation by accentual quantity is also easily susceptible to lexical and grammatical interferences. For example, the first two occurrences of the sentence testing *grȁd - grâd* resulted in Belgrade and Zagreb (native) in C while the test of *pȁs - pâs* under the same conditions resulted in B. In Zagreb (native), moreover, the test of *pèro - Péro* resulted in D, and *zòra - Zóra* in F, while Belgrade scored B in both cases; almost all students in Gacko, Stolac and Travnik successfully identified the difference between short rising and long rising accent in these two pairs.

The relative success of accentual quantity in many areas in Yugoslavia has an interesting aspect which was disclosed by the striking discrepancy between the students' ability to identify accentual quantity in Brozović's and Alerić's usage and their inability to implement it properly in the local production. For example, some local speakers in Belgrade and all local speakers in Zagreb appeared in Alerić's analysis as lacking adequate distinctions between short and long accents as well as between rising and falling tones in the accented position, e.g. *pás - pás* for the expected *pȁs - pâs;* *kónja - kónja* or *kónja - kónja* for the expected *kònja - kónjā*. In spite of this prosodic neutralization, which appeared quite consistently in all Zagreb local voices, the local representatives Dubravko P. and Nevenka Ž. identified both Brozović's and Alerić's *pȁs - pâs* perfectly. The same is true for Milenko P., the local speaker in Belgrade, who articulated *pás - pás* and *kónja - kónja* although he correctly identified Brozović's and Alerić's *pȁs - pâs* and *kònja - kónjā* and most of the other cases of accentual quantity in the test. This discrepancy seems to indicate that the speakers in the big cities are capable of identifying distinctions which they themselves do not implement in their own speech. Such a discrepancy should not be surprising because, in general, interdialectal communication would be impossible if the ability of phonological discrimination were to be entirely dependent on the ability of production. This aspect of the test is, of course, only a by-product which deserves special treatment by itself. The results of such study could be of importance for those theories of perception concerned with the relationship of the acoustic and articulatory aspects of speech.

3. CONCLUDING OBSERVATIONS ABOUT TONE

The test of semantic distinctions which rely on the difference between long falling and long rising accents in word initial syllable produced uneven and generally poor results. The words *Lûka*, "Luke," and *lúka*, "port," so familiar in the literature of accentology, were used in Test I in the neutral sentence frame *Evo Lûkē/lúkē u daljini*, "There's Luke/the port in the distance." The results indicate that this particular contrast in long tones is perceived well only in Gacko, Stolac, Dubrovnik, and Travnik; perception in little Sisak is far from perfect but still creditable (C-C). Another familiar pair is *râdio*, "radio," and *rádio*, "working, doing," which we use in Test II. It did well in Osijek, Novi Sad, and Split, but fared poorly in Travnik, Dubrovnik and other cities. Thus, it seems apparent that the distinctiveness assigned by the normative grammars to long rising and long falling accent is operative only in certain areas and only in certain forms. What is distinctive in terms of tone in one area is not necessarily distinctive in another area evidently because the prosodic peculiarities of Serbo-Croatian dialects continued to develop despite Daničić's codification and such development was not according to the normative expectations of Vuk's votaries. It follows that the normative claims, particularly in the usage of tone, have to be tested in each instance and specified accordingly, if the description of tone in "Standard Contemporary Serbo-Croatian" is to have any linguistic value.

The gloomiest picture by far was obtained in the testing of the distinctive power assigned to the difference between short falling and short rising accent in the word initial syllable. All pairs involving short tones resulted in unsuccessful performances in all areas including those places where other types of prosodic differentiation proved to be successful. It is certainly symptomatic that the classical example *pàra*, "steam," vs. *pàra*, "money," was found confusing even by the specialists tested, although this pair, distinguished by " vs. `, appears in Stevanović's authoritative grammar (1964) without any restriction or qualification.* Mitar Pešikan, the Belgrade language specialist, failed in the identification of the pàra - pàra contrast. Professor Kravar, a well known specialist on Serbo-Croatian accent, missed the distinction between òrao "he has been plowing" vs. òrao "eagle" as implemented by the voice of Pavle Ivić, the leading Serbo-Croatian dialectologist: Ivić's òrao and òrao were identified by Kravar as "eagle" in all four occurrences.

The almost general failure to identify the difference between short rising and short falling accent is complemented by Alerić's analysis of the local productions. While analyzing the voice of Nevenka Ž. from Zagreb, he attached the following comments about his difficulties in evaluating one system from the point of view of another system:

"In her pronunciation there is absolutely no difference between " and `, but one always hears ' (the *tromi*). The difference between ˜ and ´ is weak; these accents are often so short that they approximate the *tromi* as well."

In accordance with his evaluation, the expected sentences

I dànas pàra ìgrā ùlogu.
I dànas pàra ìgrā ùlogu.

appeared as

I danas para igra ulogu.
I danas para igra ulogu.

---

*Akcenat pojedinih reči je, međutim, drukčije prirode. On je, kao god i glas, fonološki elemenat od kojeg zavisi značenje pojedinih reči. Kao dokaz za ovo mi ćemo jednu pored druge navesti po dve reči (po dva paronima) koje vizuelno, okom posmatrane, imaju potpuno isti oblik, ali se razlikuju po akcentu, a imaju, naravno, i sasvim različna značenja. Takve su reči: . . . jàrica (žensko jare), i jàrica (pšenica koja se seje s proleća), pàra (isparavanje) i pàra (novac) . . . M. Stevanović, Savremeni srpskohrvatski jezik, Belgrade, 1964, pp. 156-7.

The *tromi* accent (which in this case can hardly be anything other than stress without quantity or tone) was also found by Alerić in the local voices in Belgrade. The analysis of the local production of one of Belgrade's speakers, Milenko P, is accompanied by the following caveat:

"In his pronunciation, there is practically no difference between " and `; his ˆ is like ˈ (the *tromi*) and his ′ is not well-expressed. His lengths are also unexpressed. Thus, the marking of his accent by means of the signs used for the literary accents cannot really be justified.

These comments reflect the difficulties of an accentologist who tried to adhere as strictly as possible to his concept of Hercegovinian prosody which he himself considers as Standard Serbo-Croatian. Implicitly, his problem illustrates the dialectal clash which takes place in many Yugoslav urban areas and in the major cities in particular. If Alerić were to face in person these local speakers from Zagreb and Belgrade, their mutual communication would undoubtedly be characterized by many ambiguities. In general terms, Alerić's dilemma is necessarily faced by any linguist who tries to evaluate the prosodic characteristics of a dialect other than his own. In the past such a dilemma must have been even worse because dialectologists did not have recording equipment for the verification of their subjective findings nor could they listen to the same sentence ten, twenty or thirty times as Alerić did while analyzing all the local voices, or as Brozović did during his hours-long analysis of some of the local speakers.

Considering the fact that the tape recorder is a rather recent tool in dialectal research, one is willy-nilly forced to question the exactness of earlier accentological studies, the results of which often support Vukovian accentual canons and many of the typological studies. This unavoidable scepticism applies particularly to the role of the short rising vs. short falling accent in the lexicon as well as in the morphological paradigms codified by Daničić and still being reclassified.

We do not claim that the failure to discriminate between short falling and short rising accent in our tests proved conclusively that such a difference is a fiction in every instance where it is assigned a distinctive role. But we have the right to claim that the results of our tests represent a serious challenge to the traditional claims and to hope that they will stimulate a thoroughgoing linguistic investigation. In this situation intensive and extensive field work is far more essential and will be much more relevant to accentual realities than *mere reshuffling of Daničić's categories.*

4. CONCLUDING OBSERVATIONS ABOUT PLACE OF ACCENT

The most successful identification, regardless of the regional dialectal background, was obtained in the testing of pairs of words, each of which was accented on a different syllable. This overall success, moreover, was confirmed by the local voices when tested or analyzed. Their analysis revealed that the place of accent is in certain areas the only distinct prosodic characteristic of the word. The local production in Belgrade and particularly in Zagreb furnished the best illustrations. Dubravko P. in Zagreb, for example, was found to distinguish in his own speech *prijatelja* from *prijatelja* instead of the expected *prȉjatelja* vs. *prijatéljā* so that in his production the difference between short falling and long rising accent, combined with postaccentual quantity, was replaced by a distinction in place of accent without any significant difference in tone and in accentual or postaccentual quantity. Thus, the expected sentences.

Sjȅćām se prȉjatelja svôg òca   vs.
Sjȅćām se prijatéljā svôg òca

appeared as

Sjěčam se prijatelja svog oca   vs.
Sjěčam se prijatelja svog oca

GENERAL CONCLUSIONS

Nevertheless the group of thirty-nine students in Zagreb, responding to Dubravko's voice, made only two errors in the identification of *prìjatelja* and 4 errors in their response to *prijatélja*.

In Belgrade two sentences, expected to be pronounced as

Štȍ se tȋčē ȉmena na vrátima, ne mògu vam pòmoći   vs.
Štȍ se tȋčē iménā na vrátima, ne mògu vam pòmoći

were found in the local production of Milenko P. as

Štò se tȉče ȉmena na vrātima, ne mògu vam pòmoći   vs.
Štò se tȉče iména na vrātima, ne mògu vam pòmoći

Thus, the expected difference between short falling and long rising accent combined with postaccentual quantity was replaced by the difference in the place of accent and in accentual quantity without any distinctive tone or postaccentual quantity. Nevertheless, the group of thirty students responding to Milenko's voice made only two errors in the identification of *ȉmena* and five errors in their response to *iménā*.

In this connection it is certainly noteworthy that the local speakers in Titograd, on the Albanian border, and in Subotica, on the Hungarian border, re-interpreted the expected difference between postaccentual length in

        G sg.   *pròfesora*   vs.
        G pl.   *pròfesōrā*

by means of the difference in place of accent:

        G sg.   *pròfesora*   vs.
        G pl.   *profesóra.*

The same replacement, combined with the length of the last vowel, was found in the local voice in Rijeka and Osijek and in one of the local voices in Belgrade (Milica V.). Among the thirty-two students in Belgrade, responding to Milica's voice, thirty-one identified her irregular plural *profesórā* as plural while in Osijek thirty out of thirty-three students identified the local irregular *profesórā* as plural. In Zagreb Dubravko D. and Marina S. replaced in their pronunciation the prescribed contrast between *rȉbāra* vs. *rȉbārā* by *rȉbara* vs. *rȉbara*. Alerić in his analysis denoted the plural form as *ribára* with the explanation that the sign ′ in that case should not be taken for the Hercegovinian long rising accent but for an accent which is neither rising nor falling but long. It is interesting that the identification of this irregular plural was in Zagreb more successful than the identification of Brozović's *rȉbārā*.

Replacement of the difference in postaccentual quantity by the difference in place of accent was also found in the local voice in Nikšić where the speaker used the irregular contrast *kònduktera* vs. *konduktérā* instead of the expected *konduktéra* vs. *konduktérā*. All nineteen students in Nikšić identified the irregular *kònduktera* as singular, although eleven misinterpreted Brozović's *konduktéra* as plural.

On the other hand, the place of accent in the local voices shows a very different picture in connection with the expected shift on to the proclitic. Both Alerić and Brozović shifted the accent in accordance with normative grammar, e.g., *nà tom brežúljku; ù našem drúštvu; nà tōj reláciji; zà vašu júhu;* most of the local speakers, however, totally disregarded the rules of the shift. In Gacko, for example, the local speaker Milan B. was found to pronounce consistently:

na tôm brežúljku
u nȁšēm drúštvu
na tôj reláciji
za vȁšu júhu

Also the local speakers in Stolac, Nikšić, Trebinje, Travnik, Banja Luka, Dubrovnik, Split, Titograd, Subotica and Novi Sad consistently used *na tôm, u nȁšem* (or *u nȁšēm*), *na tôj, za vȁšu*. In Zagreb and Belgrade, of course, none of the local speakers shifted the accent. Among all the local speakers in the places tested actually only one was found to follow the rules of the shift consistently.

GENERAL CONCLUSIONS 189

This single exception was found in Mostar in the pronounciation of Slobodanka N. Moreover, one of the local speakers in Sarajevo (Irfan H.) consistently used *nà tom brežùljku* but *u nàšem drùštvu* and *za vášu jùhu*, while he vacillated between *nà tōj reláciji* and *na tôj reláciji*. Margita P. in Osijek consistenly used *nà tom brežùljku* and *nà tōj reláciji* but always *za vášu jùhu* and *u nàšem drùštvu* (once *u nàšem drùštvu*). Since a clear majority of local speakers did not follow the normative rules of shift, it appears that any discussion of place of accent and its differentiating role should treat the shift of accent onto proclitics as a separate problem.

Excluding those situations involving a shift of accent onto proclitics, the place of accent on different syllables proved in our tests to be a prosodic device which clearly dominated the hierarchy of effectiveness and communality. Distinguishing between forms by placing the accent on different syllables was found umabiguous everywhere in contemporary Yugoslavia regardless of the local status of tone and of accentual or postaccentual quantity. In the tests this device appeared equally functional whether combined or not combined with quantitative or tonal differentiation.

In other words

Sjećam se prijatelja svog oca

vs.

Sjećam se prijatelja svog oca

in Zagreb was found to be as equally distinctive as Brozović's or Alerić's

Sjȅćām se prȉjatelja svôg òca

vs.

Sjȅćām se prijatéljā svôg òca.

Or, to use other examples,

Štȍ se tȉče ȉmena na vrátima, ne mògu vam pòmoći

vs.

Štȍ se tȉče iména na vrátima, ne mògu vam pòmoći

in Belgrade was as equally well identified as Brozović's or Alerić's

Štȍ se tȋčē ȉmena na vrátima, ne mògu vam pòmoći

vs.

Štȍ se tȋčē iménā na vrátima, ne mògu vam pòmoći.

Since pairs distinguishable by means of accent on a different syllable were easily recognized everywhere in the locations tested, regardless of their dialectal history, the place of accent appears to have greater power than all other prosodic devices, whether tonal or quantitative; it turned out to be a common denominator valid everywhere in contemporary Yugoslavia.

The second position in the hierarchy of effectiveness and communality of the characteristics tested is clearly occupied by accentual quantity, that is to say, by quantitative differentiation in the accented syllable. In this case only Niš deviated from the general pattern. As far as all other prosodic features are concerned, the tests resulted in a less clear picture. Judging from the test and the analysis of the local voices, one would have to say that the most dubious "distinction" appeared to be the difference between short falling and short rising accent, although some individuals with Bosnian and Hercegovinian background tested rather well. They were, however, in such a striking minority that it is legitimate to ask whether the language planning which promotes the classical Vukovian accentual system is not facing insurmountable obstacles. It appears that the natural and heterogeneous sources of prosodic development are defeating the language planners in a most spectacular way. In this sense contemporary Yugoslavia is not only interesting because of its incredible number of local prosodic systems but also as an arena dramatically demonstrating that the intrinsic forces of the language as a whole are stronger than the wishes of a few conservative grammarians who would like to determine its fate.

Jonke's emphasis on the aesthetic values of the Vukovian system may well have been its strongest argument for maintenance. But the situation now is such that there is real doubt that the Vukovian accentual canons are able to provide any aesthetic appeal to Yugoslav city-dwellers. Speech with the orthodox accentuation impresses residents of Belgrade and Zagreb as being *seljački,* "countryfied." What is now abundantly clear is that the accentual system presented in Serbo-Croatian grammars, dictionaries and textbooks has little or no relationship with the accentual system(s) employed in many urban areas. From the standpoint of language planning the acceptance and spread of Vuk's language system has been a success with, however, the one conspicuous failure in the matter of Vukovian accentuation. Against the background of urban accentual diversity, interurban speech resorts to a type of accentual koine which has as its chief characteristics an agreed-upon place of stress and the possibility of a short or long vowel under stress. It is perhaps too much to expect that the present Yugoslav Serbocroatianists will accept the accentological implications of this situation, yet they or their successors must face up to the accentual reality of the cities, step out from the "shadow of Vuk" and formulate Serbo-Croatian accentology in twentieth-century terms.

APPENDIX I

ACCENTED READINGS

As mentioned in previous sections, local voices reading the fifty sentences of Test II were recorded, then later accented by Danijel Alerić, an accentologist at the University of Zagreb. Readings by several Yugoslav linguists were also recorded and accented. A few of these many readings are presented here with the accentual notations of Alerić. The first reading is that of the well known Yugoslav dialectologist, Professor Dalibor Brozović; his reading accorded perfectly with the Vukovian accentual norms and so can be used to judge the other readings. The second reading is that of Professor Bratoljub Klaić, while the third is that of Professor Pavle Ivić; both Klaić and Ivić are renowned specialists in Serbo-Croatian accentology. Then follow the readings of three young men, all about 17 years old at the time of the reading (1966); Irfan H. from Sarajevo, Milenko P. from Belgrade, and Dubravko P. from Zagreb. Thus, the first three readings are those of Serbo-Croatian specialists, all mature men; the second three readings are those of unsophisticated high school boys whose readings reflect the speech habits of their respective cities, the three largest cities in Yugoslavia. The accent markings are the four Vukovian marks (" ` ˜ ´) along with Alerić's *tromi* (') which he uses for an indeterminate accent and which seems to indicate simple stress.

VOICE: Professor Dalibor Brozović

26. *I dànas pàra ȉgrā ȕlogu.*
44. *I dànas pàra ȉgrā ȕlogu.*

20. *Dȁ li je ȍrao nà tom brežúljku?*
30. *Dȁ li je ȍrao nà tom brežúljku?*
13. *Dȁ li je òrao nà tom brežúljku?*
47. *Dȁ li je òrao nà tom brežúljku?*

12. Štȍ je rȃdio ȕ našem drȗštvu?
31. Štȍ je rȃdio ȕ našem drȗštvu?
48. Štȍ je rȃdio ȕ našem drȗštvu?

40. Čȋnī se da je mȏj pȁs bȍljī nego tvȏj.
18. Čȋnī se da je mȏj pȃs bȍljī nego tvȏj.

4. Dȁ li je tȏ glȁsilo dȍbro?
39. Dȁ li je tȏ glȁsilo dȍbro?
25. Dȁ li je tȏ glásilo dȍbro?

8. Mȏj će pomȍćnȋk kȕpiti tȇ stvȃri.
22. Mȏj će pomȍćnȋk kúpiti tȇ stvȃri.

14. Ȍvō se tȋčē konduktéra nȁ tōj reláciji.
38. Ȍvō se tȋčē konduktérā nȁ tōj reláciji.

11. Zar nȇmā Gȑka u ȍvōj grȕpi?
28. Zar nȇmā Gȑka u ȍvōj grȕpi?
46. Zar nȇmā Gȑkā u ȍvōj grȕpi?

6. Fȍlklōrnī se refèrāt tȋčē kȍla šumȁdījskōg tȋpa.
27. Fȍlklōrnī se refèrāt tȋčē kȍlā šumȁdījskōg tȋpa.
36. Fȍlklōrnī se refèrāt tȋčē kȏlā šumȁdījskōg tȋpa.

43. Tȗ nȇmā kȍnja za jȁhānje.
17. Tȗ nȇmā kónjā za jȁhānje.

3. Štȍ se tȋčē sèla u ȍvō dȍba, tȏ je vèlik prȍblēm.
15. Štȍ se tȋčē sèla u ȍvō dȍba, tȏ je vèlik prȍblēm.
34. Štȍ se tȋčē sèlā u ȍvō dȍba, tȏ je vèlik prȍblēm.

16. Ȅvo kȍsti zȁ vašu júhu.
33. Ȅvo kȍsti zȁ vašu júhu.
49. Ȅvo kȍstī zȁ vašu júhu.

ACCENTED READINGS

29. *Ròditelji se bòjē stvâri tê vŕstē.*
7. *Ròditelji se bòjē stvárī tê vŕstē.*
37. *Ròditelji se bòjē stvárī tê vŕstē.*

2. *Nèstalo je rȉbāra za vrijème tê bȕrē.*
41. *Nèstalo je rȉbāra za vrijème tê bȕrē.*
21. *Nèstalo je rȉbārā za vrijème tê bȕrē.*

9. *Ȇvo ȍstrva u daljìni.*
24. *Ȇvo ȍstȓvā u daljìni.*
42. *Ȇvo ȍstȓvā u daljìni.*

1. *Dòbro se sjȅćām pròfesora ròmānskīh jȅzīkā.*
50. *Dòbro se sjȅćām pròfesora ròmānskīh jȅzīkā.*
10. *Dòbro se sjȅćām pròfesōrā ròmānskīh jȅzīkā.*
32. *Dòbro se sjȅćām pròfesōrā ròmānskīh jȅzīkā.*

19. *Štȍ se tȋčē ȉmena na vrátima, ne mògu vam pòmoći.*
35. *Štȍ se tȋčē iménā na vrátima, ne mògu vam pòmoći.*

45. *Sjȅćām se prȉjatelja svôg òca.*
5. *Sjȅćām se prijatéljā svôg òca.*
23. *Sjȅćām se prijatéljā svôg òca.*

VOICE: Professor Bratoljub Klaić

26. *I dànas[1] pàra[1] ȉgra ȕlogu.[1]*
44. *I dànas pàra ȉgra ȕlogu.[1]*

20. *Dà li je òrao nà tom brežúljku?*
30. *Dà li je òrao nà tom brežúljku?*
13. *Dà li je òrao nà tom brežúljku?*
47. *Dà li je òrao nà tom brežúljku?*

[1] Alerić notes: "The accent is not articulated very well; here it's close to a *tromi*."

12. Štȍ je râdio u nȁšem drúštvu?
31. Štȍ je râdio u nȁšem drúštvu?
48. Štȍ je rádio u nȁšem drúštvu?

40. Čȉni se da je môj pȁs bȍlji nego tvôj.
18. Čȉni se da je môj pâs bȍlji nego tvôj.

4. Dȁ li je tō glàsilo dòbro?
39. Dȁ li je tō glásilo dòbro?[1]
25. Dȁ li je to glásilo dòbro?[1]

8. Môj će pomòćnīk kȕpiti te stvâri.
22. Môj će pomòćnīk[2] kúpiti te stvâri.

14. Ȍvo se tîče konduktéra nà toj reláciji.
38. Ovo se tîče konduktérā nà toj reláciji.

11. Zar nêma Gȑka[1] u ȍvoj grȕpi?[1]
28. Zar nêma Gȑka[1] u ȍvoj grȕpi?[1]
46. Zar nêma Gȑkā u ȍvoj grȕpi?[1]

6. Fòlklōrni se refèrat tîče kȍla šumàdijskog tȋpa.
27. Fòlklōrni se refèrat tîče kȍlā šumàdijskog tȋpa.
36. Fòlklōrni se refèrat tîče kȍlā šumàdijskog tȋpa.

43. Tu nêma kònja za jȁhānje.
17. Tu nêma kónjā za jȁhānje.

3. Štȍ se tîčē sèla[1] u ȍvo dȍba, to je vèlik[1] pròblēm.
15. Štȍ se tîčē sèla u ȍvo dȍba, to je vèlik[1] pròblēm.
34. Štȍ se tîčē sèlā u ȍvo dȍba, to je vèlik[1] problēm.

16. Ȅvo kȍsti za vȁšu júhu.
33. Ȅvo kȍsti za vȁšu júhu.
49. Ȅvo kȍstī za vȁšu júhu.

[1] Alerić notes: "The accent is not articulated very well; here it's close to a *tromi.*"
[2] Alerić: "Here the length is hardly expressed."

ACCENTED READINGS

29. *Ròditelji se bòje stvâri te vr̀stē.*
7. *Ròditelji se bòje stvárī tê vr̀stē.*
37. *Ròditelji se bòje stvárī tê vr̀stē.*

2. *Nèstalo je rȉbārā za vrijème tê bùrē.*
41. *Nèstalo je rȉbārā za vrijème tê bùrē.*[1]
21. *Nèstalo je rȉbārā za vrijème te bùrē.*[1]

9. *Ȅvo ȍstrva u daljìni.*
24. *Ȅvo ȍstȓvā u daljìni*
42. *Ȅvo ȍstȓvā u daljìni.*

1. *Dòbro se sjȅćam pròfesora ròmanskih jȅzīkā.*
50. *Dòbro se sjȅćam pròfesora ròmanskih jȅzīkā.*
10. *Dòbro se sjȅćam pròfesōrā ròmānskih jȅzīkā.*
32. *Dòbro se sjȅćam pròfesōrā ròmānskih jȅzīkā.*

19. *Štȍ se tȉče ȉmena na vrátima, ne mògu vam pòmoći.*
35. *Štȍ se tȉče iménā na vrátima, ne mògu vam pòmoći.*

45. *Sjȅćam se prȉjatelja svôg òca.*[1]
5. *Sjȅćam se prijatéljā svôg òca.*[1]
23. *Sjȅćam se prijatéljā svôg òca.*[1]

VOICE: Professor Pavle Ivić

26. *I dànas pàra ȉgra ùlogu.*
44. *I dànas pàra ȉgra ùlogu.*

20. *Dà li je ȍrao nà tom brežúljku?*
30. *Dà li je ȍrao nà tom brežúljku?*
13. *Dà li je òrao nà tom brežúljku?*
47. *Dà li je òrao nà tom brežúljku?*

[1] Alerić notes: "The accent is not articulated very well; here it's close to a *tromi*."

12. Štà je râdio ù našem drúštvu?
31. Štà je râdio ù našem drúštvu?
48. Štà je rádio ù našem drúštvu?

40. Čìnī se da je môj pàs bȍljī nego tvôj.
18. Čìnī se da je môj pâs bȍljī nego tvôj.

4. Dà li je to glàsilo dòbro?
39. Dà li je tō glásilo dòbro?
25. Da̓ li je tō glásilo dòbro?

8. Môj će pomòćnīk kùpiti te stvâri.
22. Môj će pomòćnīk kúpiti te stvâri.

14. Òvō se tȋčē konduktéra na tôj reláciji.
38. Òvō se tȋčē konduktéra nà tōj reláciji.

11. Zar nêma Gȓka u òvōj grȕpi?
28. Zar nêma Gȓka u ȍvōj grȕpi?
46. Zar nêma Gȓka u o̓voj grȕpi?

6. Fòlklōrni se refèrāt tȋčē kȍla šumàdījskōg tîpa.
27. Fòlklōrni se refèrāt tȋčē kôlā šumàdījskōg tîpa.
36. Fòlklōrni se refèrāt tȋčē kôlā šumàdījskōg tîpa.

43. Tu nêma kònja za jȁhānje.
17. Tû nêmā kónjā za jȁhānje.

3. Što̓ se tȋčē sèla u o̓vo dȍba, tô je vèlik pròblēm.
15. Što̓ se tȋčē sèla u o̓vo dȍba, tô je vèlik pròblēm.
34. Što̓ se tȋčē sēlā u o̓vo dȍba, tô je vèlik pròblēm.

16. Ȅvo kȍsti za vȁšu čórbu.
33. Ȅvo kȍsti za vȁšu čórbu.
49. Ȅvo kòstijū za vȁšu čórbu.

29. Ròditelji se bòjē stvâri te vr̀stē.
7. Ròditelji se bòjē stvári te vr̀stē.
37. Ròditelji se bòjē stvâri tê vr̀stē.

2. Nèstalo je rȉbāra za vréme te bȕrē.
41. Nèstalo je rȉbāra za vréme tē bȕrē.
21. Nèstalo je rȉbāra za vréme te bȕrē.

9. Ȅvo ȍstrva u daljìni.
24. Ȅvo ȍstȓvā u daljìni.
42. Ȅvo ȍstȓva u daljìni.

1. Dòbro se sȅćām pròfesora ròmānskīh jȅzīkā.
50. Dòbro se sȅćam pròfesora ròmānskih jȅzīkā.
10. Dòbro se sȅćām pròfesōra ròmānskih jȅzīkā.
32. Dòbro se sȅćam pròfesōra ròmanskih jȅzīkā.

19. Štȍ se tîče ȉmena na vrátima, ne mògu vam pomòći.
35. Štȍ se tîče iména na vrátima, ne mògu vam pomòći.

45. Sȅćam se prȉjatelja svôg òca.
5. Sȅćām se prijatéljā svôg òca.
23. Sȅćam se prijatélja svôg òca.

VOICE: Irfan H. (Sarajevo)

26. I dànas pàra ìgrā ȕlogu.
44. I dànas pàra ìgrā ȕlogu.

20. Dà li je òrao nà tom brežúljku?
30. Dà li je òrao nà tom brežúljku?
13. Dà li je òrao nà tom brežúljku?
47. Dà li je òrao nà tom brežúljku?

12. Štà je râdio u nȁšem drúštvu?
31. Štò je rádio u nȁšem drúštvu?
48. Štò je rádio u nȁšem drúštvu?

40. Čìnī se da je môj pȁs bȍljī nego tvôj.
18. Čìnī se da je môj pâs bȍljī nego tvôj.

4. Dà li je to glàsilo dòbro?
39. Dà li je tô glàsilo dòbro?
25. Dà li je tô glàsilo dòbro?

8. Môj će pomòćnīk kùpiti tê stvâri.
22. Môj će pomòćnīk kúpiti tê stvâri.

14. Ȍvo se tȋčē konduktéra na tôj reláciji.
38. Ȍvo se tȋče konduktéra nà tōj reláciji.

11. Zar nêma Gȑka u ȍvōj grȕpi?
28. Zar nêma Gȑka u ȍvōj grȕpi?
46. Zar nêma Gȑkā u ȍvōj grȕpi?

6. Fòlklōrnī se refèrat tȋčē kȍla šumàdījskōg tîpa.
27. Fòlklōrnī se refèrat tȋčē kôla šumàdījskōg tîpa.
36. Fòlklōrnī se refèrat tȋče kōlā šumàdījskōg tîpa.

43. Tu nêmā kònja za jȁhānje.
17. Tû nêma kònja za jȁhānje.

3. Štȍ se tȋče sèla u ȍvō dôba, tô je vȅlik prȍblēm.
15. Što se tȋče sèla u ȍvo dôba, tô je vȅlik prȍblēm.
34. Štò se tȋče sélā u ȍvō dôba, tô je vȅlik prȍblēm.

16. Ȅvo kȍsti za vȁšu jùhu.
33. Ȅvo kȍsti za vȁšu jùhu.
49. Ȅvo kȍsti za vȁšu jùhu.

29. Ròditelji se bòje stvárī tê vȑstē.
7. Ròditelji se bòjē stvárī tê vȑstē.
37. Ròditelji se bòje stvárī tê vȑstē.

ACCENTED READINGS

2. *Nèstalo je rȉbāra za vrjéme tê bȕrē.*
41. *Nèstalo je rȉbāra za vrjéme tê bȕrē.*
21. *Nèstalo je rȉbāra za vrjéme tê bȕrē.*

9. *Ȅvo òstrva u daljìni.*
24. *Ȅvo ȍstrvā u daljìni.*
42. *Ȅvo ȍstrvā u daljìni.*

1. *Dòbro se sjȅćām prȍfesōra ròmānskīh jȅzīkā.*
50. *Dòbro se sjȅćām prȍfesora ròmānskīh jȅzīkā.*
10. *Dòbro se sjȅćām prȍfesōrā ròmānskīh jȅzīkā.*
32. *Dòbro se sjȅćām prȍfesōrā ròmānskīh jȅzīkā.*

19. *Štò se tîče ȉmena na vrátima, ne mògu vam pòmoći.*
35. *Štò se tîčē ȉmena na vrátima, ne mògu vam pòmoći.*

45. *Sjȅćām se prȉjatelja svôg òca.*
5. *Sjȅćām se prȉjatēljā svôg òca.*
23. *Sjȅćām se prȉjatēljā svôg òca.*

VOICE: Milenko P. (Belgrade)*

26. *I dànas pàra ȉgra ȕlogu.*
44. *I dànas pàra ȉgra ȕlogu.*

20. *Dà li je òrao na tôm brežúljku?*
30. *Dà li je òrao na tôm brežúljku?*
13. *Dà li je òrao na tôm brežúljku?*
47. *Dà li je òrao na tôm brežúljku?*

12. *Štà je rȃdio u nȁšem drúštvu?*
31. *Štà je rȃdio u nȁšem drúštvu?*
48. *Štà je rȃdio u nȁšem drúštvu?*

*Alerić notes: "In his pronunciation there is practically no difference between " and ' ; his ˆ is like ' (tromi), and his ' is not well expressed. His lengths are also unexpressed. Thus, the marking of his accents by means of the signs used for the literary accents cannot really be justified."

40. Čìni se da je môj pȁs bȍlji nego tvôj.
18. Čìni se da je môj pȁs bȍlji nego tvôj.

4. Dà li je tô glàsilo dòbro?
39. Dà li je to glásilo dòbro?
25. Dà li je tô glásilo dòbro?

8. Môj će pomòćnīk kúpiti¹ tê stvâri.
22. Môj će pomòćnīk kúpiti   tê stvâri.

14. Òvō se tȉče konduktéra na tôj reláciji.
38. Ȍvo se tȉče kondùktéra na tôj reláciji.

11. Zar nêma Grka u ȍvoj grȕpi?
28. Zar nêma Grka u ȍvoj grȕpi?
46. Zar nêma Grka u ȍvoj grȕpi?

6. Fòlklōrni se refèrat tȉče kȍla šumàdījskōg tȉpa.
27. Fȍlklorni se refèrat tȉče kôla šumàdījskōg tȉpa.
36. Fòlklorni se refèrat tȉče kôla šumàdījskōg tȉpa.

43. Tû nêma kȍnja za jȁhānje.
17. Tu nêma kónjā za jȁhānje.

3. Štȍ se tȉče sèla u òvō dôba, tô je vèlik pròblēm.
15. Štȍ se tȉče sèla u òvo dôba, tô je vèlik pròblēm.
34. Štȍ se tȉče sela u ȍvo dôba, tô je vèlik pròblēm.

16. Ȅvo kȍsti za vašu čȏrbu.
33. Ȅvo kȍsti za vašu čȏrbu.
49. Ȅvo kȍsti za vašu čȏrbu.

29. Ròditelji se bòje stvâri tê vŕstē.
7. Ròditelji se bòje stvárī tê vŕstē.
37. Ròditelji se bòje stvári tê vŕstē.

[1] Alerić: "Poorly expressed rising accent."

WORD ACCENT

2. Nèstalo je rȉbāra za vréme tê bȕrē.
41. Nèstalo je rȉbara za vréme tê bȕrē.
21. Nèstalo je rȉbara za vréme tê bȕrē.

9. Ȅvo ȍstrva u daljȉni.
24. Ȅvo ȍstrva u daljȉni.
42. Ȅvo ȍstrva u daljȉni.

1. Dòbro se sȅćam pròfesora ròmānskīh jȅzīkā.
50. Dòbro se sȅćam pròfesora ròmānskīh jȅzīkā.
10. Dòbro se sȅćam pròfesora ròmānskīh jȅzīkā.
32. Dòbro se sȅćam pròfesora ròmānskīh jȅzīkā.

19. Štȍ se tȋče ȉmena na vrátima, ne mògu vam pòmoći.
35. Štȍ se tȋče iména na vrátima, ne mògu vam pòmoći.

45. Sȅćam se prijatélja¹ svôg òca.
5. Sȅćam se prijatélja svôg òca.
23. Sȅćam se prijatélja svôg òca.

VOICE: Dubravko P. (Zagreb)

26. I dànas pàra ȉgra ȕlogu.
44. I dànas pàra ȉgra ȕlogu.

20. Dà li je òrao na tȍm brežùljku?
30. Dà li je òrao na tȍm brežùljku?
13. Dà li je òrao na tȍm brežùljku?
47. Dà li je òrao na tȍm brežùljku?

12. Štȍ je râdio u nȁšem drùštvu?
31. Štȍ je râdio u nȁšem drùštvu?
48. Štȍ je râdio u nȁšem drùštvu?

---

[1] Alerić: "Poorly expressed rising accent."

40. Čini se da je môj pȁs bȍlji nego tvôj.
18. Čini se da je môj pȁs bȍlji nego tvôj.

4. Dȁ li je to glȁsilo dȍbro?
39. Dȁ li je to glȁsilo dȍbro?
25. Dȁ li je to glȁsilo dȍbro?

8. Môj če pomȍčnȋk kȕpiti[1] te stvȃri.
22. Môj če pomȍčnik kȕpiti te stvȃri.

14. Ȍvo se tȉče konduktȅra na tȏj relȁciji.
38. Ȍvo se tȉče konduktȅra na tȏj relȁciji.

11. Zar nȇma Gȑka u ȍvoj grȕpi?
28. Zar nȇma Gȑka u ȍvoj grȕpi?
46. Zar nȇma Gȑka u ȍvoj grȕpi?

6. Fȍlklorni se refȅrat tȉče kȍla šumȁdijskog tȋpa.
27. Fȍlklorni se refȅrat tȉče kȍla šumȁdijskog tȋpa.
36. Fȍlklorni se refȅrat tȉče kȍla šumȁdijskog tȋpa.

43. Tu nȅma kȍnja za jȁhānje.
17. Tu nȅma kȍnja za jȁhānje.

3. Štȍ se tȉče sȅla u ȍvo dȏba, tȏ je vȅlik prȍblēm.
15. Štȍ se tȉče sȅla u ovo dȍba, to je vȅlik prȍblēm.
34. Štȍ se tȉče sȅla u ȍvo dȍba, tȏ je vȅlik prȍblēm.

16. Ȅvo kȍsti[2] za vȁšu jȕhu.
33. Ȅvo kȍsti za vȁšu jȕhu.
49. Ȅvo kȍsti za vȁšu jȕhu.

---

[1] Alerić notes: "As also in other forms the sign ′ does not mean Hercegovinian ′, and the sign ˆ does not mean Hercegovinian ˆ, but both signs denote accents which somewhat approach Hercegovinian ′ and ˆ respectively. Sometimes Zagreb ′ and ˆ approach ǃ (the tromi)."

[2] Alerić: "Here the accent is similar to Hercegovinian ˝ ."

ACCENTED READINGS

29. Ròditelji se bòje stvȃri te vȑstē.
7. Ròditelji se bòje stvȃri te vȑstē.
37. Ròditelji se bòje stvȃri te vȑstē.

2. Nèstalo je ribára¹ za vrjéme¹ te bȗrē.
41. Nèstalo je ribára za vrjéme te bȗrē.
21. Nèstalo je rȉbara za vrjéme te bȗrē.

9. Ȇvo ȍstrva² u daljìni.
24. Ȇvo òstrva u daljìni.
42. Ȇvo òstrva u daljìni.

1. Dòbro se sjȅčam pròfesora ròmanskih jȅzikā.
50. Dòbro se sjȅčam pròfesora ròmanskih jȅzikā.
10. Dòbro se sjȅčam pròfesora ròmanskih jȅzikā.
32. Dòbro se sjȅčam pròfesora ròmanskih jȅzikā.

19. Štò se tȉče ȉmena na vrátima, ne mògu vam pòmoći.
35. Štò se tȉče iména na vrátima, ne mògu vam pòmoći.

45. Sjȅčam se prȉjatelja svog òca.
5. Sjȅčam se prijatélja svog òca.
23. Sjȅčam se prȉjatelja svog òca.

---

¹Alerić notes: "As also in other forms the sign ′ does not mean Hercegovinian ′, and the sign ˉ does not mean Hercegovinian ˉ, but both signs denote accents which somewhat approach Hercegovinian ′ and ˉ respectively. Sometimes Zagreb ′ and ˉ approach ‵ (the *tromi*)."

²Alerić: "Here the accent is similar to Hercegovinian ‶."

APPENDIX II

BIBLIOGRAPHY

Perhaps the most complete bibliography of works on Serbo-Croatian accentology is that contained in Josip Matešić, *Der Wortakzent in der serbokroatischen Schriftsprache,* Heidelberg: Carl Winter, 1970, pp. 265-281. Matešić lists 408 titles. Another useful bibliography is that found in Karl-Heinz Pollok, *Der neuštokavische Akzent und die Struktur der Melodiegestalt der Rede,* Göttingen: Vandenhoeck und Ruprecht, 1964, pp. 131-139. Pollok's list of 202 titles deals not only with Serbo-Croatian accentology but also with theoretical problems of prosody and with prosodic phenomena of languages other than Serbo-Croatian. The reference books listed below are those which have proved of value in the foregoing study; Part I contains the titles of reference works, grammars, and articles, while Part II lists the titles of relevant dictionaries.

PART I - ARTICLES, BOOKS

Stjepan Babić, "U čemu je ljepota hrvatskosrpskog jezika," *Jezik* 4 (1963-1964), pp. 117-125.

Aleksandar Belić, *Osnovi istorije srpskohrvatskog jezika* I, Fonetika, Beograd: Nolit, 1960.

Aleksandar Belić, *Savremeni srpskohrvatski književni jezik* I, Glasovi i akcenat, Beograd: Naučna knjiga, 1951.

Charles E. Bidwell, "The Phonemics and Morphophonemics of Serbo-Croatian Stress," *Slavic and East European Journal* 7 (1963), pp. 160-165.

Ivan Brabec, Mate Hraste, Sreten Živković, *Gramatika hrvatskosrpskog jezika*, 6th edition, Zagreb: Školska knjiga, 1965.

E. W. Browne and J. D. McCawley, "Srpskohrvatski akcenat," *Zbornik za filologiju i lingvistiku* 8 (1965), pp. 147-151.

Dalibor Brozović, "O fonološkom sustavu suvremenog standardnog hrvatskog jezika," *Radovi*, (razdio lingvističko-filološki 4), Filozofski fakultet u Zadru, 1968, pp. 20-39.

Đuro Daničić, *Srpski akcenti*, Srpska kraljevska akademija, posebna izdanja, knjiga LVIII, Filosofski i filološki spisi, knjiga 16, Beograd-Zemun: Grafički zavod "Makarije" A.D., 1925.

Paul Garde, "Les propriétés accentuelles des morphèmes serbocroates," *Scando-Slavica* 12 (1966), pp. 152-172.

Paul Garde, *L'accent*, Paris: Presses Universitaires de France, 1968.

Paul Garde, "Fonctions des oppositions tonales dans les langues slaves du Sud, *Bulletin de la Société de Linguistique de Paris* 61 (1966), pp. 42-56.

Josip Hamm, *Kratka gramatika hrvatskosrpskog književnog jezika za strance*, Zagreb: Školska knjiga, 1967.

Josip Hamm, *Grammatik der serbokroatischen Sprache*, Wiesbaden: Otto Harrassowitz, 1967.

Carleton T. Hodge, "Serbo-Croatian Stress and Pitch," *General Linguistics* 3 (1958), pp. 43-54.

Carleton T. Hodge, "Serbo-Croatian Phonemes," *Language* 22 (1946), pp. 112-120.

Pavle Ivić, "The Functional Yield of Prosodic Features in the Patterns of Serbocroatian Dialects," *Word* 17 (1961), pp. 293-308.

Pavle Ivić, *Die serbokroatischen Dialekte*, Ihre Struktur und Entwicklung, I, Allgemeines und die štokavische Dialektgruppe, 's-Gravenhage: Mouton & Co., 1958.

Pavle Ivić, "Prozodijski sistem savremenog srpskohrvatskog standardnog jezika," *Symbolae linguisticae in honorem Georgii Kuryłowicz*, Warsaw: Polska Akademia Nauk, 1965, pp. 135-144.

Stjepan Ivšić, *Prilog za slavenski akcenat* (preštampano iz 187. knjige "Rada" Jugoslavenske akademije znanosti i umjetnosti), Zagreb: Tisak Dioničke tiskare, 1911.

Roman Jakobson, "Die Betonung und ihre Rolle in Wort- und Syntagmaphonologie," *Travaux du Cercle linguistique de Prague* IV, 1931, pp. 164-182; reprinted in Roman Jakobson, *Selected Writings* I, 's-Gravenhage: Mouton, 1962, pp. 115-136.

Roman Jakobson, "On the identification of phonemic entities, *Travaux du Cercle linguistique de Copenhague* V, 1949, pp. 205-213; republished in Roman Jakobson, *Selected Writings* I, 's-Gravenhage: Mouton, 1962, pp. 418-425.

Roman Jakobson, "Opyt fonologičeskogo podxoda k istoričeskim voprosam slavjanskoj akcentologii," *American Contributions to the Fifth International Congress of Slavists*, The Hague: Mouton, 1963, pp. 153-178.

Ljudevit Jonke, *Književni jezik u teoriji i praksi*, 2nd. edition, Zagreb: Znanje, 1965.

Ilse Lehiste, "Some Acoustic Correlates of Accent in Serbo-Croatian," *Phonetica* 7 (1961), pp. 114-147.

Ilse Lehiste and Pavle Ivić, *Accent in Serbocroatian*, Michigan Slavic Materials No. 4, Ann Arbor: Department of Slavic Languages and Literatures (Univ. of Michigan), 1963.

Werner Lehrfeldt, Božidar Finka, "Das Akzentverhalten im Serbokroatischen dargestellt an den Substantiven," *Die Welt der Slaven* 14:I (1969), pp. 26-46.

Werner Lehrfeldt, Božidar Finka, "Das Akzentverhalten im Serbokroatischen dargestellt an den Verben," *Die Welt der Slaven* 14:2 (1969), pp. 174-192.

A. Leskien, *Grammatik der serbo-kroatischen Sprache* 1. Teil: Lautlehre, Stammbildung, Formenlehre, Heidelberg: Carl Winter's Universitätsbuchhandlung, 1914.

Horace G. Lunt, "On the Study of Slavic Accentuation," *Word* 19 (1963), pp. 82-99.

Thomas F. Magner, "Post-Vukovian Accentual Norms in Modern Serbo-Croatian," *American Contributions to the Sixth International Congress*, Volume I - Linguistic Contributions, ed. by Henry Kučera, The Hague: Mouton, 1968, pp. 227-247.

T. Maretić, *Gramatika hrvatskoga ili srpskoga književnog jezika*, 3rd. edition, Zagreb: Matica Hrvatska, 1963.

Leonhard Masing, *Die Hauptformen des serbisch-chorwatischen Accents*, Mémoires de l'académie impériale des sciences de St.-Pétersbourg, VIIe Série, Tome XXIII, No. 5, St.-Pétersbourg, 1876.
Ladislav Matejka, "Generative and Recognitory Aspects in Phonology," *Phonologie der Gegenwart*, ed. J. Hamm, Wien: Hermann Böhlaus, 1967, pp. 242-253.
Ladislav Matejka, "Czech quantity in paradigmatic and syntagmatic procedures," *Proceedings of the Sixth International Congress of Phonetic Sciences*, Prague: Academia Publ. House, 1970, pp. 621-623.
Branko Miletić, *Osnovi fonetike srpskog jezika*, Beograd: Naučna knjiga, 1960.
Branko Miletić, "Uticaj rečeničke melodije na intonaciju reči," *Zbornik u čast A. Belića*, Belgrade: Izdanje "Mlada Srbija," 1937, pp. 219-223.
Asim Peco, "Valeur phonologique des accents serbocroates," *Proceedings of the Fifth International Congress of Phonetic Sciences*, Basel: S. Karger, 1965, pp. 453-457.
Asim Peco and Mitar Pešikan, *Informator o savremenom književnom jeziku sa rečnikom*, Beograd: Mlado pokolenje, 1967.
Karl-Heinz Pollok, *Der neuštokavische Akzent und die Struktur der Melodiegestalt der Rede*, Göttingen: Vandenhoeck und Ruprecht, 1964.
Ivan Popović, *Geschichte der serbokroatischen Sprache*, Wiesbaden: Otto Harrassowitz, 1960.
Peter Rehder, *Beiträge zur Erforschung der serbokroatischen Prosodie*, München: Otto Sagner, 1968.
George Y. Shevelov, *A Prehistory of Slavic*, New York: Columbia University Press, 1965 (printed Heidelberg: Winter, 1964).
Christian S. Stang, *Slavonic Accentuation*, Oslo: Universitetsforlaget, 1957.
Edward Stankiewicz, "The Accent Patterns of the Slavic Verb," *American Contributions to the Sixth International Congress of Slavists.* Vol. I: Linguistics, The Hague: Mouton, 1968, pp. 359-377.
M. Stevanović, *Savremeni srpskohrvatski jezik (gramatički sistemi i književnojezička norma)* I, Beograd: Naučno delo, 1964.

George L. Trager, "Serbo-Croatian Accents and Quantities," *Language* 16 (1940), pp. 29-32.
N. S. Trubetzkoy, *Grundzüge der Phonologie,* Prague, 1939 = Travaux du Cercle linguistique de Prague 7.

PART II - DICTIONARIES

F. Iveković i Ivan Broz, *Rječnik hrvatskog jezika,* I(A-O), II(P-Ž), Zagreb: Štamparija Karla Albrechta (Jos. Wittasek), 1901.
Vuk Stef. Karadžić, *Srpski rječnik,* Vienna, 1818, reprinted as vol. II of *Sabrana dela Vuka Karadžića* with *pogovor* [Epilogue] by Pavle Ivić, Beograd: Prosveta, 1966.
Vuk Stef. Karadžić, *Srpski rječnik,* 4th edition, Beograd: Štamparija kraljevina Jugoslavije, 1935.
Miloš Moskovljević, *Rečnik savremenog srpskohrvatskog književnog jezika s jezičkim savetnikom,* Beograd: Tehnička knjiga - Nolit, 1966.
Pravopis hrvatskosrpskog književnog jezika s pravopisnim rječnikom, Zagreb - Novi Sad: Matica Hrvatska - Matica Srpska, 1960.
Pravopis srpskohrvatskog književnog jezika s pravopisnim rečnikom, Novi Sad - Zagreb: Matica Srpska - Matica Hrvatska, 1960.
Rečnik srpskohrvatskoga književnog jezika, I(A-E), II(Ž-K), III (K-O), Novi-Sad - Zagreb: Matica Srpska - Matica Hrvatska, 1967-1969.
Rečnik srpskohrvatskog književnog i narodnog jezika, I(A-Bogoljub), II(bogoljub - Vražogrnci), III(vraznuti - guščurina), IV(d - dugulja), V(dugulja - zaključiti), VI(zaključnica - zemljen), Beograd: Srpska akademija nauka i umetnosti, 1959-1969.
Rječnik hrvatskosrpskoga književnog jezika, I(A-F), II(G-K), Zagreb - Novi Sad: Matica Hrvatska - Matica Srpska, 1967.